The Holocaust

PROBLEMS IN EUROPEAN
CIVILIZATION SERIES

The Holocaust

Problems and Perspectives of Interpretation

Fourth Edition

Edited by

Donald L. Niewyk
Southern Methodist University

WADSWORTH
CENGAGE Learning

Australia • Brazil • Japan • Korea • Mexico • Singapore • Spain • United Kingdom • United States

WADSWORTH
CENGAGE Learning™

The Holocaust: Problems and Perspectives of Interpretation, Fourth Edition

Donald L. Niewyk

Senior Acquisitions Editor:
Nancy Blaine

Development Manager:
Jeffrey Greene

Editorial Assistant:
Emma Goehring

Marketing Manager:
Diane Wenckebach

Marketing Communications Manager:
Christine Dobberpuhl

Content Project Management:
Pre-PressPMG

Senior Art Director: Cate Barr

Print Buyer: Rebecca Cross

Senior Rights Acquisition Account Manager:
Katie Huha

Text Permissions Editor:
Tracy Metivier

Production Service:
Pre-PressPMG

Image Permissions Editor:
Jennifer Meyer Dare

Photo Researcher:
Bruce Carson

Cover Designer:
Alwyn R. Velásquez

Cover Image: Bildarchiv Preussischer Kulturbesitz/ © Art Resource, NY

Compositor: Pre-PressPMG

For product information and technology assistance, contact us at **Cengage Learning Customer & Sales Support, 1-800-354-9706**

For permission to use material from this text or product, submit all requests online at **www.cengage.com/permissions.**
Further permissions questions can be e-mailed to **permissionrequest@cengage.com.**

Library of Congress Control Number: 2009936593

ISBN-13: 978-0-547-18946-8
ISBN-10: 0-547-18946-X

Wadsworth
20 Davis Drive
Belmont, CA 94002-3098
USA

Cengage Learning is a leading provider of customized learning solutions with office locations around the globe, including Singapore, the United Kingdom, Australia, Mexico, Brazil, and Japan. Locate your local office at: **international.cengage.com/region**

Cengage Learning products are represented in Canada by Nelson Education, Ltd.

For your course and learning solutions, visit **www.cengage.com.**

Purchase any of our products at your local college store or at our preferred online store **www.cengagebrain.com**

Printed in the United States of America
3 4 5 6 7   22 21 20 19 18

Contents

Preface

Literature on the Holocaust, already vast when the first edition of this book appeared fourteen years ago, continues to grow. Today it is rare to encounter earlier views of Nazi genocide as either unworthy of special attention—"just another German atrocity"—or else too horrible to understand or even imagine by those who were not there. If the former belittled the Holocaust, the latter led to its mystification. But today, more than ever before, students and the public at large sense that much depends on coming to terms with the Holocaust. For who can say who the victims might be next time?

This volume brings together some of the most important and stimulating contributions to our understanding of Nazi genocide. These readings have been selected for the purpose of acquainting students with a variety of views, some of classic stature, others very recent. After an introduction that contains a brief historical overview of the Holocaust, Part I explores problems of definition and origins. Part II looks at the motivations of Holocaust perpetrators. Part III compares conflicting views about the victims' survival strategies and women's experience of the camps. Part IV examines charges that the victims failed to put up any significant resistance to their tormentors. Part V inquires into the attitudes and actions of bystanders while the victims were being murdered. Finally, Part VI considers the possibilities that some Jews might have been saved from the gas chambers through military action or intercession by outside forces.

This edition reflects new directions in Holocaust scholarship and also incorporates some classic interpretations not previously included in this anthology. Part I begins with an essay by John Weiss that locates the origins of Nazi genocide in the long history of European and German anti-Semitism, inviting debate on the relative importance of Hitler and Nazi racism, more broadly conceived, in bringing on the Holocaust. Part II replaces the now somewhat discredited Goldhagen thesis with Omer Bartov's assessment of German army involvement in genocide on the Eastern Front. Part III tests the rival views of Bettelheim and Des Pres concerning Holocaust survival with material drawn from Primo Levi's exploration of prisoner functionary "gray zones" and Zoe Waxman's recent rethinking of women in the Holocaust. Part IV provides a nuanced reappraisal by Dan Diner of the impossible position of the Jewish Councils under German rule.

Readers should be aware that for reasons of space the original notes do not appear in the excerpts contained in this anthology. Questions about documentation can be answered by consulting the original publications.

I am grateful to Eliza Ablovatski, Kenyon College; G. Jan Colijn, The Richard Stockton College of New Jersey; Robert Franciosi, Grand Valley State University; Federico Finchelstein, The New School; Moshe Gershovich, University of Nebraska–Omaha; and Susannah Heschel of Dartmouth College for their valuable advice in selecting the content of this edition. Naturally no two scholars would be likely to choose exactly the same readings on any complex topic such as this one, and any failings with regard to the selections included in this volume must be attributed to me.

For their expert assistance in assembling this anthology, I want to thank my editors at Wadsworth/Cengage Learning, Nancy Blaine and Jeff Greene, and Pradhiba Kannaiyan, production editor.

Editor's Preface to Instructors

There are many ways to date ourselves as teachers and scholars of history: the questions that we regard as essential to ask about any historical development, the theorists whose words we quote and whose names appear in our footnotes, the price of the books purchased for courses that are on our shelves. Looking over my own shelves, it struck me that another way we could be dated was by the color of the oldest books we owned in this series, which used to be published by D.C. Heath and then by Houghton Mifflin. I first used a "Heath series" book—green and white, as I recall—when I was a freshman in college in a modern European history course. That book, by Dwight E. Lee on the Munich crisis, has long since disappeared, but several Heath books that I acquired later as an undergraduate are still on my shelves. Those that I used in graduate school, including ones on the Renaissance and Reformation, are also there, as well as several that I assigned to my students when I first started teaching or have used in the years since. Of course, as with any system of historical periodization, this method of dating a historian is flawed and open to misinterpretation. When a colleague retired, he gave me some of his even older Heath series books, in red and black, which had actually appeared when I was still in elementary and junior high school, so that a glance at my shelves might make me seem ready for retirement.

The longevity of this series, despite its changing cover design and its transition from D.C. Heath to Houghton Mifflin to Wadsworth/Cengage Learning, could serve as an indication of several things. One might be that historians are conservative, unwilling to change the way they approach the past or teach about it. The rest of the books on my shelves suggest that this is not the case, however, for many of the them discuss topics that were unheard of as subjects of historical investigation when I took that course as a freshman thirty years ago: memory, masculinity, visual culture, and sexuality.

Another way to account for the longevity of this series is that several generations of teachers have found it a useful way for their students to approach historical subjects. As teachers, one of the first issues we confront in any course is what materials we will assign our students to read. (This is often, in fact, the very first thing we must decide, for we have to order books months before the class begins.) We may include a textbook to provide an overview of the subject matter covered in the course, and often have a number from which to choose. We may use a reader of original sources, or several sources in their entirety, because we feel that it is important for our students to hear the voices of people of the past directly. We may add a novel from the period, for fictional works often give one details and insights that do not emerge from other types of sources. We may direct our students to visual materials, either in books or on the Web, for artifacts, objects, and art can give one access to aspects of life never mentioned in written sources.

Along with these types of assignments, we may also choose to assign books such as those in this series, which present the ideas and opinions of scholars on a particular topic. Textbooks are, of course, written by scholars with definite opinions, but they are designed to present material in a relatively bland manner. They may suggest areas about which there is historical debate (often couched in phrases such as "scholars disagree about . . . ") but do not participate in those debates themselves. By contrast, the books in this series highlight points of dispute and cover topics and developments about which historians often disagree vehemently. Students who are used to the textbook approach to history may be surprised at the range of opinion on certain matters, but we hope that the selections in each of these volumes will allow readers to understand why there is such a diversity. Each volume covers several issues of interpretive debate and highlights newer research directions.

Variety of interpretation in history is sometimes portrayed as a recent development, but the age of this series in its many cover styles indicates that this account is not accurate. Historians have long realized that historical sources are produced by particular individuals with particular interests and biases that consciously and unconsciously shape their content. They have also long—one is tempted to say "always"—recognized that different people approach the past differently, making choices about which topics to study, which sources to use, which developments and individuals to highlight. This diversity in both sources and methodologies is part of what makes history exciting for those of us who study it, for new materials and new approaches allow us to see things that have never been seen before, in the same way that astronomers find new stars with better tools and new ways of looking at the universe.

The variety and innovation that is an essential part of good historical scholarship allow this series both to continue and to change. Some of the volumes now being prepared have the same titles as those I read as an undergraduate, but the scholarship on that topic has changed so much in the last several decades that they had to be completely redone, not simply revised. Some of the volumes now in print examine topics that were rarely covered in undergraduate courses when the series began publication, and a few former volumes are no longer in print as the topics they investigated now show up rarely. We endeavor to keep the series up-to-date and welcome suggestions about volumes that would prove helpful for teaching undergraduate and graduate courses. You can contact us at http://cengage.com/highered.

Merry E. Wiesner

Editor's Preface to Students

History is often presented as facts marching along a timeline, and historical research viewed as the unearthing of information so that more facts can be placed on the timeline. Like geologists in cave or physicists using elaborate microscopes, historians discover new bits of data that allow them to recover more of the past.

To some degree this is an accurate model. Like laboratory scientists, historians do conduct primary research, using materials in archives, libraries, and many other places to discover new things about the past. Over the last thirty years, for example, the timeline of history has changed from a story that was largely political and military to one that includes the experiences of women, peasants, slaves, children, and workers. Even the political and military story has changed, and now includes the experiences of ordinary soldiers and minority groups, rather than simply those of generals, rulers, and political elites. This expansion of the timeline has come in part through intensive research in original sources, which has vastly increased what we know about people of the past.

However, original research is only part of what historians do, in the same way that laboratory or field research is only part of science. Historical and scientific information is useless until someone tries to make sense of what is happening—tries to explain why and how things developed the way they did. In making these analyses and conclusions, however, both historians and scientists often come to disagree vehemently about the underlying reasons for what they have observed or discovered and sometimes about the observations themselves. Certain elements of those observations are irrefutable—a substance either caught fire or it did not, a person lived and died or he or she did not—but many more of them are open to debate: Was the event (whether historical or scientific) significant? Why and how did it happen? Under what circumstances might it not have happened? What factors influenced the way that it happened? What larger consequences did it have?

The books in this series focus on just those types of questions. They take one particular event or development in European history, and present the analyses of a number of historians and other authors regarding this issue. In some cases the authors may disagree about what actually happened — in the same way that eyewitnesses of a traffic accident or crime may all see different things — but more often they disagree about the interpretation. Was the Renaissance a continuation of earlier ideas, or did it represent a new way of looking at the world? Was nineteenth-century European imperialism primarily political and economic in its origins and impact, or were cultural and intellectual factors more significant? Was ancient Athens a democracy worthy of emulation, an expansionary state seeking to swallow its neighbors, or both? Within each volume there are often more specific points of debate, which add complexity to the main question and introduce you to further points of disagreement.

Each of the volumes begins with an introduction by the editor, which you should read carefully before you turn to the selections themselves. This introduction sets out the *historical* context of the issue, adding depth to what you may have learned in a textbook account or other reading and also explains the *historiographical* context; that is, how historians (including those excerpted in the volume) have viewed the issue over time. Each volume also includes a timeline of events and several reference maps that situate the issue chronologically and geographically. These may be more detailed than the timelines and maps in your textbook, and consulting them as you read will help deepen your understanding of the selections.

Some of the volumes in the series include historical analyses that are more than a century old, and all include writings stretching over several decades. The editors include this chronological range not only to allow you to see that interpretations change, but also to see how lines of argument and analysis develop. Every historian approaching an issue depends not only on his or her own original research, but also on the secondary analyses of those who have gone before, which he or she then accepts, rejects, modifies, or adapts. Thus, within the book as a whole, or within each section, the selections are generally arranged in chronological order. Reading them in the order they are presented will allow you to get a better sense of the historiographical development and to make comparisons among the selections more easily and appropriately.

The description of the scholarly process noted previously is somewhat misleading, for in both science and history, research and analysis are not sequential but simultaneous. Historians do not wander around archives looking for interesting bits of information, but turn to their sources with specific questions in mind, questions that have often been developed by reading earlier historians. These questions shape where they will look, what they will pay attention to, and therefore what conclusions they will make. Thus the fact that we now know so much more about women, peasants, or workers than we did several decades ago did not result primarily from sources on these people suddenly appearing where there had been none, but from historians going back to the same archives and libraries that had yielded information on kings and generals with new questions in mind. The same is true in science. Of course, scientists examining an issue begin with a hypothesis and then test it through the accumulation of information, reaching a conclusion that leads to further hypotheses.

In both history and science, one's hypotheses can sometimes be so powerful that one simply cannot see what the sources or experiments show, which is one reason there is always opportunity for more research or a reanalysis of data. A scholar's analysis may also be shaped by many other factors, and in this volume the editor may have provided you with information about individual authors, such as their national origin, intellectual background, or philosophical perspective, if these factors are judged important to your understanding of their writings or points of view. You might be tempted to view certain of these factors as creating "bias" on the part of an author and thus reduce the value of his or her analysis. It is important to recognize, however, that every historian or commentator has a particular point of view and writes at a particular historical moment. Very often what scholars view as complete objectivity on their own part is seen as subjective bias by those who disagree. The central aim of this series over its forty plus years of publication has been to help students understand how and why the analyses and judgments of historians have differed and changed over time — to see that scholarly controversy is at the heart of the historical enterprise. The instructor in your course may have provided you with detailed directions for using this book, but here are some basic questions that you can ask yourself as you read the selections:

- What is the author's central argument?
- What evidence does the author put forward to support this argument?
- What is the significance of the author's argument?
- What other interpretation might there be of the evidence that the author presents?
- How does each author's argument intersect with the others in the chapter? In the rest of the book?
- How convincing do you find the author's interpretation?

These questions are exactly the same as those professional historians ask themselves, and in analyzing and comparing the selections in this book, you, too, are engaged in the business of historical interpretation.

Merry E. Wiesner

Chronology
of Events

1933	January–March	Hitler and his Nazi Party take over Germany.
	April 1	One-day boycott of Jewish stores throughout Germany.
1935	September 15	The Nuremberg Laws deprive German Jews and Gypsies of civil liberties.
1938	November 9–10	The Crystal Night pogrom destroys Jewish property throughout Germany.
1939	September 1	Nazi Germany attacks Poland, beginning World War II.
	September–December	Polish Jews from areas annexed to Germany expelled to central Poland.
	October–November	First ghettos established in Poland.
1940	January 4	Start of "Euthanasia" Program—handicapped people gassed in Germany.
	January 30	Gypsies ordered deported from Germany to occupied Poland.
	April 27	Himmler orders creation of Auschwitz concentration camp.
	October 12	Warsaw ghetto established.
1941	June 22	Nazi Germany invades the Soviet Union and unleashes mobile killing units.
	July 31	Göring orders Heydrich to formulate a "comprehensive solution to the Jewish Problem."
	August 24	Hitler calls a halt to the "Euthanasia" Program.
	September 3	First experimental gassings of Soviet POWs at Auschwitz.

	September 29–30	Mass murder of Jews at Babi Yar, near Kiev.
	October 23	Jewish emigration ordered halted.
	December 8	Gassings begin at Chelmno.
1942	January 20	Wannsee Conference outlines measures to exterminate Jews.
	March–July	Exterminations begin at Auschwitz, Belzec, Sobibor, and Treblinka.
	June–November	Deportations of Jews and Gypsies from Western Europe begin.
	September	Start of mass gassings at Maidanek.
	December 16	Gypsies ordered sent to Auschwitz.
	December 17	Allies denounce Nazi genocide.
1943	March–June	Large gas chambers and crematoria begin operations at Auschwitz-Birkenau.
	April 19– May 16	Warsaw ghetto uprising.
	June 21	Himmler orders liquidation of Polish and Russian ghettos.
	August 2	Revolt at Treblinka.
	October	7,500 Danish Jews saved.
	October 14	Revolt at Sobibor.
	October 19	"Operation Reinhard" declared complete; Belzec, Sobibor, and Treblinka cease functioning.
1944	January 22	War Refugee Board established.
	March–July	Germany occupies Hungary; Jews and Gypsies deported to Auschwitz.
	July 23	Soviet troops liberate Maidanek.
	August	The last ghetto, Lodz, liquidated.
	August 20	The American Airforce bombs Auschwitz factories for the first time.
	October 7	Revolt by *Sonderkommando* at Auschwitz.
	November 2	Himmler orders end to gassings.
1945	January 27	Soviet troops liberate Auschwitz.
	April 11	Buchenwald is first concentration camp in Germany to be liberated by the Allies.
	May 7	Nazi Germany surrenders.

Glossary

AK	"Home Army," the main Polish underground army.
Einsatzgruppen	"Special Action Squads"; mobile killing units of the SS.
Gauleiter	"District Leader(s)"; high Nazi Party official(s).
General Government	Nazi-occupied central Poland during World War II.
Judenrat	Jewish Council.
Kapos	Prisoner foremen.
Katyn Forest	Site of Soviet massacre of Polish officers, 1941.
KdF	Chancellory of the Führer (i.e., Hitler's private office).
Luftwaffe	The German airforce.
NSDAP	"National Socialist German Workers Party"; the Nazi Party.
Operation Barbarossa	The German plan to attack the USSR in 1941.
Operation Reinhard	The German plan to kill all the Jews in the General Government.
Protectorate	"The Protectorate of Bohemia and Moravia," the German-occupied Czech lands during World War II.
RSHA	"Reich Security Main Office," the SS agency that coordinated police affairs.
Reichskristallnacht	"Crystal Night," or the "November pogrom" of 1938.
SD	"Security Service," the SS intelligence agency.
Sonderkommando	"Special Detail" of prisoners or of German units.
SS	"Security Detachments," the chief instrument of police terror in Nazi Germany and occupied Europe.

T4	The program to subject German handicapped people to euthanasia, or "mercy killing."
Vichy	The collaborationist government in France.
Waffen SS	"Armed SS"; military units of the SS.
Wehrmacht	The German armed services.
Zegota	"Council for Aid to Jews," an underground group of Poles and Jews.
ZOB	"Jewish Fighting Organization" in Poland.

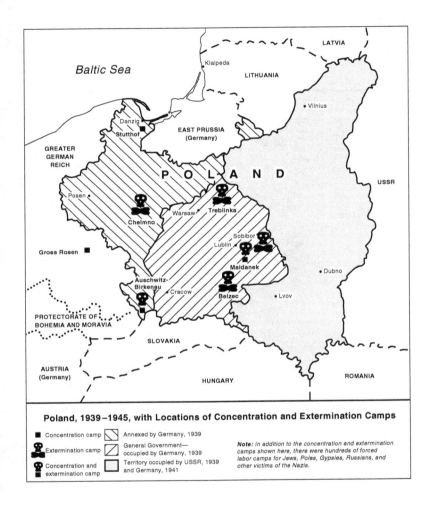

Poland, 1939–1945, with Locations of Concentration and Extermination Camps

■ Concentration camp

Extermination camp

Concentration and
extermination camp

Annexed by Germany, 1939

General Government—
occupied by Germany, 1939

Territory occupied by USSR, 1939
and Germany, 1941

*Note: In addition to the concentration and extermination
camps shown here, there were hundreds of forced
labor camps for Jews, Poles, Gypsies, Russians, and
other victims of the Nazis.*

Estimated Jewish Deaths in the Holocaust

	Pre-Holocaust Population	Low Estimate	High Estimate
Austria	191,000	50,000	65,500
Belgium	60,000	25,000	29,000
Bohemia/Moravia	92,000	77,000	78,300
Denmark	8,000	60	116
Estonia	4,600	1,500	2,000
France	260,000	75,000	77,000
Germany	566,000	135,000	142,000
Greece	73,000	59,000	67,000
Hungary	725,000	502,000	569,000
Italy	48,000	6,500	9,000
Latvia	95,000	70,000	72,000
Lithuania	155,000	130,000	143,000
Luxembourg	3,500	1,000	2,000
Netherlands	112,000	100,000	105,000
Norway	1,700	800	800
Poland	3,250,000	2,700,000	3,000,000
Romania	441,000	121,000	287,000
Slovakia	89,000	60,000	71,000
USSR	2,825,000	700,000	1,100,000
Yugoslavia	68,000	56,000	65,000
Totals	9,067,800	4,869,860	5,894,716

Note: There is uncertainty about these statistics because they must be drawn from fragmentary and sometimes inaccurate German records, Jewish sources, and various prewar and postwar census data. Border changes and diverse ways of defining Jews further complicate the estimates. These statistics are drawn from Raul Hilberg, *The Destruction of the European Jews* (New York: Holmes and Meier, 1985), pp. 1201–1220; Israel Gutman and Robert Rozett, "Estimated Jewish Losses in the Holocaust," in Israel Gutman, ed., *Encyclopedia of the Holocaust* (New York: Macmillan, 1990), vol. IV, pp. 1797–1802; and Wolfgang Benz, *Dimension des Völkermords: Die Zahl der jüdischen Opfer des Nationalsozialismus* (Munich: R. Oldenbourg, 1991).

Estimated Gypsy Deaths in the Holocaust

	Pre-Holocaust Population	Low Estimate	High Estimate
Austria	11,200	6,800	8,250
Belgium	600	350	500
Bohemia/Moravia	13,000	5,000	6,500
Estonia	1,000	500	1,000
France	40,000	15,150	15,150
Germany	20,000	15,000	15,000
Greece	?	50	50
Hungary	100,000	1,000	28,000
Italy	25,000	1,000	1,000
Latvia	5,000	1,500	2,500
Lithuania	1,000	500	1,000
Luxembourg	200	100	200
Netherlands	500	215	500
Poland	50,000	8,000	35,000
Romania	300,000	19,000	36,000
Slovakia	80,000	400	10,000
USSR	200,000	30,000	35,000
Yugoslavia	100,000	26,000	90,000
Totals	947,500	130,565	285,650

Note: Statistics on Gypsy losses are especially unreliable and controversial. These figures are based on necessarily rough estimates compiled in Rüdiger Vossen, *Zigeuner: Roma, Sinti, Gitanos, Gypsies zwischen Verfolgung and Romantisierung* (Frankfurt: Ullstein, 1983), pp. 83–86; and Michael Zimmermann, *Rassenutopie und Genozid: Die Nationalsozialistische "Lösung der Zigeunerfrage"* (Hamburg: Christians, 1996), pp. 235–292, 381–383.

The Holocaust

Introduction

The Nazi slaughter of Jews, Gypsies, and other "racial undesirables" during World War II, commonly referred to as the Holocaust,[1] occupies a special place in recent history. The genocide of innocents by one of the world's most advanced nations mocks our optimism about human reason and progress. It raises doubts about our ability to live together on the same planet with people of other cultures and persuasions.

Before it happened, virtually no one thought such a slaughter likely or even possible. To be sure, for many centuries religious and ethnic prejudice had been widespread throughout Europe. Devout Christians had viewed the Jews as Christ killers and deliberate misbelievers, but conversion was considered the inevitable cure, however long it might be delayed. Following the Jews' emancipation from discriminatory laws in the nineteenth century, the old religious antisemitism was joined by secular nationalisms that challenged the Jews' qualifications for membership in the nations in which they lived. Secular antisemites objected when the Jews, newly freed from persecution, often tied their destinies to growing capitalist economies; to liberal and socialist political movements; and to modernist trends in music, literature, architecture, and the theater. Success in banking, business, politics, and culture rendered the Jews far more visible than their small numbers ordinarily would have warranted. Europeans who felt threatened by modernity, and especially those who lost status as the result of economic changes and the spread of democracy, sometimes blamed the Jews for their plight.

Political parties that advocated antisemitism rarely won victories before 1914, but anti-Jewish attitudes became fairly commonplace in many European countries and in North America. If the "good" German (or Frenchman, or Russian) was viewed as pious, conservative, patriotic, and trusting, "the Jew" was stereotyped as materialistic, left-leaning, cosmopolitan, and manipulative. Antisemitism before World War I was more a war of words and a way to define one's own national identity ("we are the opposite of everything the Jews are") than a program for

---

[1]The word *Holocaust*, first used in the late 1950s to refer to the Jewish tragedy during World War II, means "a burnt sacrifice offered solely to God." The problems with that meaning are obvious, but no other term has succeeded in taking its place. It has become a convention, and we will have to make do with it.

radical action. Antisemitic minorities that took the "Jewish problem" seriously advocated solving it by assimilating the Jews into the larger population or else repealing their emancipation and restoring the old discriminatory laws. Even the most inveterate antisemites, those who postulated a Jewish conspiracy to dominate the civilized world, recommended expulsion as a remedy of last resort. Only a few marginal figures hinted darkly at the need for more radical measures. Hence antisemitism was a necessary precondition for the Holocaust but did not make it inevitable.

If anything, Gypsies were even less popular than the Jews. A predominantly poor and nonliterate people of color who had originated in northern India, the Gypsies (or Roma and Sinti) lived mostly nomadic lives as blacksmiths, metal workers, horse dealers, and fortune-tellers. Their reputation as beggars and petty thieves made them unwelcome everywhere.

An ominous development of the late nineteenth century was the rise of modern biological racial "science." This now discredited offshoot of Darwinism assumed the primacy and permanence of inherited racial characteristics, leading some people to view Jews and Gypsies as irredeemably depraved. But even those who played dangerously with racist ideas probably had no thought of racial annihilation, or genocide. When it became known that the Turks had committed genocide against the Armenians during World War I, Europeans dismissed it as the act of non-Christian barbarians acting in the fury of war. Western civilization, they supposed, had risen above such savagery.

After World War I, Europe experienced severe economic and political upheavals that intensified antisemitism almost everywhere. Added to the old charges that Jews were unpatriotic and greedy was the accusation that they were behind the spread of Communism. The participation of a few Jewish intellectuals and politicians in the Bolshevik Revolution in Russia and in Communist revolts elsewhere rendered this plausible. In Germany, Adolf Hitler, who had been exposed to racial antisemitism as a youth in his native Austria, made attacks on the Jews from the beginning of his career in the Nazi Party in postwar Munich. Such attacks became staples of Nazi propaganda throughout his rise to power, but they were not employed consistently. In their efforts to be all things to all Germans, Hitler and his followers played up opposition to the Jews when it helped them, and played it down when it did not. As a result, no one could be sure what, if anything, the Nazis would do to the Jews in a future Third Reich. Germans who supported Hitler did so less because he was an antisemite than because he seemed to provide a clear alternative to the failed German republic and a means of defense against a threatening Communist movement. And yet, antisemitism was sufficiently commonplace in Germany to be at least acceptable to the 44 percent of Germans who voted for the Nazis in the last election held before Hitler became dictator in 1933.

Once in power, the Nazis showed that they were sincere racists from the start. Jews were fired from government jobs and subjected to discriminatory laws, sporadic economic boycotts, and physical violence, all designed to make them despair of a future in Germany and leave the country. In 1935 the infamous Nuremberg Laws made the Jews second-class citizens and outlawed marriage and sexual relations between Jews and "Aryans." The Gypsies were liable to the same laws and were also confined to special camps. Handicapped Germans were subjected to compulsory sterilization to prevent them from passing on their "tainted" genes. But the Nazis did not press too hard against the Jews at first, fearing to upset the German economy, which was still recovering from the Great Depression, and worrying that fierce antisemitism would spawn costly foreign boycotts of German goods. Jews were sent to concentration camps only if they had been active in anti-Nazi political parties. As they moved toward the 1936 Berlin Olympics, Hitler and his lackeys were on their best behavior in order to make a positive impression on the world.

After 1936 the ever more self-confident Nazis increasingly cracked down on what was left of the Jewish community in Germany. The Third Reich was moving toward war and wanted to rid itself of its Jewish "fifth column" as soon as possible. More and more Jewish firms were "Aryanized," that is, expropriated by the state at a fraction of their value, and Jews were banned from most occupations. On the night of November 9–10, 1938, the Nazis used the excuse of a revenge attack by a Jewish teenager on a German diplomat in Paris to unleash a nationwide pogrom against the Jews. Named the "Crystal Night" for the broken windowglass that littered the streets and sidewalks in Jewish neighborhoods, it resulted in the burning of hundreds of synagogues and the beatings and arrests of thousands of Jews, several of whom were murdered. For the first time large numbers of Jews were sent indiscriminately to concentration camps and released only if they promised to leave Germany promptly. Most wanted desperately to go. The problem was finding countries that would admit them. Nazi confiscation of Jewish wealth meant that they would be penniless refugees seeking shelter in a world still sunk in depression. The democracies, preoccupied with their own problems, showed only limited understanding of the plight of the German Jews. Palestine was then a British mandate with an Arab majority that fiercely resisted any increase in the Jewish presence there. Never very particular about legalities, the Nazis resorted to "dumping" groups of Jews without papers across borders or aboard outward-bound ships. By the outbreak of the Second World War in September 1939, only about half of the approximately 757,000 German and Austrian Jews had managed to emigrate from Hitler's expanding empire.

Emigration or else deportation remained the Nazi solutions to the "Jewish problem" for more than a year after the outbreak of war. Nazi officials discussed sending all of Europe's Jews to the French-held island of Madagascar in the Indian Ocean or else to Siberia as soon as victory was won. Hence the large numbers of Polish Jews who had come under Nazi control were concentrated in cities and large towns and subjected to brutal forced labor, but rarely anything worse. But in Germany the government began secretly to gas its own physically and mentally handicapped citizens. Unofficially named "T4," this "Euthanasia" Program was designed to purify the German race from within and free resources for the war effort. Although word leaked out and Hitler formally called it off in August 1941, it continued informally until the end of the war and took a total of 150,000 lives.

Meanwhile, Jews in Hitler's enlarged "Greater Germany" began to be removed to ghettos in occupied Poland or, in smaller numbers, to France for eventual deportation abroad. What ultimately made such deportation impossible was Hitler's failure to bring his war to a successful conclusion. Unable to defeat or reach a negotiated settlement with Great Britain, Hitler turned his armies against the Soviet Union in June 1941. At the same time the mass murder of Soviet Jews began. The German forces that swept across eastern Poland and into the USSR were followed immediately by the mobile killing units called *Einsatzgruppen* (special action groups) under the command of the SS, which was the chief agency of terror throughout Nazi-dominated Europe. These units were assigned the task of liquidating all known or potential enemies of the Third Reich, especially political officials, Communist party functionaries, Gypsies, and Jews. Typically the *Einsatzgruppen* herded their victims into fields to be shot and buried in mass graves, as happened to 33,000, most of them Jews, at Babi Yar just outside Kiev on September 29–30, 1941. Occasionally the killers enlisted local nationalists to help do their work for them. Altogether the 3,000 members of the *Einsatzgruppen* took the lives of between one and two million Jews and Gypsies.

Although the *Einsatzgruppen* continued their murderous sweeps on the eastern front into the later war years, they were never adequate to cope with all of the potential victims. As early as July 1941 Hermann Göring ordered Reinhard Heydrich, after Heinrich Himmler the most powerful SS leader, to formulate a "comprehensive solution to the Jewish problem." Heydrich's plan, presented in secrecy at a conference of top Nazi officials held in the Berlin suburb of Wannsee in January 1942, called for the SS to deport all the European Jews to Eastern Europe and force them to work in ghettos and labor camps. Those who were too young, too old, too weak, or simply not needed for work were sent to newly constructed extermination centers according to carefully calculated timetables corresponding to the camps' capacities. Although not mentioned in the original plan, many Gypsies came to share the same fate as the Jews.

The Jewish ghettos of such cities as Warsaw, Lodz, Vilna, and Minsk were hideously overcrowded places of starvation, backbreaking labor, disease, and death. Smuggling alone enabled their inhabitants to survive. The exception, and then only in relative terms, was the Theresienstadt ghetto in Czechoslovakia, where prominent prisoners were held under model conditions to fool the International Red Cross and other inquisitive foreigners. The Germans assigned control of the ghettos to Jewish Councils that governed with the aid of Jewish police. The Germans maintained overall control by executing uncooperative Jewish leaders and by holding the ghetto residents to "collective responsibility," shooting the family and friends of those who resisted or escaped. Only rarely did the Jewish Councils themselves resist, preferring to buy time by producing goods that were badly needed by the Nazi war machine. The one major ghetto uprising, that in Warsaw in April and May 1943, came only after most of its occupants had been transported to extermination camps. Hopes of saving at least a remnant of the Jewish communities were dashed when the last of the ghettos were liquidated in the summer of 1944, shortly before the arrival of the Soviet Army. Their pitiful remnants were sent to labor and extermination camps closer to Germany.

The extermination centers, all located in territory conquered from Poland, were of two kinds. Chelmno and the "Operation Reinhard" camps[2] of Treblinka, Belzec, and Sobibor were devoted exclusively to

---

[2]They came to be so-named for Reinhard Heydrich after his assassination by Czech resistance fighters near Prague in May 1942.

extermination. Except for small crews of slave workers who disposed of the corpses, the victims were gassed immediately on their arrival. The Nazis were already experienced in the use of gas chambers, having employed them in the T4 "Euthanasia" Program. Experimental gassings of Soviet POWs at Auschwitz and of Jews and Gypsies at Chelmno had occurred late in 1941. By the time all four extermination centers were shut down late in 1943, they had claimed approximately 1,900,000 lives. The great majority of the victims were Jews.

Auschwitz and Maidanek, on the other hand, were both killing and slave labor centers. New arrivals were selected for work or immediate death. Auschwitz, by far the larger of the two, had been founded in 1940 as a concentration camp for first Polish and then Soviet POWs. During the Holocaust it grew to occupy several square miles covered by huge synthetic rubber and oil factories, various smaller military industries, administration buildings, and barracks for the more than 70,000 prisoners. At Auschwitz-Birkenau, gas chambers and crematoria disposed of at least a million victims, most of them Jewish, before they ceased to function in November 1944. A few of the prisoners were chosen by SS doctors for hideous medical experiments that resulted in painful deaths and permanent mutilations. For those selected for work, labor in the factories and the outlying farms and coal mines was hell.

Similar conditions prevailed in hundreds of forced labor camps scattered throughout German-dominated Europe. Tens of thousands of prisoners were literally worked to death, to be replaced from the constant inflow of new slaves. Some were resourceful enough, or lucky enough, to land desirable positions in the camp kitchens, offices, or medical wards. All were deprived of adequate food, clothing, rest, privacy, and human dignity.

As Hitler's empire crumbled, the pathetic survivors of the camps were force-marched to concentration and slave labor facilities in Germany itself. There, in the final frantic days of the war their food was cut off, and many died of starvation and disease. When British and American forces liberated such camps as Bergen-Belsen, Dachau, and Buchenwald, the grounds were strewn with the dead and dying. Estimates of the Jewish dead from all causes—shootings, gassings, overwork, and general privation—range from just under five million to nearly six million. These were not the only innocent victims of Nazi racial madness. Tens of thousands of Gypsies and millions of Eastern European civilians and Soviet POWs died at German hands.

The enormity of the Holocaust was not fully apparent to the world in the immediate postwar years. At the Nuremberg trials of the major German war criminals it was treated as part of Nazi crimes against humanity in general. Survivors set down their experiences in memoirs, and the Yad Vashem research institute established in Jerusalem in 1953 painstakingly assembled documentary evidence of Nazi efforts to eradicate the Jews. But not until the 1960s did the Holocaust become genuinely visible to scholars, students, and the general public.

The trial of Adolf Eichmann in 1961 is usually regarded as the turning point. Eichmann, the SS expert on Jewish affairs who had organized the transportation of Jews and Gypsies from all over Europe to the extermination camps, escaped to Argentina after the war. He was discovered and kidnapped by Israeli agents, and his trial in Jerusalem created a sensation. Also in the year of the Eichmann trial Raul Hilberg's *The Destruction of the European Jews* made its appearance. The first massively documented history of the Holocaust, it remains today in a revised version one of the standard works on the subject. Since then thousands of books and articles on the Holocaust have appeared, making it one of the best-documented events in recent history. Efforts to deny that it ever happened can safely be regarded as the work of malicious zealots.

With the main features of the Holocaust clearly visible to all but the willfully blind, historians have turned their attention to aspects of the story for which the evidence is incomplete or ambiguous. These are not minor matters by any means, but turn on such issues as the origins and scope of the Holocaust, Jewish responses to persecution, and reactions by onlookers both inside and outside Nazi-controlled Europe. This anthology presents selected points of view on these issues with the goal of sketching the broad outlines of the debates and the trends in historiography. Readers are urged to suppress the perhaps natural inclination to suppose that all of these well-crafted arguments are equally valid, since, as we shall see, historians sometimes evaluate the evidence in very different ways. Nor should anyone feel compelled arbitrarily to adopt one position or another. Comparing historical interpretations sheds light on the process by which we come closer to the truth through inquiry and debate. If, as is hoped, it stimulates thought and curiosity about the Holocaust, useful titles are given in the "Suggestions for Additional Reading" at the end of this volume.

Jews and Gypsies were systematically segregated and humiliated in Nazi Germany. Here a non-Jewish woman and her Jewish boyfriend are forced to wear degrading signs admitting their "racial crimes." Photograph © Keystone / The Image Works

Origins of the Holocaust

Variety of Opinion

> [Anti-Semitism made Hitler] the most popular leader of the most popular party modern Germany had ever seen. It is time to stop believing that "without Hitler, no Holocaust."
>
> John Weiss

> [W]ithout Hitler, and the unique regime he headed, the creation of a programme to bring about the physical extermination of the Jews of Europe would have been unthinkable.
>
> Ian Kershaw

> The entire killing enterprise had started in January 1940 with the murder of . . . institutionalized handicapped patients, had expanded in 1941 to include Jews and Gypsies, and had by 1945 cost the lives of at least 6 million men, women and children.
>
> Henry Friedlander

What brought the Holocaust about? Some scholars have sought the answer to this question in long-term historical trends, and especially in the long history of European antisemitism. Others locate the key to the Holocaust in more immediate factors, such as the pathological personality of Adolf Hitler and the influence of modern "scientific" racism.

John Weiss traces the outrages of modern antisemitism and the Holocaust to the negative image of the Jews that was deeply ingrained over many centuries. He identifies five major sources of stereotypes that had made Jews an unpopular minority throughout Europe and, he argues, especially in Germany and Austria. Locating the primary sources of the Holocaust in a culture of hatred that was a specific feature of German history, Weiss attributes Hitler's rise to power to his success at blaming the Jews for everything: defeat, inflation, depression, and Communism. Antisemitism was the key to Nazi appeals to German voters. Hitler was less the author of genocide than the tool chosen by the German masses to eliminate the Jews; Weiss specifically repudiates the view that no one but Hitler would have carried out the Holocaust. This is an influential but controversial argument. If Germans harbored such intense loathing for the Jews, why were no substantial steps taken against them before Hitler came to power in 1933?

Ian Kershaw argues that the key to the Holocaust lies in Adolf Hitler's murderous racial hatred combined with his absolute control over Germany. Without Hitler antisemitism probably would have ended in legal discrimination, not genocide. Other scholars have argued that Hitler was in some ways a "weak dictator" who concentrated on military and foreign affairs while leaving racial matters to other party and state officials. It was they, these scholars suggest, who engaged in a competitive process of "cumulative radicalization" that in 1941 culminated in the Holocaust. Kershaw disagrees. He admits that there were escalating lower-level initiatives, but he stresses Hitler's personal knowledge and approval of policies designed to eliminate the Jews. The dictator may not consciously have planned genocide all along, but the mass murder of the Jews was always latent in his thinking. Only wartime conditions were required to make it manifest. In the portion of Kershaw's Hitler biography included here, a discussion of Hitler's behavior at the time of Crystal Night (the "November Pogrom" of 1938) broadens into a general analysis of his obsession with the Jews, particularly in the fall of 1941 when their fate was being determined. In disagreement with historians who have argued that Hitler decided on genocide in his euphoria in victory during the first few months of his invasion of the USSR (June–October, 1941),

Kershaw sees the gradual emergence of an annihilation plan from then into 1942. It was beginning to dawn on Hitler that the Soviet Union was not a pushover and victory was no longer certain. The Jews would have to pay!

Henry Friedlander broadens the definition of the Holocaust by pointing out that the first victims of Nazi genocide were physically and mentally handicapped Germans. They and the Gypsies shared with the Jews the fate of exclusion from the German community and eventual gassing, and for the same reason—heredity. The handicapped, viewed by Nazis as carriers of defective genes, had to be prevented from passing them on to subsequent generations. The Gypsies, considered racially degenerate but less dangerous than the Jews, were at first persecuted selectively. But by 1943, says Friedlander, they were in practice treated in the same way as the Jews. All three groups were biologically selected for mass murder. In tracing the Holocaust to modern "scientific" racism and its view that society can be improved by eliminating *all* undesirable elements from the gene pool, Friedlander insists that we view Nazism as a coherent whole, aimed at the total racial purification of the Third Reich. Such a view may also shed light on the fate of other "racially undesirable" groups, including millions of Soviet POWs and Eastern European civilians who died at the hands of the Germans during World War II. Friedlander questions whether we can fully understand the Holocaust if we confine our attention to antisemitism and the fate of the Jews. His critics, however, aver that only the Jews were singled out by the Nazis for total annihilation and warn against anything that might detract from the particular dimensions and characteristics of the Jewish tragedy.

Antisemitism, Hitler, and "scientific" racism must be included in any explanation of Holocaust origins, but they may not all be equally crucial. Simply listing them leaves important questions unanswered. Is antisemitism by itself a sufficient explanation of the Holocaust? Does focusing on Hitler risk reducing Nazi genocide to the product of a single diseased mind? Does acknowledging Nazism's broadly biological-racist ideology oblige us to widen our definition of the Holocaust to include other victims besides the Jews?

John Weiss

Anti-Semitism Through the Ages

For more than a thousand years Jews have been accused of following a false and immoral religion and preferring deceitful commercial practices and usurious moneylending to honest work in field and factory. Jews have been accused of being loyal only to their own people and to enemies of any nation foolish enough to grant them hospitality or citizenship. The most extreme anti-Semites have insisted that throughout history the Jews have waged war against Gentiles, that they are international conspirators whose depraved traits are innate, "racial," and unchangeable. Such stereotypes still exist, of course, but only among those who, in the West at least, rate lowest in education, achievement, and political power. Consequently it is extremely difficult for educated and tolerant Westerners to imagine the dangerous power that anti-Semitism has enjoyed in modern Europe and impossible to grasp how it could have led to the unique and unimaginable horrors of the Holocaust.

A study of the origins and history of anti-Semitism by itself helps but little. To fully grasp the dangerous potential of racism we must also know the relationships between the fantasies of the anti-Semites and the long-term historical development of various nations, relationships that gave or denied racists the power to harm their Jewish communities. It is important to witness and remember, but it is essential to explain. Without more knowledge of its long-term historical causes, the Holocaust may well end as an inexplicable enigma, a searing and bitter memory of horror kept alive chiefly within the Jewish community. As such, the Holocaust will offer little help to those who hope to learn from its causes possible ways to avoid future if lesser mass murders with different killers and victims.

In European civilization there were five major sources of anti-Semitism. Christian anti-Semitism was the first, though today the vast majority of Christians reject it, and hostility to Jews was obviously never the message of Christ. As he said, it is not enough to love your neighbor, "You must love your enemies . . ." (Matthew 5:44–46). And of course he never thought of his own people as his enemies, only some of their religious leaders. The earliest Christians were Jews who believed that Jesus was the Messiah promised by the Hebrew Scriptures, the Christian Old Testament. They followed Jewish law, attended synagogue, and hoped to persuade their coreligionists that Christ was the awaited Messiah whose sacrifice on the cross would redeem the sins of all who accepted him as their savior.

The breach between the two communities began when St. Paul preached that obedience to Jewish law was futile without faith in Christ. By the end of the second century, Gentiles dominated the church and ignored Jewish law, but they did not believe Christianity was a new religion. For them Jesus was the culmination of Judaism, and those who accepted him were the new chosen people. The vast majority of Jews rejected Christ, of course, and thus the seeds of antagonism were sown, for the truth of Christianity seemed to depend on Old Testament prophecy, yet the Jewish community regarded Christ as a heretic and false Messiah.

In those days history seemed to be a scenario written by God, as the extreme fundamentalists and ultra-orthodox of the major religions still believe. Thus the failure of the Jews to accept Christ, St. Paul contended, must be the work of the Lord Himself; mere men could not possibly resist his divine truth. Until the Jews converted, they would suffer a bitter fate, a lesson to all who refused to accept Christ. Eventually the Lord would bring the Jews to convert, the ultimate proof of Christianity and a necessary prelude to Judgment Day.

The first Christians expected the conversion of the Jews and Christ's Second Coming momentarily. But by the third and fourth centuries after Christ, many of the most famous and saintly Christian leaders found no insult too gross to hurl at the Jews, denouncing them as an obstinate, arrogant people who denied their own God, dangerous examples to Christians if allowed to live among them. With time, the fury of the Christian masses intensified, for the truth of Christianity still seemed to depend on the conversion of the Jews. By the tenth century ordinary Christians, priests, and many higher clergy believed the Jews were literally a satanic people. Where else could they gain the power to resist the will of their own Messiah? Had they not called for Christ's death after a Jewish court convicted him of heresy? (There is no evidence that these events actually occurred. The Gospels are theology, not history, and were written long after Christ's death by persons who could not have known him.)

It did not help to tell ordinary Christians, as church leaders did, that the fate of the Jews must be left to the Lord, for they also taught that the Lord works through the deeds of mankind. Yet according to Christian theology, Christ's death was not caused by human will; the Lord foreordained his crucifixion and the miracle of his resurrection. In addition, during Christ's lifetime most Jews did not live in Palestine and had never heard of Christ. Too, his apostles were Jews, and the Gospels tell of large crowds greeting him when he entered Palestine. Nevertheless to ordinary Christians unaccustomed to theological niceties, the charge of "Christ-killers" echoed down through the ages to cause the Jews countless miseries. Thus the burst of religious passion that brought the Crusades of the later Middle Ages nearly destroyed the Jewish communities of Western Europe.

In the latter half of the twentieth century even those mainstream Christian leaders who believed Judaism to be a false religion no longer accused "the Jews" of having killed Christ; liberal Christian theologians now reject the idea out of hand. Wherever strong traditions of toleration and humanism prevail, the clergy of all but a few obscure cults today oppose harming Jews. Nor should Christian anti-Semites be confused with those who believe Jews to be innately evil because of their "blood" or "race." Even during the Crusades, Jews could save themselves by converting, something racists do not admit. And during the Holocaust, innumerable Christians of all denominations protested the killings, and thousands risked death to aid the Jews of Europe. Still, in the nineteenth century Christian hostility reinforced racist anti-Semitic movements, and in some nations—notably Poland and Austria—it helped create a culture that allowed them to flourish.

A second major source of anti-Semitism in Europe was commercial. Jews were plagued for centuries by accusations that they innately preferred to exploit and manipulate others through dishonest commercial practices and usurious moneylending. The accusations confuse the results of oppression with alleged racial traits. Jews originally migrated to Europe as traders from the advanced civilizations of the East. As centuries passed, many became peasants, warriors, craftsmen, and even nobles—as Jews were in the East. But after the fall of Rome, the dominant European feudal authorities, influenced by the clergy, gradually excluded Jews from state and military service and landowning. Heretics and Christ-killers, clerics insisted, could not hold positions of power over Christians.

Jews were also forbidden to join artisans' guilds. Composed of skilled craftsmen and small merchants, the guilds were the dominant form of enterprise in pre-industrial Europe, authorized to license those who entered a trade and to control market share, prices, wages, and product quality. Although the guilds had Christian patron saints and rituals, their basic motive was to restrict Jewish competition and persuade rulers to support the restrictions. In medieval Europe and later, Christian small businessmen could rarely compete with Jewish traders who had maintained mercantile and linguistic connections with the East, where the most desired products and commercial skills were located. Consequently European Jews were gradually limited to petty commerce and moneylending, barring a handful who served as financial agents for princes. The general population, illiterate and ignorant, easily confused the results of past oppression with innate Jewish traits. By the seventeenth century, ghettos were common and Jews assumed to be fit only for the lowest forms of commerce.

The eighteenth-century Enlightenment challenged traditional attitudes toward Jews. Basing their ideas on the new science of the seventeenth century, the new thinkers inferred that religious mythology was not divinely revealed but a human creation. Hence they argued for religious toleration and the separation of church and state. They believed that environment, experience, and education, not innate or "racial" traits, formed character. They valued free enterprise and wanted entrepreneurs freed from guild restrictions. Increasingly a burgeoning and pragmatic middle class in France, Great Britain, Italy, Scandinavia, and colonial America supported these ideas. Inspired by the Enlightenment, the leaders of the French Revolution of 1789 legislated equality before the law and attacked the old order of absolute monarchs, privileged aristocrats, guild monopolies, serfdom, and the extensive secular powers of a wealthy church. When the Revolution turned more radical in 1791, the Jews of France were liberated from all legal disabilities. By the 1860s the Jews of Western Europe were liberated, though still subject to much informal discrimination.

The association of Jews with liberal and progressive movements in modern Europe was a third source of anti-Semitism. Secular liberalism offered Jews freedom from religious persecution while their new status as free citizens offered the prospect of eventual full assimilation in a future democratic society. Aided by liberal free enterprise, Jews were no longer limited to marginal economic pursuits. They easily adapted to the new commercial expansion because of their extensive experience in commerce and trade.

In the 1870s and later, aristocrats, clergy, and guilds organized to defend their powers and values against the threatened rise of an urban, commercial, and democratic social order, and often held Jews responsible because of their prominence in commerce, the professions, and liberal and progressive movements. Royalists, aristocratic landowners, high civil servants, and military officers discriminated against Jews and used anti-Semitism to gain popular support. In Austria, Germany, and Eastern Europe, guild artisans supported extremist anti-Semitic movements, blaming Jews for the threat that free enterprise posed to their old monopolies and the new technology that made their traditional skills obsolete. Excluded from guilds, Jews had pioneered in new products, sales techniques, and large-scale merchandising beyond guild control. Small-scale merchants and handicraft shops often lacked the capital, the capability, or the will to adjust. When liberal politicians denounced guild restrictions that hindered economic growth, conservatives defended them as necessary for economic stability. By the 1800s, anti-Semitic movements tried to boycott, limit, or outlaw Jewish enterprises. But many progressives welcomed new enterprises because they lowered consumer prices and helped them challenge the power and privileges of their aristocratic opponents.

In the later nineteenth century, subsistence peasants and small landowners found it difficult to adjust to the opening of national and international markets created by railways and ocean transport. In Germany and Eastern Europe, Jews—for centuries excluded from landowning—were often dealers in cattle, farm machinery, fertilizer, and agrarian products. The naturally antagonistic relationship between buyers and sellers easily translated into anti-Semitism when hard times brought low prices for farm products and high prices for farm needs, and when cheap agrarian imports flooded the market. Peasants often fell into debt to finance the production of cash crops for new markets, and established bankers found it far too risky to lend to them. Consequently middlemen—often Jewish—were lenders of last resort, and charged high interest to cover their many losses through defaults, reinforcing the image of the usurious Jew.

The strong presence of Jews in the modern sectors of the new capitalist economies also made it convenient for anti-Semites to persuade those with no knowledge of economic complexities that Jews were responsible for depressions. But the small number of Jews — about 1 percent (excluding the Austrian Empire with just over 4 percent) — made it impossible for them to dominate the economy, and in any event capitalists follow the laws of the market, not unique ethnic or religious rules.

Physicians, lawyers, and students often supported anti-Semitism when faced with strong competition from Jewish students who, liberated from the ghetto, flocked to the study of law and medicine. Private practice freed them from the discrimination often found in state and corporate bureaucracies, the military, teaching, and the judiciary. Science and mathematics also attracted Jewish students. Scientific skills are portable and hard to ignore; the language of math and physics is international, not ethnic. But the study of history and literature was strongly nationalistic in the nineteenth century, and many academics refused to believe that a Jew could truly understand the historical or literary expression of the unique spirit of Christian peoples. Hence the predominance of assimilated German and Hungarian Jews in physics and mathematics at the turn of the century, and the prominence of assimilated European Jews among winners of the Nobel Prize.

Anthropology was a fourth source of European anti-Semitism and racism in the nineteenth century. Academics and best-selling writers believed there were different races with different physical characteristics and inborn intellectual and even moral capacities. They ignored the force of thousands of years of group isolation, sexual selection, climatic influences, and the power of society, experience, and upbringing on character, intelligence, and morality. Geneticists now know that differences between ethnic groups are tiny, including IQ, as compared to the vast variations within ethnic groups. Ethnic differences in test scores, for example, are either marginal or the result of individual inheritance as well as education, class advantage, social experience, and family influence. But only since the 1950s have most intellectuals and cultural leaders discredited the idea of fixed races with inherent traits. Historical experience has also forced changes. In Israel, for example, Jews work in almost every occupation and trade and possess the widest possible range of abilities, incomes, and physical types of perhaps any nation.

But in the later nineteenth century, anthropology gave scientific validity to educated people who wished to use racism to justify imperialism, competitive capitalism, discrimination, segregation, slavery, and conquest in war—the ultimate struggle for survival of the "most favored races." Long before the Nazis, anthropologists popularized invidious comparisons between, among others, Semites and Aryans. Textbooks often featured such ideas, and in some nations—notably Germany, Austria, and Eastern Europe—university students and high school teachers were quite prominent among the leaders and followers of anti-Semitic movements. Those who read the textbooks of the time do not wonder why so many well-educated people could support racism and anti-Semitism.

The fifth source of anti-Semitism, especially powerful in Central and Eastern Europe, was ethnic nationalism. Until the 1850s the French Revolution had determined that demands for national liberation would be accompanied by calls for human rights and democratic reforms. But when revolutionary and idealistic liberal nationalists in the East were defeated by the armies of the Ottoman, Austrian, and Russian empires, many intellectuals among the oppressed minority nations turned to an exclusive and harshly militant ethnic nationalism. Reviving the ancient language, culture, and customs of their peoples, they lauded their ancestors as a race of sturdy peasants and valiant warriors who battled to forge a free nation against tyrannical imperialists. Popular writers enshrined these idealized heroic deeds and names in stirring and bloody epics, poems, and songs; many are used still today to inspire "ethnic cleansers" in the Balkans. Ancient claims to a "greater Serbia," a "greater Hungary," or a "greater Poland," among others, were resurrected. But such claims and counterclaims necessarily encompassed territories containing other ethnic minorities with their own demands for independence. With the decay of the tsarist, Habsburg, and Ottoman empires, ethnic conflicts against them gave way to ethnic struggles among the minorities themselves, as newly free ethnic groups sought to assimilate minorities within their territories by force.

Jews were more vulnerable than other ethnic groups. They could claim no territories of their own, followed a despised religion, composed only about 10 percent of the population in the East, and were extremely prominent in the modern sectors of the economy.

Consequently ethnic nationalists denounced the influence of Jewish financiers, bankers, merchants, teachers, journalists, and cultural activists, reviling the Jews' alleged rootless urban cosmopolitanism, subversive values, and pacifism. Above all they insisted that the blood of the people must be kept pure—an impossible notion with fatal implications. Jews were even more at risk in the 1914–1918 war and after when governments inflamed all kinds of ethnic antagonisms to justify terrible civilian sacrifices, while postwar border settlements inevitably favored one ethnic group at the expense of another.

Democratic socialism, influential by the 1890s, was a counterforce to ethnic nationalism and religious discrimination. Defiantly secular, socialists blamed the capitalist system, not any ethnic group, for social misery and rejected ethnic nationalism as a delusion. Although he was an anti-Semite in his youth, Karl Marx did not embody anti-Semitism in Marxism, and he also rejected nationalism. As he wrote in the Communist Manifesto, "The Proletariat has no Fatherland." In 1890 Friedrich Engels, Marx's partner, declared anti-Semitism a reactionary attempt to divert attention away from the evils of capitalism—the official Marxist and Social Democratic position. Reactionaries, as Hitler would later do, insisted that socialism was an invention of unpatriotic and rootless Jews who manipulated honest "Aryan" workers in order to subvert and dominate traditional society. To make the case, one had to ignore the fact that some 90 percent of Western European Jewry supported liberal—not socialist—parties except in the Austrian Empire and the East, where liberalism was effectively dead long before 1914 because of raging ethnic conflicts.

With the important exception of Italian fascism, the most extreme anti-Semites in Europe tended to join fascist movements. The basis for fascist ideology was created in late-nineteenth-century Germany, Austria, and Eastern Europe. Race and blood, nationalists held, determined that they were descended from forest tribes composed of noble warriors and productive peasants. Semites were their natural enemies, a people that originated in the hostile and sterile deserts of the Middle East and were therefore drawn to the city and "parasitic" commerce. As revolutionary reactionaries, fascists hoped to launch violent and ultra-nationalist attacks against liberalism, democracy, socialism, and communism—condemned as the work of subversive Jews hoping to destroy traditional values and even pollute the blood of Aryans through racial mixing.

Like almost everyone except socialists, fascists despised women's liberation and homosexuality, but they blamed both on leftist "Hebrew women" and cowardly Jewish males trying to destroy the patriarchal institutions needed for a stable society and a strong military. Gypsies were (and still are) despised, but fascists believed them to be a degenerate race unworthy of life; the Nazis tried to exterminate both Gypsies and homosexuals. When Bolsheviks overthrew the new democratic Russian government in 1917, anti-Semites, not only fascists, added "Judeo-bolshevism" to the stereotype of the evil Jew. But fascists should not be confused with authoritarian nationalist leaders, men like Francisco Franco of Spain or Miklos Horthy of Hungary. Unlike authoritarian nationalists, including Benito Mussolini, fascists wished to reduce Jews to a ghetto existence, drive them from the nation, or worse. When threats to the powers and interests of traditional reactionary elites arose, however, authoritarian nationalists often supported fascism.

Fascists did not, as is commonly thought, regard the Jews as subhuman but as a powerful, cunning, and dangerous race who had survived and even prospered in spite of centuries of Christian persecution. German, Austrian, Romanian, Hungarian, Polish, and Croatian fascists alike insisted that the inevitable racial war against the Jews could be won only by ignoring traditional humanitarian illusions in order to destroy a people that would otherwise create and inevitably dominate a degenerate democratic, liberal, and commercial society. For fascists, war embodied heroic idealism and the nobility of sacrifice for the common good, as opposed to the liberal bourgeois desire for individualism, creature comforts, and endless ignoble compromises with their antagonists. Peace was seen as a despicable notion of Jewish merchants and leftists who knew they could never conquer "Aryans" except by economic manipulation and political subversion. Consequently many military officers and veterans supported fascist movements—men who, like Hitler, viewed politics as a military confrontation with enemies who must be destroyed.

Those who have grown up in liberal societies find the grisly terror of Nazis, fascists, and contemporary "ethnic cleansers" impossible to understand; thus we often view the murderers as small groups of psychotic criminals. Many even argue that all of us have the same potential for evil. True or not, it still takes specific historical circumstances to foster this alleged potential. Others attribute the murderous crimes of fascists to the rise to power in times of social trauma of a few obsessed, charismatic leaders who can manipulate hatreds. But this does not explain why such high percentages of the population in the 1930s—one-third in Germany, and more in Austria and Eastern Europe—eagerly believed that the Jews were responsible for all social and economic ills, and wanted them stopped, one way or another. However difficult it may be, we must recognize that even the Nazis were not psychotic brutes but often highly educated, sincere believers who led ordinary lives in spite of their unbelievably bloody deeds against "racial" enemies.

Whatever the myths or goals of anti-Semites and fascists, their hope for political power was directly related to the general history of the nation in which they lived, including, of course, the history and place of the Jewish community within it. It is not enough simply to narrate the history of anti-Semitic ideas or estimate how many believed them. Nor are different forms of anti-Semitism of equal impact. Christian anti-Semitism, for example, was distinctly unpopular among the Lutheran and Calvinist clergy of Scandinavian nations, and racism was rejected by the majority of Christians, including Pope Pius XI, though Judaism was not accepted as a valid religion. Nor do ethnic hatreds thrive simply because they have a long history; they must be encouraged by demagogues and manipulated by politicians. Even where millions of anti-Semites exist, as in France and the United States from 1919 to 1939, they often belong to groups and classes that cannot unite or gain access to power. Above all, anti-Semitism can thrive only where the ideas and values that oppose it are too weak to oppose the racism of rulers and electorates.

That is why we must know the relationships between political anti-Semitism, fascism, and the general history of nations. Therein lie the answers to our questions: Why did Germany initiate the Holocaust? Why did Austrians supply so many killers? Why is it that a million French fascists could not gain sufficient power to help destroy the Jews until the German conquest put the Vichy government in power? Why did fascist Italy not cooperate in the massacre of the Jews until Mussolini had lost the war? Why was anti-Semitism, as Poland illustrates, far stronger in Eastern than in Western Europe? The answers will help us understand why the politics of racial hate succeeds, and what can be done about it. The Holocaust was unique, but its historical origins tell us much that can help us in the battle against present and future horrors by other perpetrators with different victims. . . .

Their endless attacks on the Jews brought the Nazis the high-est percentage of votes in modern German history, a mandate for violence. From the earliest years, no Nazi campaign appeal, if only indirectly, failed to hold the Jews responsible for all of Germany's problems. Inventing nothing new, the Nazis' secret was their ability to integrate traditional racism with the practical demands of traditional lower-middle- and upper-class conservatives, and thereby coopt the constituencies of numerous rival movements that spoke only to a single class. In the elections of [1928] small anti-Semitic parties, middle-class or peasant, won more than fifty seats in the Reichstag; in 1932 they were wiped out—their voters had moved to Hitler. In the Sudeten-land, Henlein's Sudeten German party, even more anti-Semitic than the Nazis, won 60 percent of the vote in 1934. There is no longer any reason to doubt the crucial role racism played in Nazi victories. Any German who could read or hear knew that for the Nazis, all issues were racial issues. And their campaign literature bristled with metaphors of death: the Jews were a virus, a cancer, a plague infecting every social organ. Germany's miseries were the symptoms, the Jews were the dis-ease. There could be no cure as long as the Jews remained. In spite of laws against it, some posters called for death: "Annihilate the gravedig-gers of the *Mittelstand!*" "Our day of reckoning with the Jews . . . [will come] when we have the power of the state in our hands to carry out a thorough annihilation of this international racial parasite." By 1930 one could not live in Berlin, Munich, Vienna, or the smallest village without knowing the Nazis would take revenge on the Jews, a promise trumpeted again and again in thousands of rallies and millions of leaf-lets and posters. "Death to the Jews" was a common chant at Nazi ral-lies; *Juda verrecka!* was *the* Nazi slogan, a crude phrase referring to the slaughter of beasts. The very reason for choosing the Nazis rather than older reactionaries was their activism and violence, evidence of their sincerity. Some may not have believed them, and none could predict the scale of the Final Solution because it depended on success in war. But no German could be ignorant of the Nazis' promise to destroy the Jews. It was never a secret.

Those who later protested that they supported the Nazis without suspecting how far they might go presume on our liberal conscious-ness, which finds it impossible to imagine the deliberate murder of millions of innocents. Those Germans—and there were millions, in-cluding Jews and socialists—who shared liberal values and an inability to imagine such a horror, never supported the Nazis. For the others, it was not difficult to imagine the probable fate of the Jews. The Nazis said it again and again: Jews would not own land, banks, or businesses, they would be driven from commerce, government service, teaching, law, and medicine, their citizenship would be taken from them, their young would not be educated, their wealth and property would be expropriated; if they left Germany, they would leave penniless.

Did Nazi voters, who must have thought all reasonable people were anti-Semites, really imagine the world would welcome masses of penniless Jewish refugees? What did Nazi supporters think would happen to the Jews? Forced emigration, prison camps, or death were the only alternatives. And even forced emigration only added to the power of "world Jewry," as Hitler and Eichmann declared when saddled with millions of Jews in the east. Given Nazi campaign literature and rhetoric, their voters, we can safely assume, voted for a racial revolution that meant physical harm to the Jews. To these voters, without such a revolution no German problem could be resolved. Anti-Semitism was never just one issue among many; indeed, it would be less of a distortion to say there were no other issues. And with that issue, by 1932 Hitler became the most popular leader of the most popular party modern Germany had ever seen. It is time to stop believing that "without Hitler, no Holocaust."

Ian Kershaw

Hitler's Decisive Role

The open brutality of the November Pogrom, the round-up and incarceration of some 30,000 Jews that followed it, and the draconian measures to force Jews out of the economy had, Goebbels's diary entries make plain, all been explicitly approved by Hitler even if the initiatives had come from others, above all from the Propaganda Minister himself.

To those who saw him late on the evening of 9 November, Hitler had appeared to be shocked and angry at the reports reaching him of what was happening. Himmler, highly critical of Goebbels, was given the impression that Hitler was surprised by what he was hearing when Himmler's chief adjutant Karl Wolff informed them of the burning of the Munich synagogue just before 11.30 that evening. Nicolaus von Below, Hitler's Luftwaffe adjutant, who saw him immediately on his return to his apartment from the "Old Town Hall," was convinced that there was no dissembling in his apparent anger and condemnation of the destruction. Speer[1] was told by a seemingly regretful and somewhat embarrassed Hitler that he had not wanted the "excesses." Speer thought Goebbels had probably pushed him into it. Rosenberg,[2] a few weeks after the events, was convinced that Goebbels, whom he utterly detested, had "on the basis of a general decree (*Anordnung*) of the Führer ordered the action as it were in his name." Military leaders, equally ready to pin the blame on "that swine Goebbels," heard from Hitler that the "action" had taken place without his knowledge and that one of his Gauleiter had run out of control.

Was Hitler genuinely taken aback by the scale of the "action," for which he had himself given the green light that very evening? The agitated discussion with Goebbels in the Old Town Hall, like many other instances of blanket verbal authorization given in the unstructured and non-formalized style of reaching decisions in the Third Reich, probably left precise intentions open to interpretation. And certainly, in the course of the night, the welter of criticism from Göring, Himmler, and other leading Nazis made it evident that the "action" had got out of hand, become counter-productive, and had to be stopped—mainly on account of the material damage it had caused.

But when he consented to Goebbels's suggestion to "let the demonstrations continue," Hitler knew full well from the accounts from Hessen what the "demonstrations" amounted to. It took no imagination at all to foresee what would happen if active encouragement were given for a free-for-all against the Jews throughout the Reich. If Hitler had not intended the "demonstrations" he had approved to take such a course, what, exactly, had he intended? Even on the way to the Old Town

---

[1]Albert Speer, Hitler's architect and court favorite. —Ed.

[2]Alfred Rosenberg, the Nazi Party philosopher and Hitler's racial theorist. —Ed.

Hall, it seems, he had spoken against tough police action against anti-Jewish vandals in Munich. The traditional Stoßtrupp Hitler, bearing his own name, had been unleashed on Jewish property in Munich as soon as Goebbels had finished speaking. One of his closest underlings, Julius Schaub, had been in the thick of things with Goebbels, behaving like the Stoßtrupp fighter of old. During the days that followed, Hitler took care to remain equivocal. He did not praise Goebbels, or what had happened. But nor did he openly, even to his close circle, let alone in public, condemn him outright or categorically dissociate himself from the unpopular Propaganda Minister. Indeed, within a week Hitler was seen again in Goebbels's presence at a performance of *Kabale und Liebe* ("Intrigue and Love") at the opening of the Schiller Theatre, and stayed that night at the Goebbels's villa at Schwanenwerder. On that occasion, too, he "spoke harshly about the Jews." Goebbels had the feeling that his own policy against the Jews met with Hitler's full approval.

None of this has the ring of actions being taken against Hitler's will, or in opposition to his intentions. Rather, it seems to point, as Speer presumed, to Hitler's embarrassment when it became clear to him that the action he had approved was meeting with little but condemnation even in the highest circles of the regime. If Goebbels himself could feign anger at the burning of synagogues whose destruction he had himself directly incited, and even ordered, Hitler was certainly capable of such cynicism. What anger Hitler harboured was purely at an "action" that threatened to engulf him in the unpopularity he had failed to predict. Disbelieving that the Führer could have been responsible, his subordinate leaders were all happy to be deceived. They preferred the easier target of Goebbels, who had played the more visible role. From that night on, it was as if Hitler wanted to draw a veil over the whole business. At his speech in Munich to press representatives on the following evening, 10 November, he made not the slightest mention of the onslaught against the Jews. Even in his "inner circle," he never referred to "*Reichskristallnacht*" during the rest of his days. But although he had publicly distanced himself from what had taken place, Hitler had in fact favoured the most extreme steps at every juncture.

The signs are that "Crystal Night" had a profound impact upon Hitler. For at least two decades, probably longer, he had harboured feelings which fused fear and loathing into a pathological view of Jews as the incarnation of evil threatening German survival. Alongside the pragmatic reasons why Hitler agreed with Goebbels that the time was opportune to unleash the fury of the Nazi Movement against Jews ran the deeply embedded ideological urge to destroy what he saw as Germany's most implacable enemy, responsible in his mind for the war and its most tragic and damaging consequence for the Reich, the November Revolution. This demonization of the Jew and fear of the "Jewish world conspiracy" was part of a world-view that saw the random and despairing act of Herschel Grynszpan[3] as part of a plot to destroy the mighty German Reich. Hitler had by that time spent months at the epicentre of an international crisis that had brought Europe to the very brink of a new war. In the context of continuing crisis in foreign policy, with the prospect of international conflict never far away, "Crystal Night" seems to have re-invoked—certainly to have re-emphasized—the presumed links, present in his warped outlook since 1918–19 and fully expounded in *Mein Kampf*, between the power of the Jews and war.

He had commented in the last chapter of *Mein Kampf* that "the sacrifice of millions at the front" would not have been necessary if "twelve or fifteen thousand of these Hebrew corrupters of the people had been held under poison gas." Such rhetoric, appalling though the sentiments were, was not an indication that Hitler already had the "Final Solution" in mind. But the implicit genocidal link between war and the killing of Jews was there. Göring's remarks at the end of the meeting on 12 November had been an ominous pointer in the same direction: "If the German Reich comes into foreign-political conflict in the foreseeable future, it can be taken for granted that we in Germany will think in the first instance of bringing about a great showdown with the Jews."

With war approaching again, the question of the threat of the Jews in a future conflict was evidently present in Hitler's mind. The idea of using the Jews as hostages, part of Hitler's mentality, but also advanced in the SS's organ *Das Schwarze Korps* in October and November 1938, is testimony to the linkage between war and idea of a "world conspiracy." "The Jews living in Germany and Italy are the hostages which fate has placed in our hand so that we can defend ourselves effectively against the attacks of world Jewry," commented *Das Schwarze Korps* on 27 October 1938, under the headline "Eye for an Eye, Tooth for a Tooth." "Those

---

[3]The Jewish teenager whose assassination of a German diplomat in Paris had provided the pretext for Crystal Night.—Ed.

Jews in Germany are a part of world Jewry," the same newspaper threatened on 3 November, still days before the nationwide pogrom was unleashed. "They are also responsible for whatever world Jewry undertakes against Germany, and—they are liable for the damages which world Jewry inflicts and will inflict on us." The Jews were to be treated as members of a warring power and interned to prevent their engagement for the interests of world Jewry. Hitler had up to this date never attempted to deploy the "hostage" tactic as a weapon of his foreign policy. Perhaps promptings from the SS leadership now reawakened "hostage" notions in his mind. Whether or not this was the case, the potential deployment of German Jews as pawns to blackmail the western powers into accepting further German expansion was possibly the reason why, when stating that it was his "unshakeable will" to solve "the Jewish problem" in the near future, and at a time when official policy was to press for emigration with all means possible, he showed no interest in the plans advanced by South African Defence and Economics Minister Oswald Pirow, whom he met at the Berghof on 24 November, for international cooperation in the emigration of German Jews. The same motive was probably also behind the horrific threat he made to the Czechoslovakian Foreign Minister Franzisek Chvalkovsky on 21 January 1939. "The Jews here (*bei uns*) will be annihilated (*vernichtet*)," he declared. "The Jews had not brought about the 9 November 1918 for nothing. This day will be avenged."

Again, rhetoric should not be mistaken for a plan or programme. Hitler was scarcely likely to have revealed plans to exterminate the Jews which, when they did eventually emerge in 1941, were accorded top secrecy, in a comment to a foreign diplomat. Moreover, "annihilation" (*Vernichtung*) was one of Hitler's favourite words. He tended to reach for it when trying to impress his threats upon his audience, large or small. He would speak more than once the following summer, for instance, of his intention to "annihilate" the Poles. Horrific though their treatment was after 1939, no genocidal programme followed.

But the language, even so, was not meaningless. The germ of a possible genocidal outcome, however vaguely conceived, was taking shape. Destruction and annihilation, not just emigration, of the Jews was in the air. Already on 24 November *Das Schwarze Korps*, portraying the Jews as sinking ever more to the status of pauperized parasites and criminals, had concluded: "In the stage of such a development we would therefore be faced with the hard necessity of eradicating (*auszurotten*) the Jewish underworld just as we are accustomed in our ordered state (*Ordnungsstaat*) to eradicate criminals: with fire and sword! The result would be the actual and final end of Jewry in Germany, its complete annihilation (*Vernichtung*)." This was not a preview of Auschwitz and Treblinka. But without such a mentality, Auschwitz and Treblinka would not have been possible.

In his speech to the Reichstag on 30 January 1939, the sixth anniversary of his takeover of power, Hitler revealed publicly his implicitly genocidal association of the destruction of the Jews with the advent of another war. The "hostage" notion was probably built into his comments. And, as always, he obviously had an eye on the propaganda impact. But his words were more than propaganda. They gave an insight into the pathology of his mind, into the genocidal intent that was beginning to take hold. He had no idea how the war would bring about the destruction of the Jews. But, somehow, he was certain that this would indeed be the outcome of a new conflagration. "I have very often in my lifetime been a prophet," he declared, "and was mostly derided. In the time of my struggle for power it was in the first instance the Jewish people who received only with laughter my prophecies that I would some time take over the leadership of the state and of the entire people in Germany and then, among other things, also bring the Jewish problem to its solution. I believe that this once hollow laughter of Jewry in Germany has meanwhile already stuck in the throat. I want today to be a prophet again: if international finance Jewry inside and outside Europe should succeed in plunging the nations once more into a world war, the result will be not the bolshevization of the earth and thereby the victory of Jewry, but the annihilation (*Vernichtung*) of the Jewish race in Europe!" It was a "prophecy" that Hitler would return to on numerous occasions in the years 1941 and 1942, when the annihilation of the Jews was no longer terrible rhetoric, but terrible reality. . . .

Hitler's responsibility for the genocide against the Jews cannot be questioned. Yet for all his public tirades against the Jews, offering the strongest incitement to ever more radical onslaughts of extreme violence, and for all his dark hints that his "prophecy" was being fulfilled, he was consistently keen to conceal the traces of his involvement in the murder of the Jews. Perhaps even at the height of his own power he feared theirs, and the possibility one day of their "revenge." Perhaps, sensing that the German people were not ready to learn the deadly secret, he was determined—his own general inclination to secrecy was, as always, a marked one—not to speak of it other than in horrific, but imprecise, terms. Whatever the reasons, he could never have delivered the sort of speech which, notoriously, Himmler would give in Posen two years later when he described what it was like to see 1,000 corpses lying side by side and spoke openly of "the extermination (*Ausrottung*) of the Jewish people" as a "glorious page in our history that has never been written and is never to be written." Even in his inner circle Hitler could never bring himself to speak with outright frankness about the killing of the Jews. Full knowledge of their murder was evidently not to be touched upon directly in his presence, even among the close band of criminal conspirators.

Even so, compared with the first years of the war when he had neither in public nor—to go from Goebbels's diary accounts—in private made much mention of the Jews, Hitler did now, in the months when their fate was being determined, refer to them on numerous occasions. Invariably, whether in public speeches or during comments in his late-night monologues in his East Prussian headquarters, his remarks were confined to generalities—but with the occasional menacing allusion to what was happening.

At lunch on 6 October [1941], conversation focused mainly on eliminating Czech resistance following Heydrich's appointment on 27 September as Deputy Reich Protector. Hitler spoke of ways "to make the Czechs small." Shooting ten hostages for every act of sabotage where the perpetrator could not be found was one method. Another— as usual, the carrot as well as the stick—was to improve food rations in factories where there was no case of sabotage. His third means was the deportation of the Jews. He was speaking about three weeks after he had agreed to their deportation from the Reich and the Protectorate. His comments reveal at least one of the reasons why he agreed to deport them: he continued to believe in the Jews as dangerous "fifth-columnists," spreading sedition among the population. It was exactly what he had thought of the role of the Jews in Germany during the First World War. "All Jews must be removed from the Protectorate," he declared around the lunch-table, "and not just into the General Government, but straight away further to the east. This is at present not practical merely because of the great demand of the military for means of transport. Along with the Protectorate's Jews, all the Jews from Berlin and Vienna should disappear at the same time. The Jews are everywhere the pipeline through which all enemy news rushes with the speed of wind into all branches of the population."

On 21 October, a month after the deportation order, as part of a diatribe comparing "Jewish Christianity" with "Jewish Bolshevism," he compared the fall of Rome with latter-day Bolshevization through the Jews. "If we eradicate (*ausrotten*) this plague," he concluded, "we will be carrying out a good deed for mankind, of the significance of which our men out there can have no conception." Four days later his guests were Himmler (a frequent visitor to the Wolf's Lair during these weeks) and Heydrich. The conversation again revolved mainly around the connections of Jewry and Christianity. Hitler reminded his guests and his regular entourage of his "prophecy." "This criminal race has the two million dead of the World War on its conscience," he went on, and "now again hundreds of thousands. Don't anyone tell me we can't send them into the marshes (*Morast*)! Who bothers, then, about our people? It's good when the horror (*der Schrecken*) precedes us that we are exterminating Jewry. The attempt to found a Jewish state will be a failure." These notes of Hitler's rantings were disjointed. But, although lacking coherence, they point to his knowledge of the attempts—eventually given up—in the summer to drown Jewish women by driving them into the Pripet marshes. Hitler's allocation of guilt for the dead of the First World War and the current war to the Jews, and the recourse once more to his "prophecy," underline his certainty that the destruction of Jewry was imminent. But, other than the reference to the efficacy of rumours of extermination, there was no suggestion of the looming "Final Solution." With Himmler and Heydrich as his guests, it was scarcely necessary to dissemble. However, no significance ought to be attached to the absence of any reference. By mid-October the consequences flowing from the deportation order of the previous month had still to merge into the full genocidal programme.

On the evening of 5 November, remarks about the "racial inferiority" of the English lower class led Hitler once more into a monologue about the Jews. As usual, he linked it to the war. This was the "most idiotic war" that the British had ever begun, he ranted, and would lead in defeat to an outbreak of antisemitism in Britain which would be without parallel. The end of the war, he proclaimed, would bring "the fall of the Jew." He then unleashed an extraordinary verbal assault on the lack of ability and creativity of Jews in every walk of life but one: lying and cheating. The Jew's "entire building will collapse if he is refused a following," he went on. "In one moment, it's all over. I've always said the Jews are the most stupid devils that exist. They don't have a true musician, thinker, no art, nothing, absolutely nothing. They are liars, forgers, deceivers. They've only got anywhere through the simple-mindedness of those around them. If the Jew were not washed by the Aryan, he wouldn't be able to see out of his eyes for filth. We can live without the Jews. But they can't live without us."

The links, as he saw them, between the Jews and the war that they had allegedly inspired, now also, after years in which he had scarcely mentioned the Jews, found a prominent place in his public speeches. But, whatever the rhetorical flourishes, whatever the propaganda motive in appealing to the antisemitic instincts of his hard-core supporters in the Party, there cannot be the slightest doubt, on the basis of his private comments, that Hitler believed in what he said.

In his speech to the "Old Guard" of veterans of the Putsch, on 8 November 1941, Hitler pressed home the theme of Jewish guilt for the war. Despite the victories of the previous year, he stated, he had still worried because of his recognition that behind the war stood "the international Jew." They had poisoned the peoples through their control of the press, radio, film, and theatre; they had made sure that rearmament and war would benefit their business and financial interests; he had come to know the Jews as the instigators of world conflagration. England, under Jewish influence, had been the driving force of the "world-coalition against the German people." But it had been inevitable that the Soviet Union, "the greatest servant of Jewry," would one day confront the Reich. Since then it had become plain that the Soviet state was dominated by Jewish commissars. Stalin, too, was no more than "an instrument in the hand of this almighty Jewry." Behind him stood "all those Jews who in thousandfold ramification lead this powerful empire." This "insight," Hitler suggested, had weighed heavily upon him, and compelled him to face the danger from the east.

Hitler returned to the alleged "destructive character" of the Jews when talking again to his usual captive audience in the Wolf's Lair in the small hours of 1–2 December. Again, there was a hint, but no more than that, of what Hitler saw as the natural justice being meted out to the Jews: "he who destroys life, exposes himself to death. And nothing other than this is happening to them"—to the Jews. The gas-vans of Chelmno would start killing the Jews of the Warthegau in those very days. In Hitler's warped mentality, such killing was natural revenge for the destruction caused by the Jews—above all in the war which he saw as their work. His "prophecy" motif was evidently never far from his mind in these weeks as the winter crisis was unfolding in the east. It would be at the forefront of his thoughts in the wake of Pearl Harbor. With his declaration of war on the USA on 11 December, Germany was now engaged in a "world war"—a term used up to then almost exclusively for the devastation of 1914–18. In his Reichstag speech of 30 January 1939, he had "prophesied" that the destruction of the Jews would be the consequence of a new world war. That war, in his view, had now arrived.

On 12 December, the day after he had announced Germany's declaration of war on the USA, Hitler addressed the Reichsleiter and Gauleiter—an audience of around fifty persons—in his rooms in the Reich Chancellery. Much of his talk ranged over the consequences of Pearl Harbor, the war in the east, and the glorious future awaiting Germany after final victory. He also spoke of the Jews. And once more he evoked his "prophecy."

"With regard to the Jewish Question," Goebbels recorded, summarizing Hitler's comments, "the Führer is determined to make a clear sweep of it (*reinen Tisch zu machen*). He prophesied that, if they brought about another world war, they would experience their annihilation (*Vernichtung*). That was no empty talk (*keine Phrase*). The world war is there. The annihilation of Jewry must be the necessary consequence. This question is to be viewed without any sentimentality. We're not there to have sympathy with the Jews, but only sympathy with our German people. If the German people has again now sacrificed around 160,000 dead in the eastern campaign, the originators of this bloody conflict will have to pay for it with their own lives."

The tone was more menacing and vengeful than ever. The original "prophecy" had been a warning. Despite the warning, the Jews—in Hitler's view—had unleashed the world war. They would now pay the price.

Hitler still had his "prophecy" in mind when he spoke privately to Alfred Rosenberg, Reich Minister for the Eastern Territories, on 14 December, two days after his address to the Gauleiter. Referring to the text of a forthcoming speech, on which he wanted Hitler's advice, Rosenberg remarked that his "standpoint was not to speak of the extermination (*Ausrottung*) of Jewry. The Führer approved this stance and said they had burdened us with the war and brought about the destruction so it was no wonder if they would be the first to feel the consequences."

The party chieftains who had heard Hitler speak on 12 December in the dramatic context of war now against the USA and unfolding crisis on the eastern front understood the message. No order or directive was necessary. They readily grasped that the time of reckoning had come. On 16 December, Hans Frank reported back to leading figures in the administration of the General Government. "As regards the Jews," he began, "I'll tell you quite openly: an end has to be made one way or another." He referred explicitly to Hitler's "prophecy" about their destruction in the event of another world war. He repeated Hitler's expression in his address to the Gauleiter that sympathy with the Jews would be wholly misplaced. The war would prove to be only a partial success should the Jews in Europe survive it, Frank went on. "I will therefore proceed in principle regarding the Jews that they will disappear. They must go," he declared. He said he was still negotiating about deporting them to the east. He referred to the rescheduled Wannsee Conference in January, where the issue of deportation would be discussed. "At any event," he commented, "a great Jewish migration will commence." "But," he asked: "what is to happen to the Jews? Do you believe they'll be accommodated in village settlements in the *Ostland?* They said to us in Berlin: why are you giving us all this trouble? We can't do anything with them in the *Ostland* or in the Reich Commissariat [Ukraine] either. Liquidate them yourselves! . . . We must destroy (*vernichten*) the Jews wherever we find them and wherever it is possible to do so . . ." A programme for bringing this about was evidently, however, still unknown to Frank. He did not know how it was to happen. "The Jews are also extraordinarily harmful to us through their gluttony," he continued. "We have in the General Government an estimated 2.5 million—perhaps with those closely related to Jews and what goes with it, now 3.5 million Jews. We can't shoot these 3.5 million Jews, we can't poison them, but we must be able to take steps leading somehow to a success in extermination (*Vernichtungserfolg*) . . ."

The "Final Solution"—meaning the physical extermination of the Jews of Europe—was still emerging. The ideology of total annihilation was now taking over from any lingering economic rationale of working the Jews to death. "Economic considerations should remain fundamentally out of consideration in dealing with the problem" was the answer finally given on 18 December to Lohse's inquiry about using skilled Jewish workers from the Baltic in the armaments industry. On the same day, in a private discussion with Himmler, Hitler confirmed that in the east the partisan war, which had expanded sharply in the autumn, provided a useful framework for destroying the Jews. They were "to be exterminated as partisans (*Als Partisanen auszurotten*)," Himmler noted as the outcome of their discussion. The separate strands of genocide were rapidly being pulled together.

On 20 January 1942, the conference on the "final solution," postponed from 9 December, eventually took place in a large villa by the Wannsee. Alongside representatives from the Reich ministries of the Interior, Justice, and Eastern Territories, the Foreign Office, from the office of the Four-Year Plan, and from the General Government, sat Gestapo chief SS-Gruppenführer Heinrich Müller, the commanders of the Security Police in the General Government and Latvia, Karl Schoengarth and Otto Lange, together with Adolf Eichmann (the RSHA's deportation expert, who had the task of producing a written record of the meeting).

Heydrich opened the meeting by recapitulating that Göring had given him responsibility—a reference to the mandate of the previous July—for preparing "the final solution of the European Jewish question." The meeting aimed to clarify and coordinate organizational arrangements. (Later in the meeting an inconclusive attempt was made to define the status of part-Jews (*Mischlinge*) in the framework of deportation plans.) Heydrich surveyed the course of anti-Jewish policy, then declared that "the evacuation of the Jews to the east has now emerged, with the prior permission of the Führer, as a further possible solution instead of emigration." He spoke of gathering "practical experience" in the process for "the coming final solution of the Jewish question," which would embrace as many as 11 million Jews across Europe (stretching, outside German current territorial control, as far as Britain and Ireland, Switzerland, Spain, Turkey, and French north African colonies). In the gigantic deportation programme, the German-occupied territories would be combed from west to east. The deported Jews would be put to work in large labour gangs. Many—perhaps most—would die in the process. The particularly strong and hardy types who survived would have "to be dealt with accordingly."

Though there was, as Eichmann later testified, explicit talk at the conference—not reflected in the minutes—of "killing and eliminating and exterminating (*Töten und Eliminieren und Vernichten*)," Heydrich was not orchestrating an existing and finalized programme of mass extermination in death camps. But the Wannsee Conference was a key stepping-stone on the path to that terrible genocidal finality. A deportation programme aimed at the annihilation of the Jews through forced labour and starvation in occupied Soviet territory following the end of a victorious war was rapidly giving way to the realization that the Jews would have to be systematically destroyed before the war ended—and that the main locus of their destruction would no longer be the Soviet Union, but the territory of the General Government.

That the General Government should become the first area to implement the "Final Solution" was directly requested at the conference by its representative, State Secretary Josef Bühler. He wanted the 2½ million Jews in his area—most of them incapable of work, he stressed—"removed" as quickly as possible. The authorities in the area would do all they could to help expedite the process. Bühler's hopes would be fulfilled over the next months. The regionalized killing in the districts of Lublin and Galicia was extended by spring to the whole of the General Government, as the deportation trains began to ferry their human cargo to the extermination camps of Belzec, Sobibor, and Treblinka. By this time, a comprehensive programme of systematic annihilation of the Jews embracing the whole of German-occupied Europe was rapidly taking shape. By early June a programme had been constructed for the deportation of Jews from western Europe. The transports from the west began in July. Most left for the largest of the extermination camps by this time in operation, Auschwitz-Birkenau in the annexed territory of Upper Silesia. The "final solution" was under way. The industrialized mass murder would now continue unabated. By the end of 1942, according to the SS's own calculations, 4 million Jews were already dead.

Hitler had not been involved in the Wannsee Conference. Probably he knew it was taking place; but even this is not certain. There was no need for his involvement. He had signalled yet again in unmistakable terms in December 1941 what the fate of the Jews should be now that Germany was embroiled in another world war. By then, local and regional killing initiatives had already developed their own momentum.

Heydrich was more than happy to use Hitler's blanket authorization of deportations to the east now to expand the killing operations into an overall programme of Europe-wide genocide.

On 30 January 1942, the ninth anniversary of the "seizure of power," Hitler addressed a packed Sportpalast. As he had been doing privately over the past weeks, he invoked once more—how often he repeated the emphasis in these months is striking—his "prophecy" of 30 January 1939. As always, he wrongly dated it to the day of the outbreak of war with the attack on Poland. "We are clear," he declared, "that the war can only end either with the extermination of the aryan peoples or the disappearance of Jewry from Europe." He went on: "I already stated on 1 September 1939 in the German Reichstag—and I refrain from over-hasty prophecies—that this war will not come to an end as the Jews imagine, with the extermination of the European-Aryan peoples (*nämlich daß die europäisch-arischen Völker ausgerottet werden*), but that the result of this war will be the annihilation (*Vernichtung*) of Jewry. For the first time the old Jewish law will now be applied: an eye for an eye, a tooth for a tooth . . . And the hour will come when the most evil world-enemy of all time will have played out its role, at least for a thousand years."

The message was not lost on his audience. The SD—no doubt picking up comments made above all by avid Nazi supporters—reported that his words had been "interpreted to mean that the Führer's battle against the Jews would be followed through to the end with merciless consistency, and that very soon the last Jew would disappear from European soil."

When Goebbels spoke to Hitler in March, the death mills of Belzec had commenced their grisly operations. As regards the "Jewish Question," Hitler remained "pitiless," the Propaganda Minister recorded. "The Jews must get out of Europe, if need be through use of the most brutal means," was his view.

A week later, Goebbels left no doubt what "the most brutal means" implied. "From the General Government, beginning with Lublin, the Jews are now being deported to the east. A fairly barbaric procedure, not to be described in any greater detail, is being used here, and not much more remains of the Jews themselves. In general, it can probably be established that 60 per cent of them must be liquidated, while only 40 per cent can be put to work . . . A judgement is being carried out on the Jews which is barbaric, but fully deserved. The prophecy which the Führer gave them along the way for bringing about a new world war is beginning to become true in the most terrible fashion. No sentimentality can be allowed to prevail in these things. If we didn't fend them off, the Jews would annihilate (*vernichten*) us. It's a life-and-death struggle between the aryan race and the Jewish bacillus. No other government and no other regime could produce the strength to solve this question generally. Here, too, the Führer is the unswerving champion and spokesman of a radical solution . . ."

Goebbels himself had played no small part over the years in pushing for a "radical solution." He had been one of the most important and high-placed of the Party activists pressing Hitler on numerous occasions to take radical action on the "Jewish Question." The Security Police—Heydrich's role was, if anything, probably more important even than Himmler's—had been instrumental in gradually converting an ideological imperative into an extermination plan. Many others, at different levels of the regime, had contributed in greater or lesser measure to the continuing and untrammelled process of radicalization. Complicity was massive, from the Wehrmacht leadership and captains of industry down to Party hacks, bureaucratic minions, and ordinary Germans hoping for their own material advantage through the persecution then deportation of a helpless, but unloved, minority which had been deemed to be the inexorable enemy of the new "people's community."

But Goebbels knew what he was talking about in singling out Hitler's role. This had often been indirect, rather than overt. It had consisted of authorizing more than directing. And the hate-filled tirades, though without equal in their depth of inhumanity, remained at a level of generalities. Nevertheless, there can be no doubt about it: Hitler's role had been decisive and indispensable in the road to the "Final Solution." Had he not come to power in 1933 and a national-conservative government, perhaps a military dictatorship, had gained power instead, discriminatory legislation against Jews would in all probability still have been introduced in Germany. But without Hitler, and the unique regime he headed, the creation of a programme to bring about the physical extermination of the Jews of Europe would have been unthinkable.

Henry Friedlander

The Opening Act of Nazi Genocide

Nazi genocide did not take place in a vacuum. Genocide was only the most radical method of excluding groups of human beings from the German national community. The policy of exclusion followed and drew upon more than fifty years of scientific opposition to the equality of man. Since the turn of the century, the German elite—that is, the members of the educated professional classes—had increasingly accepted an ideology of human inequality. Geneticists, anthropologists, and psychiatrists advanced a theory of human heredity that merged with the racist doctrine of ultra-nationalists to form a political ideology based on race. The Nazi movement both absorbed and advanced this ideology. After their assumption of power in 1933, the Nazis created the political framework that made it possible to translate this ideology of inequality into a policy of exclusion. At the same time, the German bureaucratic, professional, and scientific elite provided the legitimacy the regime needed for the smooth implementation of this policy.

The growing importance of the biological sciences in the nineteenth century, following the discoveries of Charles Darwin, led most scientists to advance theories of human inequality as matters of scientific fact. In the middle of the century, a widely accepted theory maintained that there was a causal relationship between the size of the human brain and human intelligence. In 1861 the anthropologist Paul Broca thus asserted that "there is a remarkable relationship between the development of intelligence and the volume of the brain," and he argued that studies based on this premise showed that "in general, the brain is larger in mature adults than in the elderly, in men than in women, in eminent men than in men of mediocre talent, in superior races than in inferior races."

Belief in inequality coexisted with the principles of equality proclaimed by American and French revolutionaries. Scientists, themselves products of their times, constructed "rank-order or value-judgment hierarchies" that placed human beings on a single scale of intelligence, thus incorporating popular prejudices into their theories. As proof they offered meaningless, but carefully compiled, correlations between the size of the brain and presumed intelligence. But such scientific data, "no matter how numerically sophisticated, have recorded little more than social prejudice." Popular prejudice accepted that males were more intelligent than females, and in 1879 Gustave Le Bon, the founder of social psychology, concurred: "In the most intelligent races, as among the Parisians, there are a large number of women whose brains are closer in size to those of gorillas than to the most developed male brains. This inferiority is so obvious that no one can contest it for a moment; only its degree is worth discussion."

Popular prejudice also accepted as self-evident the superiority of the white race over all others, placing blacks at the bottom of a ranking order of races. In 1864 the German anatomist Carl Vogt reflected this prejudice by stating that "the grown-up Negro partakes, as regards his intellectual faculties, of the nature of the child, the female, and the senile white." Finally, the prejudices of the scientists themselves led them to conclude that the wealthy and the educated inherited greater intelligence than the lower socioeconomic classes. The American paleontologist E. D. Cope thus "identified four groups of lower human forms," including—along with women, nonwhites, and Jews—all "lower classes within superior races."

In this way, the biological sciences of the nineteenth century simply recorded traditional prejudices. Without any evidence, scientists concluded that human differences were hereditary and unalterable, and in doing so, they "precluded redemption" because they imposed "the additional burden of intrinsic inferiority upon despised groups." Science thus showed "the tenacity of unconscious bias and the surprising malleability of 'objective,' quantitative data in the interest of a preconceived idea." . . .

The term "eugenics" was coined in 1881 by the British naturalist and mathematician Francis Galton and described by the leading American eugenicist, Charles B. Davenport, as "the science of the improvement of the human race by better breeding." Eugenics developed within the larger movement of Social Darwinism, which applied Darwin's "struggle for survival" to human affairs. In the United States, Social Darwinism was used to justify unbridled economic competition and the "survival of the fittest" as a law of nature. Eugenics provided a biological basis for these ideas. Recruited from the biological and social sciences, or what today may be called the life sciences, eugenicists firmly believed that just as the Mendelian laws governed the hereditary transmission of human traits like color blindness or a particular blood group, these laws also determined the inheritance of social traits. . . .

. . . These professionals—biologists, geneticists, engineers, social workers, psychologists, and sociologists—wanted to introduce rational social planning into human affairs and believed that biological manipulation would achieve their ends.

The eugenics movement in the United States and elsewhere pursued two connected policies. First, it sponsored research to investigate the transmission of social traits, especially undesirable ones, and undertook to classify individuals, groups, and nations on a scale of human worth. Second, it proposed biological solutions to social problems and lobbied for their implementation. . . .

Eugenic research, both anthropological fieldwork and psychological testing, was designed to isolate and record individuals with inferior intelligence and other social disabilities. Eugenicists claimed that their research on individuals and families proved the inferiority of entire groups. Using mass testing, the psychologists classified the American population by IQ on a ranking scale, predictably placing the wealthy and professionals at the top of the scale as the most intelligent. The psychologist Henry H. Goddard, director of research at the Vineland Training School for Feeble-Minded Girls and Boys in New Jersey, who had introduced the Binet scale to the United States and had coined the term "moron," believed that "democracy means that the people rule by selecting the wisest, most intelligent and most human to tell them what to do to be happy." But apart from several investigations of the intelligent—for example, the "project to record the IQ of past geniuses"—eugenicists concentrated their research on the lower classes. They used their findings to "prove" that class differences reflected intelligence. Stanford psychologist Lewis M. Terman, creator of the Stanford-Binet test, argued that "class boundaries had been set by innate intelligence"; his analysis of test scores led him to jump to the conclusion that "the children of successful and cultured parents test higher than children from wretched and ignorant homes for the simple reason that their heredity is better."

Eugenicists focused attention on the feebleminded—labeled as idiots, imbeciles, or morons—and argued that their findings proved the existence of a relationship between low intelligence and both immorality and crime. They saw the cause of the social problems of their time, such as alcoholism and prostitution, as inherited feeblemindedness and viewed the manifestations of poverty, such as intermittent unemployment and chronic illness, as a hereditary degeneracy. Terman thus concluded: "Not all criminals are feebleminded, but all feeble-minded persons are at least potential criminals. That every feeble-minded woman is a potential prostitute would hardly be disputed by anyone." Considering the acceptance of the connection between low intelligence and degenerate behavior, it is hardly surprising that Goddard, one of the scientists whose works were published by the ERO, commented, "How can there be such a thing as social equality with this wide range of mental capacity?"

The eugenicists ascribed degeneracy not only to class but also to race and ethnic group. Yerkes concluded that the U.S. Army test scores proved that the "darker peoples of southern Europe and the Slavs of eastern Europe are less intelligent than the fair peoples of western and northern Europe" and that the "Negro lies at the bottom of the scale" of intelligence. Convinced of the inferiority and even criminality of other races, the eugenicists wanted to maintain the purity of the American pioneer stock and opposed marriages between people of different races. The ERO director, Harry Hamilton Laughlin, "compared human racial crossing with mongrelization in the animal world" and argued that "immigrants from southern and eastern Europe, especially Jews, were racially so different from, and genetically so inferior to, the current American population that any racial mixture would be deleterious."

Confronted with low test scores of Jewish immigrants examined at Ellis Island and in the U.S. Army on the one hand and the achievements of Jewish intellectuals on the other, Princeton psychologist Brigham theorized that "the able Jew is popularly recognized not only because of his ability, but because he is able and a Jew," concluding that "our figures, then, would rather tend to disprove the popular belief that the Jew is highly intelligent." . . .

The research results of the eugenicists were accepted not only by fellow scientists but also by national policy makers. Pointing to their findings as proof of human inequality, eugenicists in Britain and the United States campaigned for changes in public policy to halt the degeneration of society. In Britain, this led to the introduction of the eleven-plus examinations, designed to exclude the unfit from higher education. In the United States, eugenicists labeled groups from southern and eastern Europe as inferior and campaigned to restrict the immigration of members of those ethnic groups. Their research and lobbying assured passage of the 1924 Johnson Act (Immigration Restriction Act), which imposed quotas that severely limited immigration from countries whose inhabitants were identified as unfit.

Individuals from inferior races and ethnic groups could be prohibited from entering the country, but other solutions had to be found to deal with feebleminded individuals who already resided in the United States. Goddard advocated "colonization," a term he used to disguise incarceration in closed institutions, and Terman proposed "permanent custodial care." But this was not a permanent solution to the problem of the unfit. The favorite solution proposed by the eugenicists was sterilization. Eugenicists viewed individuals with mental disabilities as a burden to society and a threat to civilization. In 1910 Charles Davenport thus advocated sterilization "to dry up the springs that feed the torrent of defective and degenerate protoplasm." Similarly, in 1914 Goddard, who regarded handicapped individuals as immoral beings totally unable to control their sexual urges, stated a position that reflected universal eugenic opinion: "If both parents are feeble-minded all the children will be feebleminded. It is obvious that such matings should not be allowed. It is perfectly clear that no feeble-minded person should ever be allowed to marry or to become a parent. It is obvious that if this rule is to be carried out the intelligent part of society must enforce it."

The political campaign of the eugenics movement in favor of sterilization was relatively successful. In 1907 Indiana enacted the first sterilization law, and by the middle of the 1930s, more than half of the states had passed laws that authorized the sterilization of "inmates of mental institutions, persons convicted more than once of sex crimes, those deemed to be feeble-minded by IQ tests, 'moral degenerate persons,' and epileptics." In 1927, one such law, a Virginia statute, which authorized directors of state institutions to order the compulsory sterilization of handicapped patients diagnosed as suffering from "an hereditary form of insanity or imbecility," reached [and was upheld by] the Supreme Court. . . .

In the United States, eugenics eventually lost scientific acceptance and public support. New scientific discoveries led to the rejection of eugenic research results. Moreover, events in Nazi Germany during the 1930s, and the close cooperation between American and German eugenicists, seriously damaged the standing of the American eugenics movement, and the revelation of Nazi crimes in the 1940s discredited eugenic theories.

The development of eugenics in Germany resembled developments in the United States, but there were differences. In Germany, university scientists enjoyed far greater status than they did in the United States, and they played a more active role in the eugenics movement. Most scientists in the eugenics movement were physicians, medical education being the preferred career path for research in biology and anthropology at the turn of the century. . . .

. . . As early as 1920, two eminent scholars proposed the most radical solution to the problem posed by institutionalized handicapped patients in Germany. In that year, Karl Binding and Alfred Hoche published a polemical work entitled *Die Freigabe der Vernichtung lebensunwerten Lebens* (Authorization for the destruction of life unworthy of life). Karl Binding, a widely published legal scholar who died just before the book appeared, argued that the law should permit the killing of "incurable feebleminded" individuals. Alfred Hoche, a psychiatrist and specialist in neuropathology, analyzed Binding's arguments from a "medical perspective." . . .

Hoche did not accept the traditional obligation of physicians to do no harm. Dismissing the Hippocratic oath as a "physician's oath of ancient times," he argued that physicians always balance benefits against risks and thus protect "higher values." He did not expect opposition from the medical profession, pointing out that young physicians no longer follow absolute ethical rules but orient themselves according to the teachings of their professors and the opinions of their peers.

In two areas of special concern to physicians, Hoche added to the arguments advanced by Binding. First, he insisted that physicians must be protected against prosecution for euthanasia, because even relatives who ask for the death of patients sometimes change their minds. Second, he argued that the killing of defective patients would expand research opportunities, particularly brain research.

In conclusion, Binding discussed the procedures necessary to implement the destruction of unworthy life. The handicapped patient, the physician, or the patient's relatives could apply for euthanasia, but Binding reserved the right to authorize the killing to the state, which would appoint an "authorization committee" composed of one jurist and two physicians to make an "objective expert evaluation." Binding added a number of further requirements: the decision had to rest on advanced scientific knowledge, the means to accomplish the killing had to be appropriate and "absolutely painless," and only an expert (*Sachverständiger*) could actually kill. Binding acknowledged the possibility of error (*Irrtumsrisiko*), except perhaps with "idiots," but he argued that "humanity loses due to error so many members, that one more or less really does not make a difference."

The Binding-Hoche polemic was followed by other publications favoring euthanasia for those deemed unworthy of life, and, although the idea was never officially accepted during the Weimar Republic, it was widely discussed in German medical circles. In the United States and Great Britain, where public discussion of euthanasia centered on mercy killing for terminal patients and not the killing of unworthy life, the Binding-Hoche polemic made no impression. In Germany, however, it was very influential; eventually the Nazi killers would adopt many of its arguments and later use them as justification. Although the German race hygienists did not originally advocate eugenic euthanasia, they did accept it as "the logical outgrowth of the cost-benefit analysis at the heart of race hygiene."

We might ask why American eugenics withered and died while German race hygiene succeeded in imposing on society its radical vision of a biological-social utopia. The answer is politics. The political climate of the Weimar Republic, especially the ideology of the right-wing *völkisch* movements, provided a hospitable milieu where race hygiene could prosper. But most important, in January 1933 the National Socialist German Workers Party (Nationalsozialistische Deutsche Arbeiter Partei, or NSDAP) captured the German government. This assumption of power by the Nazis, the most radical *völkisch* movement, made the implementation of the race hygiene utopia possible. The Nazis had pledged to preserve the "purity of German blood," that is, they were determined to cleanse the German gene pool. To accomplish that end, the Nazi regime introduced radical social engineering designed to create a society racially homogeneous, physically hardy, and mentally healthy.

A policy of exclusion stood at the center of the Nazi utopia. Killing operations were only the most radical, final stage of exclusion. As we shall see, Adolf Hitler, who was totally committed to the politics of exclusion, ordered the killings once domestic and foreign restraints were removed. The party leaders, the uniformed party formations, and the civil service promptly implemented his orders. And the professional classes, protected by Hitler's authorization, readily cooperated in the killings.

Exclusion institutionalized human inequality. It was applied to entire groups of human beings who simply did not fit into this utopian community, including all those long designated as degenerate (*entartet*) by the teachings of race scientists. First, exclusion was applied to the handicapped, that is, the physically malformed, mentally disturbed, and intellectually retarded. In 1932 the prominent Social Democratic physician Julius Moses predicted that the medical profession under the Nazis would "destroy and exterminate" incurable patients because they were "unproductive" and "unworthy." And as race scientists had always considered criminality an outgrowth of degeneration, exclusion of the handicapped was also designed to apply to individuals considered antisocial or criminal—prostitutes, beggars, vagabonds, habitual criminals—and was later extended to include anyone whose behavior was "alien to the community [*gemeinschaftsfremd*]." The adjective "antisocial" is translated in German as *asozial*; race scientists transformed this adjective into the noun *Asozial* in order to label and stigmatize individuals and groups. One official definition of members of the *Asozialen* group described them as "human beings with a hereditary and irreversible mental attitude, who, due to this nature, incline toward alcoholism and immorality, have repeatedly come into conflict with government agencies and the courts, and thus appear unrestrained and a threat to humanity."

Second, exclusion was applied to racially alien peoples whose physical and intellectual penetration of the so-called Aryan race was also viewed as degeneration. All non-Caucasian races were to be excluded, but the policy primarily concerned two ethnic groups residing in Germany and designated as alien (*artfremde*) races: Jews and Gypsies. Although they may have emphasized different dangers posed by specific groups, the Nazis thus applied exclusion to exactly the same groups that had been targeted by the Aryan supremacist wing of the race hygiene movement. During the 1930s, exclusion became official German government policy.

Exclusion was applied differently to each group. The exclusion of the handicapped, who were for the most part already institutionalized, did not pose a serious administrative problem. In the Weimar Republic, psychiatrists and others in the race hygiene movement had argued that cost containment must apply to institutions caring for the handicapped, and in 1932 Prussia reduced support for so-called defectives. During the 1930s, conditions imposed on the institutionalized handicapped deteriorated precipitously because physicians considered it "obvious" that incurable patients should receive less food than those able to return to work. During the war, conditions became even worse when institutions for the disabled, the senile, alcoholics, and others were denied the additional food regular hospitals received. Antisocial individuals were committed to concentration camps as early as 1933 and were sent to the camps in growing numbers after 1937. During the war, psychiatrists even sought to transfer troublesome handicapped patients from state hospitals to concentration camps. Also, in 1932 the Weimar bureaucracy drafted a voluntary sterilization law for the handicapped, which the Nazi regime implemented in 1933 as a compulsory law.

The method of exclusion applied to those considered aliens on the basis of race depended on the size and importance of the group. For example, the small number of German blacks—children of black French soldiers and German women—were sterilized during the 1930s to prevent future black offspring. This sterilization, illegal even under German law in the Nazi era, was validated by scientific recommendations from Eugen Fischer, Fritz Lenz, Hans F. K. Günther, Alfred Ploetz, and others. Against the larger group of German Gypsies—Roma and Sinti—the regime simply intensified existing discriminatory laws traditionally enforced by the police. In 1936 German scientists embarked on a massive effort to register and classify all Gypsies, while the police severely limited their mobility and incarcerated large numbers in special Gypsy camps.

These simple methods of exclusion could not be imposed as easily on Jews, members of the largest and most visible minority considered alien on the basis of race. Although Hitler and the Nazi movement were fixated on the threat supposedly presented by "international Jewry," they found it difficult to reverse immediately the legal, social, and economic integration of Jews into German society. The process of exclusion required a number of years and involved both domestic and foreign policy considerations. Racial laws and regulations, as well as general harassment, slowly excluded Jews from active participation in the life of the nation. But during the 1930s, the party and state bureaucracy considered the emigration of Jews from Germany as the most promising and the most feasible form of total exclusion.

The Nazi regime issued numerous laws and regulations during the 1930s to implement its eugenic and racial program, and, as we shall see, the practitioners of race hygiene—anthropologists, geneticists, psychiatrists, and physicians—were involved in drafting and applying them. Of course, their role had changed. They profited from being governed by a regime that favored race hygiene, but they also had to accommodate themselves to the regime's political needs. They continued to consider the Nazis "vulgar and ordinary" and Nazi antisemitism somewhat extreme, but they accepted, even applauded, Nazi policies because they reflected an ideology they as individuals and as scientists had long supported. But even though they may have tried to maintain a certain scientific detachment, their assistants and students enthusiastically embraced all aspects of Nazi ideology. . . .

German science was rapidly synchronized (*gleichgeschaltet*) with Nazi ideology after 1933, especially after scientists opposed to the new regime, as well as those with the wrong ethnic background, were fired. There was no effective resistance. . . .

The scientists of race hygiene thus rapidly adjusted to the new political realities, adopting the language and tenor of the new regime. Neither the scientists nor the Nazi leadership saw a distinction between racial and eugenic policies. They joined hands in their common struggle against "degeneration." Newly empowered party and government officials . . . admired the work and supported the goals of the scientists. In turn, leading scientists . . . adopted the harsh position on race espoused by the Nazi movement. Spreading the gospel of race hygiene, the scientists offered courses on race and eugenics to public health officers, SS physicians, teachers, nurses, and civil servants. Profiting from the increased demand for genealogies created by the new race laws, they provided anthropological, racial evaluations of individuals—both living and dead—to prove or disprove Aryan descent. They fully supported the regime's policy of exclusion, designed to improve the racial stock of the German nation. In the language used by both the Nazis and the scientists, this policy was called "*Aufartung durch Ausmerzung*," which can be translated as "improvement through exclusion." But this translation does not fully transmit the perversion and brutality of the phrase. A better translation is "physical regeneration through eradication," that is, the Nazi regime and its scientists wanted to improve the stock of the German *Volk* through the eradication of its inferior members and of the racial aliens dwelling among them.

The policy of exclusion required precise definitions of groups and individuals, which only race science could provide. However arbitrary, the "criteria for selection" had to be scientific, and the cooperation of the scientists was an important prerequisite for the successful implementation of the policy of exclusion. Scientific exactitude provided *Rechtssicherheit*, that is, legal reassurance for the masses that the law would protect their own security.

Exclusion not only stripped individuals of rights and standing but also barred them from receiving the state's assistance. Of course, the removal of the safety net for inferiors had always been one of the central themes of eugenics, both in Germany and elsewhere, and opposition to public welfare expenditures had become even more vocal during the depression. It is thus not surprising that the Nazi regime manipulated public welfare to exclude Jews and Gypsies.

The German public welfare system was both expensive and tightly regulated, and the regime could thus use its control of both administration and finances to bar undesirables from receiving public welfare. The Reich authorities responsible for the regulations governing welfare used them to exclude undesirable groups. Obviously, local governments responsible for paying the mandated welfare costs attempted to relieve their burden by excluding as many undesirables as possible from the welfare rolls. The Reich complied by forcing Jewish welfare agencies to assume all responsibility for Jewish welfare recipients. The Reich also decreed that Gypsies were to receive the same treatment as Jews, but because Gypsies did not possess their own welfare agencies, their level of welfare was left to the discretion of local welfare offices; however, Gypsies were to receive less aid than Aryans.

As the Nazi regime moved toward war, Hitler authorized state and party planners to proceed from the exclusionary policies of emigration, incarceration, and sterilization to the most radical exclusionary solution of killings. The first group targeted were the handicapped. They were excluded by being institutionalized, but this was not enough. Hostile to their existence, institutions reduced services and sought to cut the costs of caring for mental and disabled patients. Excluded, incarcerated, sterilized, and neglected, the handicapped were viewed as expendable, and thus a logical progression led to the killing of the handicapped in the so-called euthanasia program. The other group of undesirables—the *Asozialen*—were treated similarly: those committed to institutions by the courts were among the first killed; others were later selected for killing when euthanasia was applied within the concentration camps.

In 1940 and early 1941, when the radical killing solution was already being applied to the handicapped, the policy toward Jews did not yet include killings. At that time, limited emigration, ghettoization, and schemes calling for the establishment of Jewish reservations remained the only exclusionary policy options for Jews. But when international conditions and the progress of the war made a more radical solution possible, the killings were expanded to include Jews.

The much smaller group of Gypsies was also not at first a target of the killing solution. Gypsies were initially subjected to persecution by the police, who incarcerated them as criminals and *Asoziale* by virtue of social stereotype. Then they were studied and sterilized by anthropologists and psychiatrists, in a close collaboration between the police and health authorities. Eventually, after they had been classified by the race scientists as racially inferior, they were killed alongside Jews.

The killing operations that commenced with the start of World War II were the result of old beliefs and recent policies. Although the Nazi policies of exclusion, including compulsory sterilization, provided a crucial stepping-stone toward the implementation of the killings, old beliefs that predated Hitler's assumption of power were equally essential. As we have seen, as early as 1920 Binding and Hoche had called for the "destruction of life unworthy of life," euphemistically called euthanasia. The Nazi regime merely put their proposal into practice.

The euthanasia killings—that is, the "systematic and secret execution" of the handicapped—were Nazi Germany's first organized mass murder, in which the killers developed their killing technique. They created the method for selecting the victims. They invented techniques to gas people and burn their bodies. They employed subterfuge to hide the killings, and they did not hesitate to pillage the corpses.

The euthanasia killings proved to be the opening act of Nazi genocide. The mass murder of the handicapped preceded that of Jews and Gypsies; the final solution followed euthanasia. In euthanasia, the perpetrators recognized their limitations and, to avoid popular disapproval, transferred the killings from the Reich to the East. No substantive difference existed, however, between the killing operations directed against the handicapped, Jews, and Gypsies. The killing technique that had been developed and tested in euthanasia was used again and again. The killers who learned their trade in the euthanasia killing centers of Brandenburg, Grafeneck, Hartheim, Sonnenstein, Bernburg, and Hadamar also staffed the killing centers at Belzec, Sobibor, and Treblinka. The instigators had learned that individuals selected at random would carry out terrible crimes "without scruples." . . .

On 22 June 1941, the German Wehrmacht invaded the Soviet Union, and the Nazi regime embarked on its second, and far more ambitious, killing operation. Mobile operational units of the SS, the Einsatzgruppen of the Sipo and SD, crossed the Soviet border immediately after the battle troops. In the occupied territory of the Soviet Union, these units shot large numbers of civilians in mass executions. Their primary task was the murder of all Jews on Soviet soil. They also murdered all Gypsies and, wherever possible, the handicapped. . . .

Historians investigating Nazi genocide have long debated who gave the order to kill all Jews, when it was issued, and how it was transmitted. Even though the specific mechanism, including the approximate date, has been a matter of contention, there now appears to be general agreement that Hitler had a deciding voice, although no one has ever discovered, or is likely to discover, a smoking gun.

The chronology of Nazi killing operations provides a road map for those seeking answers to these questions. The murder of the handicapped preceded the murder of Jews and Gypsies, and it is therefore reasonable to conclude that T4's killing operation served as a model for the final solution. The success of the euthanasia policy convinced the Nazi leadership that mass murder was technically feasible, that ordinary men and women were willing to kill large numbers of innocent human beings, and that the bureaucracy would cooperate in such an unprecedented enterprise.

Just as race scientists, psychiatrists, and party ideologues had advocated killing the handicapped even before the killings commenced, German police officers and government administrators in the East proposed killing the Jews before the final solution started. But nothing so radical or unprecedented could be initiated without Hitler's approval. There is no reason to believe that the decision-making process that led to the final solution was substantially different from the one that preceded the euthanasia killings. The decision-making process thus illustrates the linkage between the two killing operations.

As Hans Heinrich Lammers testified at Nuremberg, Hitler gave a direct verbal order to start the T4 killing operation, and, as we have seen, the KdF moved quickly to implement this order. But, in the best tradition of CYA (Cover Your Ass), the bureaucrats of the KdF insisted upon written authorization from their Führer both for their own protection and to assure the collaboration of physicians and government agencies. The KdF prepared the text of the authorization, and, backdating it to the day the war had started, Hitler signed it in October 1939.

It seems eminently reasonable to assume that the decision to implement the final solution would have been made in the same way. Although no testimony has survived to document this, Hitler apparently again gave verbal orders, this time commissioning Heinrich Himmler and his SS and police to kill the Jews. However, unlike euthanasia, there was no written authorization. The reasons for this are not difficult to fathom. Too many people had read Hitler's euthanasia authorization, and such widespread knowledge could have implicated him in the T4 killings; obviously, he refused to sign another such document. In addition, the loyal SS could hardly attempt CYA by asking their Führer for an authorization. Still, Heydrich, whose RSHA had to implement the order Hitler gave to Himmler, needed some written commission to compel the cooperation of other government agencies. Hermann Göring therefore supplied a retroactive sanction in a letter dated 31 July 1941 when he authorized Heydrich to "undertake organizational, technical, and financial preparations" for the murder of the European Jews. Just as Hitler did not write but only signed the letter to Brandt and Bouhler prepared by the KdF, Göring did not initiate but only signed the authorization prepared and submitted by Heydrich. . . .

We do not know the date Hitler issued his order to kill the Jews. Obviously, that order had to precede the killings and Göring's letter, and most historians accept the spring of 1941 as the earliest possible time. But the decision on the highest level to kill handicapped Jewish patients as a group provides at least some indication that a preliminary decision might already have been reached in the spring of 1940. Further, although Hitler believed that the cover of war would make radical exclusion through killing operations possible—which he emphasized by backdating his euthanasia authorization to the day the war began—he nevertheless did not issue a definite order until he was certain that such an ambitious killing enterprise was feasible. But when international conditions, the progress of the war, and the killing capabilities demonstrated by euthanasia made radical exclusion attainable, Jews as a group were included in the killing operations.

Once the order had been given, the SS Einsatzgruppen served as the first means of implementation. In the first sweep through the Soviet Union in 1941 and early 1942, most Soviet Jews were shot; only those able to work for the Germans were permitted to live and relegated to ghettos and camps. But this primitive method of shooting the victims was too public. It also posed logistic problems for the killers, requiring a large killing staff and imposing a psychological burden on the shooters. The SS and police, therefore, soon began to search for a better killing method. They soon turned to the euthanasia program as a model. But carbon monoxide tanks were too expensive, and a dependable supply from distant factories could not be assured. The RSHA motor pool therefore combined the T4 gas van used in the Wartheland with the killing method Albert Widmann had discovered in Bielorussia to develop a gas van, which, like a perpetual motion machine, recycled exhaust fumes to kill its human cargo. . . .

Himmler's men eventually realized, just as the T4 killers had discovered several years earlier, that it was more efficient to bring the victims to a central killing place. It was only logical that these places would be modeled on the T4 centers. But the killers had also learned from the public response to euthanasia that such installations should not be established inside Germany. Therefore, the first killing center of the final solution began functioning in December 1941 at Chelmno (Kulmhof in German) in the Wartheland. Although it was a stationary killing center, it used the gas vans already tested by the Einsatzgruppen. . . .

The final solution applied to Gypsies as well as Jews. As we have seen, the SS Einsatzgruppen shot them alongside Jews. In Germany and Austria, large numbers of Gypsies had already been incarcerated in Gypsy camps, and others had been deported to Poland. And just as the European Jews were either deported to the East by the Germans or killed locally by Germany's allies, Gypsies everywhere faced death at the hands of the Germans or their local collaborators. In the Protectorate, Gypsies were incarcerated in camps—Lety in Bohemia and Hodonin in Moravia—where forced labor, malnutrition, and disease killed many; those remaining were deported to Auschwitz. In Croatia, a German ally, almost all Gypsies were murdered. In the Netherlands and in Belgium, both under German occupation, almost all Gypsies were deported to the East. . . .

Finally, on 16 December 1942, Himmler ordered the total deportation of Gypsies from the German Reich to Auschwitz. . . . Himmler's Auschwitz decree, condemning Gypsies to the concentration camps and certain death, provided for exceptions. The decree exempted "racially pure Sinti and Lalleri Gypsies." This exemption has misled some historians into believing that the Nazi regime considered some Gypsies to be Aryan relatives who must not be destroyed. But these theoretical exemptions never became reality. At the time Himmler issued his exemption, for example, Lalleri Gypsies held at the Berlin-Marzahn camp were deported to Auschwitz. . . .

We have now seen, again and again, the linkage between the killing operations against the handicapped, Jews, and Gypsies. Interpretations about the three operations have changed over the years. At the time, the murder of the handicapped led to public opposition, while the murder of Jews, and even more so Gypsies, failed to produce public opposition. Since the war, however, public interest has focused on the murder of Jews, while the murder of the handicapped and Gypsies has received little attention until recently. But one cannot explain any one of these Nazi killing operations without explaining the others. Together they represented Nazi genocide.

The linkage between the three killing operations was, as we have seen, ideological, based on the belief in human inequality and on the determination to cleanse the gene pool of the German nation. But collaboration between different segments of the bureaucracy [i.e., T4, Hitler's private chancellory, the Reich Ministry of the Interior, the SS, etc.] also established linkage. . . .

The killing technique was the most important contribution made by the T4 euthanasia program to the final solution. This technique involved both the hardware and the software of the killing process. It encompassed not only gas chambers and crematoria, but also the method developed to lure victims into these chambers, to kill them on an assembly line, and to process their corpses. These techniques, including the extraction of teeth and bridgework containing gold, were developed by T4 and exported to the East.

As we have seen, there were obvious differences. For example, the euthanasia killing centers located within the Reich used gas tanks from I. G. Farben with pure carbon monoxide, while centers in the East, where it was too expensive and time-consuming to obtain such tanks, utilized impure exhaust fumes from diesel engines. But the similarities are far more important than the differences.

First, subterfuge was used to fool the victims upon arrival with the appearance of normality. In the euthanasia centers, physicians and nurses checking medical files made the killing center look like a regular hospital, while in the camps of Operation Reinhard, the trappings of the reception area and the welcoming speech by a staff member made the killing center look like a labor camp. The victims were told in both places that they had to take showers for hygienic reasons, and the gas chambers were disguised as shower rooms, while the belongings of the victims were carefully collected and registered to maintain the illusion of normality. In both places, but especially in the East, the practice of assembly line mass murder did, however, produce a callous barbarity that usually vitiated all attempts to deceive the victims.

Second, in both the Reich and the East, the victims were crowded into the gas chambers, and their corpses were burned immediately after they had been killed. In the Reich, they used mobile crematoria; in the East, they utilized outdoor burning. At home, the German staff had to remove and burn the corpses; in Poland, they supervised Jewish prisoners who did the job. But in both places, they robbed the corpses. The system of stealing gold teeth and gold bridgework from the corpses of the murdered victims was first introduced in the euthanasia killing centers and then copied in the extermination camps of Operation Reinhard.

In Birkenau, the killing center at Auschwitz, the SS staff improved upon the extermination technique first used in the euthanasia killings. They introduced Zyklon B, which acted faster, and constructed a killing plant combining gas chambers and stationary crematoria in one building. They also identified and selected those still able to work so that they could exploit their labor before killing them. But even this had already been practiced by the euthanasia killers, who postponed the deaths of those handicapped patients still able to work.

At Auschwitz-Birkenau, and also at Majdanek, the SS did not need the help of T4 specialists. The T4 technique was a basically simple German invention, one that any organization could learn to use. The concentration camps possessed both the organization and the manpower, as well as a commitment to savage brutality, to execute the killing task. . . .

In the postwar world, Auschwitz has come to symbolize genocide in the twentieth century. But Auschwitz was only the last, most perfect Nazi killing center. The entire killing enterprise had started in January 1940 with the murder of the most helpless human beings, institution- alized handicapped patients, had expanded in 1941 to include Jews and Gypsies, and had by 1945 cost the lives of a least 6 million men, women, and children.

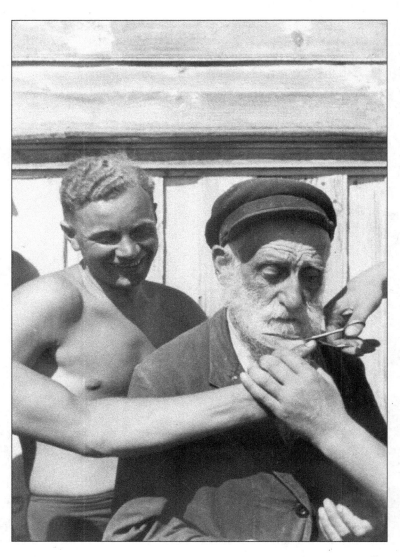

German soldiers having their fun with an elderly Jew. Poland, ca.1940. Photograph by
Joe Heydecker/Bildarchiv Preussischer Kulturbesitz/Art Resource, New York

PART

II

The Motivations
of the Killers

Variety of Opinion

*The key to understanding how Nazi doctors came to do the work of
Auschwitz is the psychological principle I call "doubling": the division
of the self into two functioning wholes, so that a part-self acts as an entire
self. An Auschwitz doctor could, through doubling, not only kill . . . but
organize . . . all aspects of his behavior.*

Robert Jay Lifton

*Anti-Semitic sentiments among the troops increased as conditions at the
front worsened and as soldiers were no longer merely exposed to racist
propaganda but also observed and in some cases participated in mass
murders of Jews.*

Omer Bartov

*To break ranks and step out, to adopt overtly nonconformist behavior,
was simply beyond most of the men. It was easier for them to shoot. . . .
If the men of Reserve Police Battalion 101 could become killers, what
group of men cannot?*

Christopher R. Browning

What drove the men who were directly involved in killing Jews, Gypsies, and others during the Holocaust? Earlier views of them as the personification of unalloyed evil have not proved very satisfying. After all, thousands of Germans (and others) participated in the killings, and they could not all have been morally depraved brutes, although some certainly were. We now know that they were not all SS men. Even those who were could be loving family men and decent human beings capable of acts of kindness to some victims. How, then, could they participate in mass murder?

Robert Jay Lifton examines the motivations of Nazi doctors who selected who would live and who would die in the camps, supervised the gassings, and performed experiments on prisoners that ended in fatal injections when the victims no longer were useful. What transformed men dedicated to healing into killers? Lifton, a leading American psychiatrist, sought to answer this question by interviewing dozens of surviving Nazi doctors and nonmedical professionals, as well as former camp inmates. He concluded that the doctors had gone through the process of "doubling," the separation of a person's self into two functioning wholes, a phenomenon he distinguished from multiple and split personalities. Lifton underscored the central role of Nazi ideology in doubling. Killing Jews, who were viewed as embodying all that was evil in the world, would heal the Aryan race. By adopting an "Auschwitz self" while simultaneously maintaining their professional identity, the doctors could murder with a clear conscience. After 1945 they could return to their "prewar self" and resume normal lives and careers— unburdened, it seems, by guilt or remorse. As Lifton makes clear, this analysis has implications that go well beyond the medical profession and the Nazi era.

Omer Bartov finds that Nazi racial ideology was equally important in motivating many of the millions of men of the German Army (the Wehrmacht) to participate in Holocaust crimes, but that it required extreme conditions on the Eastern Front to bring that about. After brief but spectacular initial victories over Soviet forces in the initial phases of "Operation Barbarossa," the German attack on the USSR that began in June, 1941, the Wehrmacht became bogged down in a dehumanizing war of attrition that inflicted staggering losses on both sides. Some German units were completely wiped out, and the Army's cohesive "primary groups" of 1941 disappeared as a flood of new recruits replaced the dead and wounded. Its unit solidarity shattered and its soldiers increasingly brutalized by primitive conditions and savage fighting, the Wehrmacht maintained discipline by inflicting draconian punishments (including thousands of executions) and giving the men a safety valve: mistreating Soviet prisoners of war as well as Jews, Gypsies, and other Soviet civilians. Inhuman conditions at the front also made German soldiers more receptive to Nazi propaganda blaming the Jews for the war. Hence ideology combined with the barbarization of warfare to draw Hitler's army into genocide.

Christopher Browning puts even greater emphasis on situational factors in his study of Reserve Police Battalion 101, made up of older men (and "ordinary men," not SS or frontline soldiers) drafted to keep order behind German lines in Eastern Europe and unexpectedly ordered to murder Jews. Although they were given the choice of other assignments in the unit and did not have to fear being punished or sent away for noncompliance, most joined in the killing and grew used to it. Browning examined their testimony to a postwar German court and found that Nazi ideology played little part in determining their behavior. Few of the men had been enthusiastic Nazis, and their ideological indoctrination had been rudimentary. In exploring the complex web of motivation, Browning concludes that deference to authority and conformity to the group are what made killers out of "ordinary men."

Some scholars have portrayed most Germans under Hitler as "willing executioners" because they allegedly were products of a deeply anti-Jewish culture, but such sweeping indictments have not proven very persuasive. It should be apparent from these essays that antisemitism and Nazi racial ideology were not uniform in their power to motivate. Readiness to kill depended on a complex of personal predispositions, experiences, and circumstances and hence varied among groups and individuals.

Robert Jay Lifton

The Nazi Doctors

In Nazi mass murder, we can say that a barrier was removed, a boundary crossed: that boundary between violent imagery and periodic killing of victims (as of Jews in pogroms) on the one hand, and systematic genocide in Auschwitz and elsewhere on the other. My argument in this study is that the medicalization of killing—the imagery of killing in the name of healing—was crucial to that terrible step. At the heart of the Nazi enterprise, then, is the destruction of the boundary between healing and killing.

Early descriptions of Auschwitz and other death camps focused on the sadism and viciousness of Nazi guards, officers, and physicians. But subsequent students of the process realized that sadism and viciousness alone could not account for the killing of millions of people. The emphasis then shifted to the bureaucracy of killing: the faceless, detached bureaucratic function originally described by Max Weber, now applied to mass murder. This focus on numbed violence is enormously important, and is consistent with what we shall observe to be the routinization of all Auschwitz functions.

Yet these emphases are not sufficient in themselves. They must be seen in relation to the visionary motivations associated with ideology, along with the specific individual-psychological mechanisms enabling people to kill. What I call "medicalized killing" addresses these motivational principles and psychological mechanisms, and permits us to understand the Auschwitz victimizers—notably Nazi doctors—both as part of a bureaucracy of killing and as individual participants whose attitudes and behavior can be examined.

Medicalized killing can be understood in two wider perspectives. The first is the "surgical" method of killing large numbers of people by means of a controlled technology making use of highly poisonous gas; the methods employed became a means of maintaining distance between killers and victims. This distancing had considerable importance for the Nazis in alleviating the psychological problems experienced (as attested

From *Nazi Doctors* by Robert Jay Lifton. Reprinted by permission of Basic Books, a member of Perseus Books, L.L.C.

over and over by Nazi documents) by the *Einsatzgruppen* troops who carried out face-to-face shooting of Jews in Eastern Europe . . . —problems that did not prevent those troops from murdering 1,400,000 Jews.

I was able to obtain direct evidence on this matter during an interview with a former *Wehrmacht* neuropsychiatrist who had treated large numbers of *Einsatzgruppen* personnel for psychological disorders. He told me that these disorders resembled combat reactions of ordinary troops: severe anxiety, nightmares, tremors, and numerous bodily complaints. But in these "killer troops," as he called them, the symptoms tended to last longer and to be more severe. He estimated that 20 percent of those doing the actual killing experienced these symptoms of psychological decompensation. About half of that 20 percent associated their symptoms mainly with the "unpleasantness" of what they had to do, while the other half seemed to have moral questions about shooting people in that way. The men had the greatest psychological difficulty concerning shooting women and children, especially children. Many experienced a sense of guilt in their dreams, which could include various forms of punishment or retribution. Such psychological difficulty led the Nazis to seek a more "surgical" method of killing.

But there is another perspective on medicalized killing that I believe to be insufficiently recognized: *killing as a therapeutic imperative.* That kind of motivation was revealed in the words of a Nazi doctor quoted by the distinguished survivor physician Dr. Ella Lingens-Reiner. Pointing to the chimneys in the distance, she asked a Nazi doctor, Fritz Klein, "How can you reconcile that with your [Hippocratic] oath as a doctor?" His answer was, "Of course I am a doctor and I want to preserve life. And out of respect for human life, I would remove a gangrenous appendix from a diseased body. The Jew is the gangrenous appendix in the body of mankind."

The medical imagery was still broader. Just as Turkey during the nineteenth century (because of the extreme decline of the Ottoman empire) was known as the "sick man of Europe," so did pre-Hitler ideologues and Hitler himself interpret Germany's post–First World War chaos and demoralization as an "illness," especially of the Aryan race. Hitler wrote in *Mein Kampf*, in the mid-1920s, that *"anyone who wants to cure this era, which is inwardly sick and rotten, must first of all summon up the courage to make clear the causes of this disease."* The diagnosis was racial. The only genuine "culture-creating" race, the Aryans, had permitted themselves to be weakened to the point of endangered survival by the "destroyers of culture," characterized as "the Jew." The Jews were agents of "racial pollution" and "racial tuberculosis," as well as parasites and bacteria causing sickness, deterioration, and death in the host peoples they infested. They were the "eternal bloodsucker," "vampire," "germ carrier," "peoples' parasite," and "maggot in a rotting corpse." The cure had to be radical: that is (as one scholar put it), by "cutting out the 'canker of decay,' propagating the worthwhile elements and letting the less valuable wither away, . . . [and] 'the extirpation of all those categories of people considered to be worthless or dangerous.'"

Medical metaphor blended with concrete biomedical ideology in the Nazi sequence from coercive sterilization to direct medical killing to the death camps. The unifying principle of the biomedical ideology was that of a deadly racial disease, the sickness of the Aryan race; the cure, the killing of all Jews.

Thus, for Hans Frank, jurist and General Governor of Poland during the Nazi occupation, "the Jews were a lower species of life, a kind of vermin, which upon contact infected the German people with deadly diseases." When the Jews in the area he ruled had been killed, he declared that "now a sick Europe would become healthy again." It was a religion of the will—the will as "an all-encompassing metaphysical principle;" and what the Nazis "willed" was nothing less than total control over life and death. While this view is often referred to as "social Darwinism," the term applies only loosely, mostly to the Nazi stress on natural "struggle" and on "survival of the fittest." The regime actually rejected much of Darwinism; since evolutionary theory is more or less democratic in its assumption of a common beginning for all races, it is therefore at odds with the Nazi principle of inherent Aryan racial virtue.

Even more specific to the biomedical vision was crude genetic imagery, combined with still cruder eugenic visions. . . . Here Heinrich Himmler, as high priest, spoke of the leadership's task as being "like the plant-breeding specialist who, when he wants to breed a pure new strain from a well-tried species that has been exhausted by too much cross-breeding, first goes over the field to cull the unwanted plants."

The Nazi project, then, was not so much Darwinian or social Darwinist as a vision of absolute control over the evolutionary process, over the biological human future. Making widespread use of the Darwinian term "selection," the Nazis sought to take over the functions of nature (natural selection) and God (the Lord giveth and the Lord taketh away) in orchestrating their own version of human evolution.

In these visions the Nazis embraced not only versions of medieval mystical anti-Semitism but also a newer (nineteenth- and twentieth-century) claim to "scientific racism." Dangerous Jewish characteristics could be linked with alleged data of scientific disciplines, so that a "mainstream of racism" formed from "the fusion of anthropology, eugenics, and social thought." The resulting "racial and social biology" could make vicious forms of anti-Semitism seem intellectually respectable to learned men and women.

One can speak of the Nazi state as a "biocracy." The model here is a theocracy, a system of rule by priests of a sacred order under the claim of divine prerogative. In the case of the Nazi biocracy, the divine prerogative was that of cure through purification and revitalization of the Aryan race: "From a dead mechanism which only lays claim to existence for its own sake, there must be formed a living organism with the exclusive aim of serving a higher idea." Just as in a theocracy, the state itself is no more than a vehicle for the divine purpose, so in the Nazi biocracy was the state no more than a means to achieve "*a mission of the German people on earth*": that of "*assembling and preserving the most valuable stocks of basic racial elements in this* [Aryan] *people . . .* [and] *. . . raising them to a dominant position.*" The Nazi biocracy differed from a classical theocracy in that the biological priests did not actually rule. The clear rulers were Adolf Hitler and his circle, not biological theorists and certainly not the doctors. (The difference, however, is far from absolute: even in a theocracy, highly politicized rulers may make varying claims to priestly authority.) In any case, Nazi ruling authority was maintained in the name of the higher biological principle.

Among the biological authorities called forth to articulate and implement "scientific racism"—including physical anthropologists, geneticists, and racial theorists of every variety—doctors inevitably found a unique place. It is they who work at the border of life and death, who are most associated with the awesome, death-defying, and sometimes death-dealing aura of the primitive shaman and medicine man. As bearers of this shamanistic legacy and contemporary practitioners of mysterious healing arts, it is they who are likely to be called upon to become biological activists.

I have mentioned my primary interest in Nazi doctors' participation in medicalized or biologized killing. We shall view their human experiments as related to the killing process and to the overall Nazi biomedical vision. At Nuremberg, doctors were tried only limitedly for their involvement in killing, partly because its full significance was not yet understood.

In Auschwitz, Nazi doctors presided over the murder of most of the one million victims of that camp. Doctors performed selections — both on the ramp among arriving transports of prisoners and later in the camps and on the medical blocks. Doctors supervised the killing in the gas chambers and decided when the victims were dead. Doctors conducted a murderous epidemiology, sending to the gas chamber groups of people with contagious diseases and sometimes including everyone else who might be on the medical block. Doctors ordered and supervised, and at times carried out, direct killing of debilitated patients on the medical blocks by means of phenol injections into the bloodstream or the heart. In connection with all of these killings, doctors kept up a pretense of medical legitimacy: for deaths of Auschwitz prisoners and of outsiders brought there to be killed, they signed false death certificates listing spurious illnesses. Doctors consulted actively on how best to keep selections running smoothly; on how many people to permit to remain alive to fill the slave labor requirements of the I. G. Farben enterprise at Auschwitz; and on how to burn the enormous numbers of bodies that strained the facilities of the crematoria.

In sum, we may say that doctors were given much of the responsibility for the murderous ecology of Auschwitz — the choosing of victims, the carrying through of the physical and psychological mechanics of killing, and the balancing of killing and work functions in the camp. While doctors by no means ran Auschwitz, they did lend it a perverse medical aura. As one survivor who closely observed the process put the matter, "Auschwitz was like a medical operation," and "the killing program was led by doctors from beginning to end."

We may say that the doctor standing at the ramp represented a kind of omega point, a mythical gatekeeper between the worlds of the dead and the living, a final common pathway of the Nazi vision of therapy via mass murder. . . .

The key to understanding how Nazi doctors came to do the work of Auschwitz is the psychological principle I call "doubling": the division of the self into two functioning wholes, so that a part-self acts as an entire self. An Auschwitz doctor could, through doubling, not only kill and contribute to killing but organize silently, on behalf of that evil project, an entire self-structure (or self-process) encompassing virtually all aspects of his behavior.

Doubling, then, was the psychological vehicle for the Nazi doctor's Faustian bargain with the diabolical environment in exchange for his contribution to the killing; he was offered various psychological and material benefits on behalf of privileged adaptation. Beyond Auschwitz was the larger Faustian temptation offered to German doctors in general: that of becoming the theorists and implementers of a cosmic scheme of racial cure by means of victimization and mass murder.

One is always ethically responsible for Faustian bargains—a responsibility in no way abrogated by the fact that much doubling takes place outside of awareness. In exploring doubling, I engage in psychological probing on behalf of illuminating evil. For the individual Nazi doctor in Auschwitz, doubling was likely to mean a choice for evil.

Generally speaking, doubling involves five characteristics. There is, first, a dialectic between two selves in terms of autonomy and connection. The individual Nazi doctor needed his Auschwitz self to function psychologically in an environment so antithetical to his previous ethical standards. At the same time, he needed his prior self in order to continue to see himself as humane physician, husband, father. The Auschwitz self had to be both autonomous and connected to the prior self that gave rise to it. Second, the doubling follows a holistic principle. The Auschwitz self "succeeded" because it was inclusive and could connect with the entire Auschwitz environment: it rendered coherent, and gave form to, various themes and mechanisms, which I shall discuss shortly. Third, doubling has a life-death dimension: the Auschwitz self was perceived by the perpetrator as a form of psychological survival in a death-dominated environment; in other words, we have the paradox of a "killing self" being created on behalf of what one perceives as one's own healing or survival. Fourth, a major function of doubling, as in Auschwitz, is likely to be the avoidance of guilt: the second self tends to be the one performing the "dirty work." And, finally, doubling involves both an unconscious dimension—taking place, as stated, largely outside of awareness—and a significant change in moral consciousness. These five characteristics frame and pervade all else that goes on psychologically in doubling. . . .

The way in which doubling allowed Nazi doctors to avoid guilt was not by the elimination of conscience but by what can be called the *transfer of conscience.* The requirements of conscience were transferred to the Auschwitz self, which placed it within its own criteria for good (duty, loyalty to group, "improving" Auschwitz conditions, etc.), thereby freeing the original self from responsibility for actions there. . . . The Auschwitz self of the Nazi doctor similarly assumed the death issue for him but at the same time used its evil project as a way of staving off awareness of his own "perishable and mortal part." It does the "dirty work" for the entire self by rendering that work "proper" and in that way protects the entire self from awareness of its own guilt and its own death.

In doubling, one part of the self "disavows" another part. What is repudiated is not reality itself—the individual Nazi doctor was aware of what he was doing via the Auschwitz self—but the meaning of that reality. The Nazi doctor knew that he selected, but did not interpret selections as murder. One level of disavowal, then, was the Auschwitz self's altering of the meaning of murder; and on another, the repudiation by the original self of *anything* done by the Auschwitz self. From the moment of its formation, the Auschwitz self so violated the Nazi doctor's previous self-concept as to require more or less permanent disavowal. Indeed, disavowal was the life blood of the Auschwitz self.

Doubling is an active psychological process, a means of *adaptation to extremity.* That is why I use the verb form, as opposed to the more usual noun form, "the double." The adaptation requires a dissolving of "psychic glue" as an alternative to a radical breakdown of the self. In Auschwitz, the pattern was established under the duress of the individual doctor's transition period. At that time the Nazi doctor experienced his own death anxiety as well as such death equivalents as fear of disintegration, separation, and stasis. He needed a functional Auschwitz self to still his anxiety. And that Auschwitz self had to assume hegemony on an everyday basis, reducing expressions of the prior self to odd moments and to contacts with family and friends outside the camp. Nor did most Nazi doctors resist that usurpation as long as they remained in the camp. Rather they welcomed it as the only means of psychological function. If an environment is sufficiently extreme, and one chooses to remain in it, one may be able to do so *only* by means of doubling.

Yet doubling does not include the radical dissociation and sustained separateness characteristic of multiple or "dual personality." In the latter condition, the two selves are more profoundly distinct and autonomous, and tend either not to know about each other or else to see each other as alien. . . .

While individual Nazi doctors in Auschwitz doubled in different ways, all of them doubled. Ernst B.,[1] for instance, limited his doubling; in avoiding selections, he was resisting a full-blown Auschwitz self. Yet his conscious desire to adapt to Auschwitz was an accession to at least a certain amount of doubling: it was he, after all, who said that "one could react like a normal human being in Auschwitz only for the first few hours;" after that, "you were caught and had to go along," which meant that you had to double. His own doubling was evident in his sympathy for Mengele[2] and, at least to some extent, for the most extreme expressions of the Nazi ethos (the image of the Nazis as a "world blessing" and of Jews as the world's "fundamental evil"). And despite the limit to his doubling, he retains aspects of his Auschwitz self to this day in his way of judging Auschwitz behavior.

In contrast, Mengele's embrace of the Auschwitz self gave the impression of a quick adaptive affinity, causing one to wonder whether he required any doubling at all. But doubling was indeed required in a man who befriended children to an unusual degree and then drove some of them personally to the gas chamber; or by a man so "collegial" in his relationship to prisoner doctors and so ruthlessly flamboyant in his conduct of selections. Whatever his affinity for Auschwitz, a man who could be pictured under ordinary conditions as "a slightly sadistic German professor" had to form a new self to become an energetic killer. The point about Mengele's doubling was that his prior self could be readily absorbed into the Auschwitz self; and his continuing allegiance to the Nazi ideology and project probably enabled his Auschwitz self, more than in the case of other Nazi doctors, to remain active over the years after the Second World War.

[1]"Dr. Ernst B." (real name Wilhelm Münch), an Auschwitz physician described as "a human being in an SS uniform," was the only death-camp doctor acquitted in a postwar trial. Former prisoners, including prisoner doctors, testified in his behalf. —Ed.

[2]Dr. Josef Mengele, a fanatical Nazi, performed macabre experiments on twins at Auschwitz. He escaped capture and died in hiding in Brazil in 1979. —Ed.

Wirth's[3] doubling was neither limited (like Dr. B's) nor harmonious (like Mengele's): it was both strong and conflicted. We see Auschwitz's chief doctor as a "divided self" because both selves retained their power. Yet his doubling was the most successful of all from the standpoint of the Auschwitz institution and the Nazi project. Even his suicide was a mark of that success: while the Nazi defeat enabled him to equate his Auschwitz self more clearly with evil, he nonetheless retained responsibility to that Auschwitz self sufficiently to remain inwardly divided and unable to imagine any possibility of resolution and renewal—either legally, morally, or psychologically.

Within the Auschwitz structure, significant doubling included future goals and even a sense of hope. Styles of doubling varied because each Nazi doctor created his Auschwitz self out of his prior self, with its particular history, and with his own psychological mechanisms. But in all Nazi doctors, prior self and Auschwitz self were connected by the overall Nazi ethos and the general authority of the regime. Doubling was a shared theme among them.

Indeed, Auschwitz as an *institution*—as an atrocity-producing situation—ran on doubling. An atrocity-producing situation is one so structured externally (in this case, institutionally) that the average person entering it (in this case, as part of the German authority) will commit or become associated with atrocities. Always important to an atrocity-producing situation is its capacity to motivate individuals psychologically toward engaging in atrocity.

In an institution as powerful as Auschwitz, the external environment could set the tone for much of an individual doctor's "internal environment." The demand for doubling was part of the environmental message immediately perceived by Nazi doctors, the implicit command to bring forth a self that could adapt to killing without one's feeling oneself a murderer. Doubling became not just an individual enterprise but a shared psychological process, the group norm, part of the Auschwitz "weather." And that group process was intensified by the general awareness that, whatever went on in other camps, Auschwitz was the great

---

[3]Dr. Eduard Wirth was chief physician at Auschwitz. A dedicated physician capable of showing compassion to individual prisoners, he also set up the camp's machinery of mass murder. He hanged himself in 1945.—Ed.

technical center of the Final Solution. One had to double in order that one's life work there not be interfered with either by the corpses one helped to produce or by those "living dead" (the *Muselmänner*) all around one. Inevitably, the Auschwitz pressure toward doubling extended to prisoner doctors, the most flagrant examples of whom were those who came to work closely with the Nazis. . . . Even those prisoner doctors who held strongly to their healing ethos, and underwent minimal doubling, inadvertently contributed to Nazi doctors' doubling simply by working with them, as they had to, and thereby in some degree confirmed a Nazi doctor's Auschwitz self.

Doubling undoubtedly occurred extensively in nonmedical Auschwitz personnel as well. Rudolf Höss[4] told how noncommissioned officers regularly involved in selections "pour[ed] out their hearts" to him about the difficulty of their work (their prior self speaking)—but went on doing that work (their Auschwitz self directing behavior). Höss described the Auschwitz choices: "either to become cruel, to become heartless and no longer to respect human life [that is, to develop a highly functional Auschwitz self] or to be weak and to get to the point of a nervous breakdown [that is, to hold onto one's prior self, which in Auschwitz was nonfunctional]." But in the Nazi doctor, the doubling was particularly stark in that a prior healing self gave rise to a killing self that should have been, but functionally was not, in direct opposition to it. And as in any atrocity-producing situation, Nazi doctors found themselves in a psychological climate where they were virtually certain to choose evil: they were propelled, that is, toward murder.

Beyond Auschwitz, there was much in the Nazi movement that promoted doubling. The overall Nazi project, replete with cruelty, required constant doubling in the service of carrying out that cruelty. The doubling could take the form of a gradual process of "slippery slope" compromises: the slow emergence of a functional "Nazi self" via a series of destructive actions, at first more incriminating, if not more murderous, than the previous ones.

---

[4]Höss was commandant of Auschwitz from 1940 to 1943. He was tried and hanged by the Poles in 1947.—Ed.

Doubling could also be more dramatic, infused with transcendence, the sense (described by a French fascist who joined the SS) of being someone entering a religious order "who must now divest himself of his past," and of being "reborn into a new European race." That new Nazi self could take on a sense of mystical fusion with the German *Volk*, with "destiny," and with immortalizing powers. Always there was the combination noted earlier of idealism and terror, imagery of destruction and renewal, so that "gods . . . appear as both destroyers and culture-heroes, just as the Führer could appear as front comrade and master builder." Himmler, especially in his speeches to his SS leaders within their "oath-bound community," called for the kind of doubling necessary to engage in what he considered to be heroic cruelty, especially in the killing of Jews.

The degree of doubling was not necessarily equivalent to Nazi Party membership; thus, Hochhuth could claim that "the great divide was between Nazis [meaning those with well-developed Nazi selves] and decent people, not between Party members and other Germans." But probably never has a political movement demanded doubling with the intensity and scale of the Nazis.

Doctors as a group may be more susceptible to doubling than others. For example, a former Nazi doctor claimed that the anatomist's insensitivity toward skeletons and corpses accounted for his friend Hirt's grotesque "anthropological" collection of Jewish skulls. . . . While hardly a satisfactory explanation, this doctor was referring to a genuine pattern not just of numbing but of medical doubling. That doubling usually begins with the student's encounter with the corpse he or she must dissect, often enough on the first day of medical school. One feels it necessary to develop a "medical self," which enables one not only to be relatively inured to death but to function reasonably efficiently in relation to the many-sided demands of the work. The ideal doctor, to be sure, remains warm and humane by keeping that doubling to a minimum. But few doctors meet that ideal standard. Since studies have suggested that a psychological motivation for entering the medical profession can be the overcoming of an unusually great fear of death, it is possible that this fear in doctors propels them in the direction of doubling when encountering deadly environments. Doctors drawn to the Nazi movement in general, and to SS or concentration-camp medicine in particular, were likely to be those with the greatest previous medical doubling. But even doctors without outstanding Nazi sympathies could well have had a certain experience with doubling and a proclivity for its further manifestations.

Certainly the tendency toward doubling was particularly strong among *Nazi* doctors. Given the heroic vision held out to them—as cultivators of the genes and as physicians to the *Volk*, and as militarized healers combining the life-death power of shaman and general—any cruelty they might perpetrate was all too readily drowned in hubris. And their medical hubris was furthered by their role in the sterilization and "euthanasia" projects within a vision of curing the ills of the Nordic race and the German people.

Doctors who ended up undergoing the extreme doubling necessitated by the "euthanasia" killing centers and the death camps were probably unusually susceptible to doubling. There was, of course, an element of chance in where one was sent, but doctors assigned either to the killing centers or to the death camps tended to be strongly committed to Nazi ideology. They may well have also had greater schizoid tendencies, or been particularly prone to numbing and omnipotence-sadism, all of which also enhance doubling. Since, even under extreme conditions, people have a way of finding and staying in situations they connect with psychologically, we can suspect a certain degree of self-selection there too. In these ways, previous psychological characteristics of a doctor's self had considerable significance—but a significance in respect to tendency or susceptibility, and no more. Considerable doubling occurred in people of the most varied psychological characteristics.

We thus find ourselves returning to the recognition that most of what Nazi doctors did would be within the potential capability—at least under certain conditions—of most doctors and of most people. But once embarked on doubling in Auschwitz, a Nazi doctor did indeed separate himself from other physicians and from other human beings. Doubling was the mechanism by which a doctor, in his actions, moved from the ordinary to the demonic. . . .

The Auschwitz self depended upon radically diminished feeling, upon one's not experiencing psychologically what one was doing. I have called the state "psychic numbing," a general category of diminished capacity or inclination to feel. Psychic numbing involves an interruption in psychic action—in the continuous creation and recreation of images and forms that constitutes the symbolizing or "formative process" characteristic of human mental life. Psychic numbing varies greatly in degree, from everyday blocking of excessive stimuli to extreme manifestations in response to death-saturated environments. But it is probably impossible to kill another human being without numbing oneself toward that victim.

The Auschwitz self also called upon the related mechanism of "derealization," of divesting oneself from the actuality of what one is part of, not experiencing it as "real." (That absence of actuality in regard to the killing was not inconsistent with an awareness of the killing policy—that is, of the Final Solution.) Still another pattern is that of "disavowal," or the rejection of what one actually perceives and of its meaning. Disavowal and derealization overlap and are both aspects of the overall numbing process. The key function of numbing in the Auschwitz self is the avoidance of feelings of guilt when one is involved in killing. The Auschwitz self can then engage in medicalized killing, an ultimate form of numbed violence.

To be sure, a Nazi doctor arrived at Auschwitz with his psychic numbing well under way. Much feeling had been blunted by his early involvement with Nazi medicine, including its elimination of Jews and use of terror, as well as by his participation in forced sterilization, his knowledge of or relationship to direct medical killing ("euthanasia"), and the information he knew at some level of consciousness about concentration camps and medical experiments held there if not about death camps such as Auschwitz. Numbing was fostered not only by this knowledge and culpability but by the admired principle of "the new spirit of German coldness." Moreover, early Nazi achievements furthered that hardness; and it is often the case that success breeds numbing. . . .

There has to be a transition from feeling to not feeling—a transition that, in Auschwitz, could be rapid and radical. It began with a built-in barrier toward psychologically experiencing the camp's main activity: killing Jews. The great majority of Jews were murdered upon arrival, without having been admitted to the camp and achieving the all-important status of having a number tattooed on one's arm, which in Auschwitz meant life, however precarious. Numbing toward victims was built in because, in Auschwitz terms, those victims never existed. The large selections brought about that massive non-existence; and the selections themselves became psychologically dissociated from other activities, relegated to a mental area that "didn't count"—that is, both derealized and disavowed. In that sense, there was a kernel of truth to Dr. B.'s claim that selections were psychologically less significant to Nazi doctors than the problems of hunger they encountered from moment to moment.

But only a kernel, since Nazi doctors knew that selections meant killing, and had to do the psychological work of calling forth a numbed Auschwitz self in order to perform them. While Nazi doctors varied in their original will, or willingness, to perform selections, they tended to have to overcome some "block" (as Dr. B. put it) or "scruple" (as Nazi literature has it). With the actual performance of one's first and perhaps second selection, one had, in effect, made a pledge to stay numbed, which meant to live within the restricted feelings of the Auschwitz self.

For this transition, the heavy drinking I have referred to has great significance on several levels. It provided, at the very beginning, an altered state of consciousness within which one "tried on" the threatening Auschwitz realities (the melodramatic, even romanticized declarations of doubts and half opposition described by Dr. B.). In this altered state, conflicts and objections need not have been viewed as serious resistance, need not have been dangerous. One could then explore doubts without making them real: one could derealize both the doubts and the rest of one's new Auschwitz life. At the same time, alcohol was central to a pattern of male bonding through which new doctors were socialized into the Auschwitz community. Men pull together for the "common good," even for what was perceived among Nazi doctors as group survival. Drinking enhanced the meeting of the minds between old-timers, who could offer models of an Auschwitz self to the newcomer seeking entry into the realm of Auschwitz killing. The continuing alcohol-enhanced sharing of group feelings and group numbing gave further shape to the emerging Auschwitz self.

Over time, as drinking was continued especially in connection with selections, it enabled the Auschwitz self to distance that killing activity and reject responsibility for it. Increasingly, the Jews as victims failed to touch the overall psychological processes of the Auschwitz self. Whether a Nazi doctor saw Jews without feeling their presence, or did not see them at all, he no longer experienced them as beings who affected him—that is, as human beings. Much of that transition process occurred within days or even hours, but tended to become an established pattern by two or three weeks.

The numbing of the Auschwitz self was greatly aided by the diffusion of responsibility. With the medical corpsmen closer to the actual killing, the Auschwitz self of the individual doctor could readily feel "It is not I who kill." He was likely to perceive what he did as a combination of military order ("I am assigned to ramp duty"), designated role ("I am expected to select strong prisoners for work and weaker ones for 'special treatment'"), and desirable attitude ("I am supposed to be disciplined and hard and to overcome 'scruples'"). Moreover, since "the Führer decides upon the life and death of any enemy of the state," responsibility lay with him (or his immediate representatives) alone. As in the case of the participant in direct medical killing ("euthanasia"), the Auschwitz self could feel itself no more than a member of a "team," within which responsibility was so shared, and so offered to higher authorities, as no longer to exist for anyone on that team. And insofar as one felt a residual sense of responsibility, one could reinvoke numbing by means of a spirit of numerical compromise: "We give them ten or fifteen and save five or six."

Numbing could become solidified by this focus on "team play" and "absolute fairness" toward other members of the team. Yet if the "team" did something incriminating, one could stay numbed by asserting one's independence from it. I have in mind one former Nazi doctor's denial of responsibility for the medical experiments done by a team to which he provided materials from his laboratory, even though he showed up on occasion at a concentration camp and looked over experimental charts and subjects. That same doctor also denied responsibility for the "team" (committee) decision to allocate large amounts of Zyklon-B for use in death camps, though he was prominent in the decision-making process, because, whatever other members of the team knew, he had not been informed that the gas would be used for killing. In this last example in particular, we sense that numbing can be willed and clung to in the face of the kind of continual involvement of the self in experiences that would ordinarily produce lots of feeling. . . .

The language of the Auschwitz self, and of the Nazis in general, was crucial to the numbing. A leading scholar of the Holocaust told of examining "tens of thousands" of Nazi documents without once encountering the word "killing," until, after many years he finally did discover the word—in reference to an edict concerning dogs.

For what was being done to the Jews, there were different words, words that perpetuated the numbing of the Auschwitz self by rendering murder nonmurderous. For the doctors specifically, these words suggested responsible military-medical behavior: "ramp duty" (*Rampendienst*) or sometimes even "medical ramp duty" (*ärztliche Rampendienst*) or "[prisoners] presenting themselves to a doctor" (*Arztvorstellern*). For what was being done to the Jews in general, there was, of course, the "Final Solution of the Jewish question" (*Endlösung der Judenfrage*), "possible solutions" (*Lösungsmöglichkeiten*), "evacuation" (*Aussiedlung* or *Evakuierung*), "transfer" (*Überstellung*), and "resettlement" (*Umsiedlung,* the German word suggesting removal from a danger area). Even when they spoke of a "gassing *Kommando*" (*Vergasungskommando*), it had the ostensible function of disinfection. The word "selection" (*Selektion*) could imply sorting out the healthy from the sick, or even some form of Darwinian scientific function having to do with "natural selection" (*natürliche Auswahl*), certainly nothing to do with killing.

The Nazi doctor did not literally believe these euphemisms. Even a well-developed Auschwitz self was aware that Jews were not being resettled but killed, and that the "Final Solution" meant killing all of them. But at the same time the language used gave Nazi doctors a discourse in which killing was no longer killing; and need not be experienced, or even perceived, as killing. As they lived increasingly within that language—and they used it with each other—Nazi doctors became imaginatively bound to a psychic realm of derealization, disavowal, and nonfeeling. . . .

Although doubling can be understood as a pervasive process present in some degree in most if not all lives, we have mainly been talking about a destructive version of it: *victimizer's doubling.* The Germans of the Nazi era came to epitomize this process not because they were inherently more evil than other people, but because they succeeded in making use of this form of doubling for tapping the general human moral and psychological potential for mobilizing evil on a vast scale and channeling it into systematic killing.

While victimizer's doubling can occur in virtually any group, perhaps professionals of various kinds—physicians, psychologists, physicists, biologists, clergy, generals, statesmen, writers, artists—have a special capacity for doubling. In them a prior, humane self can be joined by a "professional self" willing to ally itself with a destructive project, with harming or even killing others. . . .

In light of the recent record of professionals engaged in mass killing, can this be the century of doubling? Or, given the ever greater potential for professionalization of genocide, will that distinction belong to the twenty-first century? Or, may one ask a little more softly, can we interrupt the process—first by naming it?

Omer Bartov

Hitler's Army

[A] detailed reconstruction of life at the front . . . demonstrates the effects of the immense material attrition on the troops' physical condition and state of mind. It stresses that as of winter 1941–42 the majority of Germany's soldiers were forced into trench warfare highly reminiscent of the Western Front of 1914–18, while facing, however, an increasingly modernized enemy. Unable to rely on its hitherto highly successful Blitzkrieg tactics, the Wehrmacht accepted Hitler's view that this was an all-or-nothing struggle for survival, a "war of ideologies" which demanded total spiritual commitment, and thus tried to compensate for the loss of its technological superiority by intensifying the troops' political indoctrination. This in turn opened the way for an ever greater brutalization of the soldiers. . . .

The demodernization of the front had several important consequences. First, it led to such heavy losses among combat units that the traditional backbone of the German army, the "primary groups" which had hitherto assured its cohesion, were largely wiped out. Second, in order to prevent the disintegration of the army as a whole which might have resulted from the breakup of the "primary group," the Wehrmacht introduced and ruthlessly implemented an extremely harsh disciplinary system, to which was given not merely a military, but also an ideological legitimation. Yet draconian punishment did not suffice in cases where fear of the enemy was greater than fear of one's superiors. Thus in compensation for their obedience, and as a logical conclusion of the politicization of discipline, the troops were in turn given license to vent their anger and frustration on the enemy's soldiers and civilians. The demodernization of the front consequently greatly enhanced the brutalization of the troops, and made the soldiers more receptive to ideological indoctrination and more willing to implement the policies it advocated. This process was possible, however, only because a large proportion of the Wehrmacht's officers and men already shared some key elements of the National Socialist world-view. Confronted with a battlefield reality which no longer corresponded to their previous image of war, and with an enemy who could not be overcome by employing familiar military methods, German soldiers now accepted the Nazi vision of war as the only one applicable to their situation. It was at this point that the Wehrmacht finally became Hitler's army. . . .

[I]t was the unprecedented harsh discipline of the Wehrmacht which kept the units together at the front. However, the soldiers' submission to a disciplinary system which led to the execution of some 15,000 men was closely tied to the troops' own conduct toward enemy soldiers and civilians. While many of the army's criminal activities were directed from above, the troops went unpunished even when they totally disregarded orders forbidding plunder and indiscriminate shooting. By allowing unauthorized actions against individuals considered as mere "subhumans," the army created a convenient safety valve which made it possible to demand strict combat discipline. Cohesion came to depend on a perversion of the moral and legal basis of martial law. Nevertheless, when terror from the enemy became greater than fear of one's superiors, breakdowns did occur. Complete disintegration was prevented not merely by discipline, but by creating a commonly shared view of the war which made the prospect of defeat seem equivalent to a universal apocalypse. . . .

[A]t critical moments, when terror from the enemy became even greater than fear of one's superiors, incidents of breakdown among combat units did occur, and no amount of disciplinary brutality could prevent them. But what is most important about these incidents is that although they were far from infrequent, at no stage of the war save for the very last weeks did they threaten the cohesion of the army as a whole. Thus it was shown that just as brutal discipline could be accepted by the troops only because they had been taught to believe in the ideological arguments on which it was based, so too this ideological cohesion of the troops assumed a major role in preventing the organizational disintegration of the army when the disciplinary system crumbled. Paradoxically, while discipline was aimed at instilling into the troops' fear of their superiors, indoctrination increasingly terrorized the soldiers by horror tales about what they could expect from the "Judeo-Bolshevik" and "Asiatic flood" threatening the cradle of culture. Thus precisely when fear of the enemy in one point of the front overcame fear of punishment and caused local breakdowns, the overwhelming terror from the ultimate consequences of a Soviet victory rapidly isolated this incident; rather than the breakdown spreading across the front, the reaction of nearby units was to steel themselves once more and make yet another effort to halt the demonic hordes advancing from the East. Mutiny and disintegration tend to have a contagious effect on armies and to spread with remarkable speed; the Wehrmacht protected itself from most breakouts by harsh discipline, but completely inoculated its troops from a panic epidemic by huge counter-injections of terror from the enemy. Indeed, one can say that the typical *Landser* was a very frightened man, scared of his commanders, terrified of the enemy; this is probably why he seems to have enjoyed so much watching others suffer. The photographs of smiling Wehrmacht troops, each with his little camera, busily taking pictures of hanged "partisans," or of piles of butchered Jews. . . can only be understood as the ultimate perversion of the soldiers by a terroristic system of discipline, backed by a murderous ideology, which achieved its aim of preserving cohesion at the price of destroying the individual's moral fabric and thereby making possible the extermination of countless defenseless people. The troops' perception of reality and understanding of their actions was distorted by the conditions and circumstances of their existence. Yet it must be emphasized that it was the years of premilitary and army indoctrination which molded the soldiers' state of mind, prepared them for the horrors of war, and instilled into them such determination and ruthlessness. . . .

[Y]ears of premilitary and army indoctrination distorted the soldiers' perception of reality. The Wehrmacht's propaganda relied on a radical demonization of the enemy and on a similarly extreme deification of the Führer. The astonishing efficacy of these images is shown by reference to a wide array of evidence, ranging from analyses of soldiers' opinions by the regime's own agencies and leaders, to the views of its opposers, the memoirs of former generals and soldiers, the oral testimonies of workers and youths, and the private correspondence of troops from the front. It is particularly in the latter case that we find how soldiers preferred to view the reality they knew best through the ideological filters of the regime. . . .

The correspondence from the Eastern Front provides us with a particularly good opportunity to observe the manner in which German troops internalized some of the central notions of National Socialism and employed them to rationalize their predicament at the front, legitimize their criminal actions, and fortify their spirits. Naturally, much of what the soldiers wrote was heavily influenced by the

Wehrmacht's propaganda. But it is extremely revealing that they incorporated these arguments in their private correspondence, given the fact that censorship was concerned with incidents of criticism, not with the absence of Nazi phraseology. The soldiers' letters reflected the distortion of reality among the troops in two significant spheres: first, the dehumanization and demonization of the enemy on political and racial grounds, with a particular reference to the Jews as the lowest expression of human depravity; and, second, the deification of the Führer as the only hope for Germany's salvation. Intermixed with these central themes were notions regarding battle as a supreme test of character and manhood, as well as of racial and cultural superiority, and a view of the war as a holy crusade for a better future and against an infernal host of enemies sanctioned by God, who among the more pious and philosophically inclined at least partially replaced Hitler as the arbiter of German and universal destiny.

Anti-Semitic sentiments among the troops increased as conditions at the front worsened and as soldiers were no longer merely exposed to racist propaganda but also observed and in some cases participated in mass murders of Jews. Whereas concerning the Russians soldiers occasionally expressed pity, the fate of the Jews only enhanced the feeling that this was a "race" which indeed deserved total annihilation, particularly as it might otherwise take revenge on the Germans for its destruction. But from the very first weeks of "Barbarossa" many soldiers' letters revealed the impact of years of anti-Semitic indoctrination and deeply rooted prejudices. Lance-Corporal Paul Lenz maintained early on in the campaign: "Only a Jew can be a Bolshevik, for this blood-sucker there can be nothing nicer than to be a Bolshevik. . . . Wherever one spits one finds a Jew. . . . As far as I know . . . not one single Jew has worked in the workers' paradise, everyone, even the smallest blood-sucker, has a post where he naturally enjoys great privileges." In early August 1941 Lance-Corporal Herbert Nebenstreit wrote of his impression of Russia: "Only in Poland have I seen so much filth, mire, and rabble, especially Jews. I think that even there it was not half as bad as here." Private Reinhold Mahnke furnished a detailed description of Bolshevik-Jewish atrocities against the Lithuanians. Not only did they eject them from their houses and then burn them down, they also "cut off their feet and hands, tore out their tongues. . . . They even nailed men and children to walls. Had these criminals come to our country," Mahnke now realized, "they would have torn us to pieces and mangled us, that's clear. But the Lithuanians have taken revenge," he concluded, referring to the anti-Jewish pogroms conducted by the local population with the encouragement of the *Einsatzgruppen* and under the observing eye of the Wehrmacht.

Lance-Corporal Heinrich Sachs similarly noted "how the Jewish question was solved with impressive thoroughness under the enthusiastic applause of the local population." He then went on to quote Hitler's speech before the Reichstag threatening the Jews with destruction if they caused a war against Germany, and added that the "Jew should have known that the Führer was serious and must now bear the appropriate consequences." Captain Hans Kondruss, writing from Lvov (Lemberg) in mid-July had discovered ample evidence to show that "here clearly a whole people has systematically been reared into subhumanity. This is clearly the most Satanic educational plan of all times, which only Jewish sadism could have constructed and carried through." The fact that the municipal library contained the Talmud, and that among the massacred civilians there were allegedly no Jews, was to his mind "indicative of the real originators." He too was satisfied to note that the "wrath of the people has however been turned upon this people of criminals." Indeed, he asserted: "It will be necessary radically to scorch out this boil of plague, because these 'animals' will always constitute a danger." The Jews had turned the population away "from everything which to us human beings has been eternally holy," for their goal was "the brutalization [*Vertierung*] of a whole people, in order to make use of it as an instrument in the war for Judas' world domination." Lance-Corporal Paul Rubelt agreed that the "Jews were for the most part the evil doers" in the Lvov massacres, and noted that now the "culprits are shot." Indeed, Corporal K. Suffner, who maintained that the "Bolsheviks and the Jews have murdered 12,000 Germans and Ukrainians in a beastly manner," reported that "the surviving Ukrainians arrested 2000 Jews and exercised frightful revenge." He concluded: "We swear that this plague will be eradicated root and branch." Lance-Corporal Hans Fleischauer expressed similar sentiments: "The Jew is a real master in murdering, burning and massacring. . . . These bandits deserve the worst and toughest punishment conceivable." The consequences he drew from his experience with Jewish atrocities were far from untypical: "We all cannot be thankful enough to our Führer, who had protected us from such brutalities, and only for that we must follow

him through thick and thin, wherever that might be." Private von Kaull
believed that "international Jewry," already in control of the capitalist
world, had taken "as a counter-weight this proletarian insanity" as well:
"Now these two powers of destruction have been sent to the field, now
they are incited against Europe, against the heart of the West, in order
to destroy Germany." He was impressed with the scale and significance
of the conflict: "Such a huge battle has never before taken place on
earth. It is the greatest battle of the spirits ever experienced by humanity, it is waged for the existence or downfall of Western man and the
highest values which a people consciously carries on its shield." Consequently: "We must give our all to withstand this battle." Private Gregor
Lisch asked his family in the rear to "be happy that the Bolsheviks and
the Jews had not come to us," for "the Jews have destroyed these poor
people." And Private Fallnbigl, while stressing that "we should be happy
that we have not had this scourge of humanity in our own country," was
convinced that "the German world would not be prepared for such hei-
nous deeds even after years of preparation."

As the war dragged on, soldiers progressively embittered by the
endless fighting readily accepted the propagandistic line that the Jews
were to blame. As one lance-corporal exclaimed in April 1942: "These
swine of human creatures. They have clearly brought us this outrage of
a war." Typical of the inversion process common among the troops and
the sense that the murderous treatment of the Jews merely confirmed
their inhumanity was the following letter sent in July 1942:

> About events in the East concerning the Jews one could write a book.
> But it would be a waste of paper. You can be sure that they come to the
> right place, where they will no longer oppress any peoples.

The frustration caused by partisan activities also contributed to anti-
Semitic sentiments among the troops. It was the Wehrmacht's policy
to execute large numbers of civilians in retaliation for any attack on
military personnel, and the Jews were clearly the most convenient target, especially as the local population itself was often also strongly anti-
Semitic. The soldiers were quick to draw the conclusion that not only
did the Jews constitute the main support of "Bolshevism" in Russia and
had been about to overtake Germany as well, but that they were also
directly responsible for the growing number of "terroristic" guerrilla
attacks. One NCO wrote home in July 1942 that

> *the great task given us in the struggle against Bolshevism lies in the destruction of eternal Jewry. Once one sees what the Jew has done in Russia, one can well understand why the Führer began the struggle against Jewry. What sorrows would have come to our homeland, had this beast of a man had the upper hand? . . . Recently a comrade of ours was murdered in the night. He was stabbed in the back. That can only have been the Jew, who stands behind these crimes. The revenge taken for that act brought indeed a nice success. The population itself hates the Jews as never before. It realizes now, that he is guilty of everything.*

It is interesting to note that the encounter with real Jews seemed to confirm even the most pornographic and malicious anti-Semitic propaganda produced in the Third Reich. Thus while it is true that initially it was easier to create hatred and fear of an abstract enemy, once this image had been internalized soldiers applied it to real living human beings, apparently believing that they actually resembled the caricatures of "the Jew" in Nazi newspapers. As one corporal wrote,

> *although in the course of this war a little more light will have been cast on the Jewish question even for the most pigheaded philistine [Spieser], it is nevertheless still of the utmost importance that this question be further put in the necessary light, and here the "Stürmer" has, thank God, still remained true to its old positions. Just as the Eastern Jew now reveals himself in all his brutality, so have all this vicious lot, no matter whether in the West or in the East. . . .*

Increasingly during the last two years of the war, the troops at the front came to see themselves as the missionaries of the entire German nation, indeed of Western civilization as a whole. Rational evaluation and clear perception of events were replaced by intense terror from and rage against a faceless, monstrous enemy, which in turn only enhanced the men's desperate clinging to their faith in Hitler's ability to avert the apocalypse and lead the Reich to the *Endsieg* over the forces of evil. It was at this period, just as Germany was accelerating even further the implementation of its genocidal policies, that the view of the Wehrmacht as the protector of humanity gained increasing force. Paradoxically, the soldiers' awareness of the regime's criminal actions (at least at the front) made them fight with even greater determination for its survival by intensifying their fear of the consequences of defeat. Note the following letter by a Wehrmacht captain written in mid-February 1943:

> *May God allow the German people to find now the peace of mind and strength which would make it into the instrument needed by the Führer to protect the West from ruin, for what the Asiatic hordes will not destroy, will be annihilated by Jewish hatred and revenge. The belief at the front is unshakable, and we all hope that, as Göring has said, with the rising sun the fortunes of war will again return to our side.*

This was, indeed, the core German troops' ideological motivation, a combination of prejudices and phobias which made them so much into Hitler's soldiers. God was with the Führer, and the German people were God's instrument, whose goal was to save the West from Asiatic barbarism and Jewish revenge. The danger was great; but as long as belief in Hitler remained unshakable, victory was certain to come. Ironically, even men who claimed that the "time of fanaticism and intolerance of other views is over," and that "if we want to win the war, we must become more rational" concluded that all this was necessary "so that we will not be delivered to the revenge of the Jews."

Christopher R. Browning

"Ordinary Men"

In the very early hours of July 13, 1942, the men of Reserve Police Battalion 101 were roused from their bunks in the large brick school building that served as their barracks in the Polish town of Biłgoraj. They were middle-aged family men of working- and lower-middle-class background from the city of Hamburg. Considered too old to be of use to the German army, they had been drafted instead into the Order Police. Most were raw recruits with no previous experience in German occupied territory. They had arrived in Poland less than three weeks earlier.

It was still quite dark as the men climbed into the waiting trucks. Each policeman had been given extra ammunition, and additional boxes had been loaded onto the trucks as well. They were headed for their first major action, though the men had not yet been told what to expect.

The convoy of battalion trucks moved out of Biłgoraj in the dark, heading eastward on a jarring washboard gravel road. The pace was slow, and it took an hour and a half to two hours to arrive at the destination — the village of Józefów — a mere thirty kilometers away. Just as the sky was beginning to lighten, the convoy halted outside Józefów. It was a typical Polish village of modest white houses with thatched straw roofs. Among its inhabitants were 1,800 Jews.

The village was totally quiet. The men of Reserve Police Battalion 101 climbed down from their trucks and assembled in a half-circle around their commander, Major Wilhelm Trapp, a fifty-three-year-old career policeman affectionately known by his men as "Papa Trapp." The time had come for Trapp to address the men and inform them of the assignment the battalion had received.

Pale and nervous, with choking voice and tears in his eyes, Trapp visibly fought to control himself as he spoke. The battalion, he said plaintively, had to perform a frightfully unpleasant task. This assignment was

Excerpts from pp. 151–7, 159–69, 175–6, 184, 188–9 from *Ordinary Men: Reserve Police Battalion 101 and the Final Solution in Poland* by Christopher R. Browning. Copyright © 1992, 1998 by HarperCollins Publishers, Inc. Reprinted with permission.

not to his liking, indeed it was highly regrettable, but the orders came from the highest authorities. If it would make their task any easier, the men should remember that in Germany the bombs were falling on women and children.

He then turned to the matter at hand. The Jews had instigated the American Boycott that had damaged Germany, one policeman remembered Trapp saying. There were Jews in the village of Józefów who were involved with the partisans, he explained according to two others. The battalion had now been ordered to round up these Jews. The male Jews of working age were to be separated and taken to a work camp. The remaining Jews—the women, children, and elderly—were to be shot on the spot by the battalion. Having explained what awaited his men, Trapp then made an extraordinary offer: if any of the older men among them did not feel up to the task that lay before him, he could step out. . . . [Some members of the battalion rounded up three hundred able-bodied Jewish men for shipment to a slave labor camp. Other members systematically murdered the remaining Jews.]

When Trapp first made his offer early in the morning, the real nature of the action had just been announced and time to think and react had been very short. Only a dozen men had instinctively seized the moment to step out, turn in their rifles, and thus excuse themselves from the subsequent killing. For many the reality of what they were about to do, and particularly that they themselves might be chosen for the firing squad, had probably not sunk in. But when the men of First Company were summoned to the marketplace, instructed in giving a "neck shot," and sent to the woods to kill Jews, some of them tried to make up for the opportunity they had missed earlier. One policeman approached First Sergeant Kammer, whom he knew well. He confessed that the task was "repugnant" to him and asked for a different assignment. Kammer obliged, assigning him to guard duty on the edge of the forest, where he remained throughout the day. Several other policemen who knew Kammer well were given guard duty along the truck route. After shooting for some time, another group of policemen approached Kammer and said they could not continue. He released them from the firing squad and reassigned them to accompany the trucks. . . .

With the constant coming and going from the trucks, the wild terrain, and the frequent rotation, the men did not remain in fixed groups.

The confusion created the opportunity for work slowdown and evasion. Some men who hurried at their task shot far more Jews than others who delayed as much as they could. After two rounds one policeman simply "slipped off" and stayed among the trucks on the edge of the forest. Another managed to avoid taking his turn with the shooters altogether.

> *It was in no way the case that those who did not want to or could not carry out the shooting of human beings with their own hands could not keep themselves out of this task. No strict control was being carried out here. I therefore remained by the arriving trucks and kept myself busy at the arrival point. In any case I gave my activity such an appearance. It could not be avoided that one or another of my comrades noticed that I was not going to the executions to fire away at the victims. They showered me with remarks such as "shithead" and "weakling" to express their disgust. But I suffered no consequences for my actions. I must mention here that I was not the only one who kept himself out of participating in the executions. . . .*

For his first victim August Zorn was given a very old man. Zorn recalled that his elderly victim

> *could not or would not keep up with his countrymen, because he repeatedly fell and then simply lay there. I regularly had to lift him up and drag him forward. Thus, I had only reached the execution site when my comrades had already shot their Jews. At the sight of his countrymen who had been shot, my Jew threw himself on the ground and remained lying there. I then cocked my carbine and shot him through the back of the head. Because I was already very upset from the cruel treatment of the Jews during the clearing of the town and was completely in turmoil, I shot too high. The entire back of the skull of my Jew was torn off and the brain exposed. Parts of the skull flew into Sergeant Steinmetz's face. This was grounds for me, after returning to the truck, to go to the first sergeant and ask for my release. I had become so sick that I simply couldn't anymore. I was then relieved by the first sergeant. . . .*

When the men arrived at the barracks in Biłgoraj, they were depressed, angered, embittered, and shaken. They ate little but drank heavily. Generous quantities of alcohol were provided, and many of the policemen got quite drunk. Major Trapp made the rounds, trying to console and reassure them, and again placing the responsibility on higher authorities. But neither the drink nor Trapp's consolation could wash away the sense of shame and horror that pervaded the barracks. Trapp asked the men not to talk about it, but they needed no encouragement in that direction. Those who had not been there likewise had no desire to speak, either then or later. By silent consensus within Reserve Police Battalion 101, the Józefów massacre was simply not discussed. "The entire matter was a taboo." But repression during waking hours could not stop the nightmares. During the first night back from Józefów, one policeman awoke firing his gun into the ceiling of the barracks. . . .

The resentment and bitterness in the battalion over what they had been asked to do in Józefów was shared by virtually everyone, even those who had shot the entire day. The exclamation of one policeman to First Sergeant Kammer of First Company that "I'd go crazy if I had to do that again" expressed the sentiments of many. But only a few went beyond complaining to extricate themselves from such a possibility. Several of the older men with very large families took advantage of a regulation that required them to sign a release agreeing to duty in a combat area. One who had not yet signed refused to do so; another rescinded his signature. Both were eventually transferred back to Germany. The most dramatic response was again that of Lieutenant Buchmann, who asked Trapp to have him transferred back to Hamburg and declared that short of a direct personal order from Trapp, he would not take part in Jewish actions. In the end he wrote to Hamburg, explicitly requesting a recall because he was not "suited" to certain tasks "alien to the police" that were being carried out by his unit in Poland. Buchmann had to wait until November, but his efforts to be transferred were ultimately successful. . . .

In subsequent actions two vital changes were introduced and henceforth—with some notable exceptions—adhered to. First, most of the future operations of Reserve Police Battalion 101 involved ghetto clearing and deportation, not outright massacre on the spot. The policemen were thus relieved of the immediate horror of the killing process, which (for deportees from the northern Lublin district) was carried out in the extermination camp at Treblinka. Second, while deportation was a horrifying procedure characterized by the terrible coercive violence needed to drive people onto the death trains as well as the systematic killing of those who could not be marched to the trains, these actions were generally undertaken jointly by units of Reserve Police Battalion 101 and the Trawnikis, SS-trained auxiliaries from Soviet territories, recruited from the POW camps and usually assigned the very worst parts of the ghetto clearing and deportation. . . .

When the time came to kill again, the policemen did not "go crazy." Instead they became increasingly efficient and calloused executioners. . . .

With a conservative estimate of 6,500 Jews shot during earlier actions like those at Józefów and Łomazy and 1,000 shot during the "Jew hunts," and a minimum estimate of 30,500 Jews shot at Majdanek and Poniatowa, the battalion had participated in the direct shooting deaths of at least 38,000 Jews. With the death camp deportation of at least 3,000 Jews from Międzyrzec in early May 1943, the number of Jews they had placed on trains to Treblinka had risen to 45,000. For a battalion of less then 500 men, the ultimate body count was at least 83,000 Jews. . . .

Why did most men in Reserve Police Battalion 101 become killers, while only a minority of perhaps 10 percent—and certainly no more than 20 percent—did not? A number of explanations have been invoked in the past to explain such behavior: wartime brutalization, racism, segmentation and routinization of the task, special selection of the perpetrators, careerism, obedience to orders, deference to authority, ideological indoctrination, and conformity. These factors are applicable in varying degrees, but none without qualification. . . .

War, and especially race war, leads to brutalization, which leads to atrocity. . . . Except for a few of the oldest men who were veterans of World War I, and a few NCOs who had been transferred to Poland from Russia, the men of the battalion had not seen battle or encountered a deadly enemy. Most of them had not fired a shot in anger or ever been fired on, much less lost comrades fighting at their side. Thus, wartime brutalization through prior combat was not an immediate experience directly influencing the policemen's behavior at Józefów. Once the killing began, however, the men became increasingly brutalized. As in combat, the horrors of the initial encounter eventually became routine, and the killing became progressively easier. In this sense, brutalization was not the cause but the effect of these men's behavior. . . .

To what degree, if any, did the men of Reserve Police Battalion 101 represent a process of special selection for the particular task of implementing the Final Solution? . . . By age, geographical origin, and social background, the men of Reserve Police Battalion 101 were least likely to be considered apt material out of which to mold future mass killers. On the basis of these criteria, the rank and file — middle-aged, mostly working-class, from Hamburg — did not represent special selection or even random selection but for all practical purposes negative selection for the task at hand. . . . Reserve Police Battalion 101 was not sent to Lublin to murder Jews because it was composed of men specially selected or deemed particularly suited for the task. On the contrary, the battalion was the "dregs" of the manpower pool available at that stage of the war. It was employed to kill Jews because it was the only kind of unit available for such behind-the-lines duties. Most likely, Globocnik simply assumed as a matter of course that whatever battalion came his way would be up to this murderous task, regardless of its composition. If so, he may have been disappointed in the immediate aftermath of Józefów, but in the long run events proved him correct. . . .

Those who emphasize the relative or absolute importance of situational factors over individual psychological characteristics invariably point to Philip Zimbardo's Stanford prison experiment. Screening out everyone who scored beyond the normal range on a battery of psychological tests, including one that measured "rigid adherence to conventional values and a submissive, uncritical attitude toward authority" (i.e., the F-scale for the "authoritarian personality"), Zimbardo randomly divided his homogeneous "normal" test group into guards and prisoners and placed them in a simulated prison. Though outright physical violence was barred, within six days the inherent structure of prison life — in which guards operating on three-man shifts had to devise ways of controlling the more numerous prisoner population — had produced rapidly escalating brutality, humiliation, and dehumanization. "Most dramatic and distressing to us was the observation of the ease with which sadistic behavior could be elicited in individuals who were not 'sadistic types.'" The prison situation alone, Zimbardo concluded, was "a *sufficient* condition to produce aberrant, anti-social behavior."

Perhaps most relevant to this study of Reserve Police Battalion 101 is the spectrum of behavior that Zimbardo discovered in his sample of eleven guards. About one-third emerged as "cruel and tough." They constantly invented new forms of harassment and enjoyed their new-found power to behave cruelly and arbitrarily. A middle group of guards was "tough but fair." They "played by the rules" and did not go out of their way to mistreat prisoners. Only two (i.e., less than 20 percent) emerged as "good guards" who did not punish prisoners and even did small favors for them.

Zimbardo's spectrum of guard behavior bears an uncanny resemblance to the groupings that emerged within Reserve Police Battalion 101: a nucleus of increasingly enthusiastic killers who volunteered for the firing squads and "Jew Hunts"; a larger group of policemen who performed as shooters and ghetto clearers when assigned but who did not seek opportunities to kill (and in some cases refrained from killing, contrary to standing orders, when no one was monitoring their actions); and a small group (less than 20 percent) of refusers and evaders. . . .

If obedience to orders out of fear of dire punishment is not a valid explanation, what about "obedience to authority" in the more general sense used by Stanley Milgram — deference simply as a product of socialization and evolution, a "deeply ingrained behavior tendency" to comply with the directives of those positioned hierarchically above, even to the point of performing repugnant actions in violation of "universally accepted" moral norms. In a series of now famous experiments, Milgram tested the individual's ability to resist authority that was not backed by any external coercive threat. Naive volunteer subjects were instructed by a "scientific authority" in an alleged learning experiment to inflict an escalating series of fake electric shocks upon an actor/victim, who responded with carefully programmed "voice feedback" — an escalating series of complaints, cries of pain, calls for help, and finally fateful silence. In the standard voice feedback experiment, two-thirds of Milgram's subjects were "obedient" to the point of inflicting extreme pain.

Several variations on the experiment produced significantly different results. If the actor/victim was shielded so that the subject could hear and see no response, obedience was much greater. If the subject had both visual and voice feedback, compliance to the extreme fell to 40 percent. If the subject had to touch the actor/victim physically by forcing his hand onto an electric plate to deliver the shocks, obedience dropped to 30 percent. If a nonauthority figure gave orders, obedience was nil. If the naive subject performed a subsidiary or accessory task but did not personally inflict the electric shocks, obedience was nearly total. In contrast, if the subject was part of an actor/peer group that staged a carefully planned refusal to continue following the directions of the authority figure, the vast majority of subjects (90 percent) joined their peer group and desisted as well. If the subject was given complete discretion as to the level of electric shock to administer, all but a few sadists consistently delivered a minimal shock. When not under the direct surveillance of the scientist, many of the subjects "cheated" by giving lower shocks than prescribed, even though they were unable to confront authority and abandon the experiment.

Milgram adduced a number of factors to account for such an unexpectedly high degree of potentially murderous obedience to a noncoercive authority. An evolutionary bias favors the survival of people who can adapt to hierarchical situations and organized social activity. Socialization through family, school, and military service, as well as a whole array of rewards and punishments within society generally, reinforces and internalizes a tendency toward obedience. A seemingly voluntary entry into an authority system "perceived" as legitimate creates a strong sense of obligation. Those within the hierarchy adopt the authority's perspective or "definition of the situation" (in this case, as an important scientific experiment rather than the infliction of physical torture). The notions of "loyalty, duty, discipline," requiring competent performance in the eyes of authority, become moral imperatives overriding any identification with the victim. Normal individuals enter an "agentic state" in which they are the instrument of another's will. In such a state, they no longer feel personally responsible for the content of their actions but only for how well they perform.

Once entangled, people encounter a series of "binding factors" or "cementing mechanisms" that make disobedience or refusal even more difficult. The momentum of the process discourages any new or contrary initiative. The "situational obligation" or etiquette makes refusal appear improper, rude, or even an immoral breach of obligation. And a socialized anxiety over potential punishment for disobedience acts as a further deterrent.

Milgram made direct reference to the similarities between human behavior in his experiments and under the Nazi regime. He concluded, "Men are led to kill with little difficulty." Milgram was aware of significant differences in the two situations, however. Quite explicitly he acknowledged that the subjects of his experiments were assured that no permanent physical damage would result from their actions. The subjects were under no threat or duress themselves. And finally, the actor/victims were not the object of "intense devaluation" through systematic indoctrination of the subjects. In contrast, the killers of the Third Reich lived in a police state where the consequences of disobedience could be drastic and they were subjected to intense indoctrination, but they also knew they were not only inflicting pain but destroying human life.

Was the massacre at Józefów a kind of radical Milgram experiment that took place in a Polish forest with real killers and victims rather than in a social psychology laboratory with naive subjects and actor/victims? Are the actions of Reserve Police Battalion 101 explained by Milgram's observations and conclusions? There are some difficulties in explaining Józefów as a case of deference to authority, for none of Milgram's experimental variations exactly paralleled the historical situation at Józefów, and the relevant differences constitute too many variables to draw firm conclusions in any scientific sense. Nonetheless, many of Milgram's insights find graphic confirmation in the behavior and testimony of the men of Reserve Police Battalion 101.

At Józefów the authority system to which the men were responding was quite complex, unlike the laboratory situation. Major Trapp represented not a strong but a very weak authority figure. He weepingly conceded the frightful nature of the task at hand and invited the older reserve policemen to excuse themselves. If Trapp was a weak immediate authority figure, he did invoke a more distant system of authority that was anything but weak. The orders for the massacre had been received from the highest quarter, he said. Trapp himself and the battalion as a unit were bound by the orders of this distant authority, even if Trapp's concern for his men exempted individual policemen.

To what were the vast majority of Trapp's men responding when they did not step out? Was it to authority as represented either by Trapp or his superiors? Were they responding to Trapp not primarily as an authority figure, but as an individual—a popular and beloved officer whom they would not leave in the lurch? And what about other factors? Milgram himself notes that people far more frequently invoke authority than conformity to explain their behavior, for only the former seems to absolve them of personal responsibility. "Subjects deny conformity and *embrace* obedience as the explanation of their actions." Yet many policemen admitted responding to the pressures of conformity—how would they be seen in the eyes of their comrades?—not authority. On Milgram's own view, such admission was the tip of the iceberg, and this factor must have been even more important than the men conceded in their testimony. If so, conformity assumes a more central role than authority at Józefów.

Milgram tested the effects of peer pressure in bolstering the individual's capacity to resist authority. When actor/collaborators bolted, the naive subjects found it much easier to follow. Milgram also attempted to test for the reverse, that is, the role of conformity in intensifying the capacity to inflict pain. Three subjects, two collaborators and one naive, were instructed by the scientist/authority figure to inflict pain at the lowest level anyone among them proposed. When a naive subject acting alone had been given full discretion to set the level of electric shock, the subject had almost invariably inflicted minimal pain. But when the two collaborators, always going first, proposed a step-by-step escalation of electric shock, the naive subject was significantly influenced. Though the individual variation was wide, the average result was the selection of a level of electric shock halfway between no increase and a consistent step-by-step increase. This is still short of a test of peer pressure as compensation for the deficiencies of weak authority. There was no weeping but beloved scientist inviting subjects to leave the electric shock panel while other men—with whom the subjects had comradely relations and before whom they would feel compelled to appear manly and tough—stayed and continued to inflict painful shocks. Indeed, it would be almost impossible to construct an experiment to test such a scenario, which would require true comradely relations between a naive subject and the actor/collaborators. Nonetheless, the mutual reinforcement of authority and conformity seems to have been clearly demonstrated by Milgram.

If the multifaceted nature of authority at Józefów and the key role of conformity among the policemen are not quite parallel to Milgram's experiments, they nonetheless render considerable support to his conclusions, and some of his observations are clearly confirmed. Direct proximity to the horror of the killing significantly increased the number of men who would no longer comply. On the other hand, with the division of labor and removal of the killing process to the death camps, the men felt scarcely any responsibility at all for their actions. As in Milgram's experiment without direct surveillance, many policemen did not comply with orders when not directly supervised; they mitigated their behavior when they could do so without personal risk but were unable to refuse participation in the battalion's killing operations openly.

One factor that admittedly was not the focal point of Milgram's experiments, indoctrination, and another that was only partially touched upon, conformity, require further investigation. Milgram did stipulate "definition of the situation" or ideology, that which gives meaning and coherence to the social occasion, as a crucial antecedent of deference to authority. Controlling the manner in which people interpret their world is one way to control behavior, Milgram argues. If they accept authority's ideology, action follows logically and willingly. Hence "ideological justification is vital in obtaining willing obedience, for it permits the person to see his behavior as serving a desirable end."

In Milgram's experiments, "overarching ideological justification" was present in the form of a tacit and unquestioned faith in the goodness of science and its contribution to progress. But there was no systematic attempt to "devalue" the actor/victim or inculcate the subject with a particular ideology. Milgram hypothesized that the more destructive behavior of people in Nazi Germany, under much less direct surveillance, was a consequence of an internalization of authority achieved "through relatively long processes of indoctrination, of a sort not possible within the course of a laboratory hour."

To what degree, then, did the conscious inculcation of Nazi doctrines shape the behavior of the men of Reserve Police Battalion 101? Were they subjected to such a barrage of clever and insidious propaganda that they lost the capacity for independent thought and responsible action? Were devaluation of the Jews and exhortations to kill them central to this indoctrination? . . .

[T]he men of Reserve Police Battalion 101, like the rest of German society, were immersed in a deluge of racist and anti-Semitic propaganda. Furthermore, the Order Police provided for indoctrination both in basic training and as an ongoing practice within each unit. Such incessant propagandizing must have had considerable effect in reinforcing general notions of Germanic racial superiority and "a certain aversion" toward the Jews. However, much of the indoctrination material was clearly not targeted at older reservists and in some cases was highly inappropriate or irrelevant to them. And material specifically designed to harden the policemen for the personal task of killing Jews is conspicuously absent from the surviving documentation. One would have to be quite convinced of the manipulative powers of indoctrination to believe that any of this material could have deprived the men of Reserve Police Battalion 101 of the capacity for independent thought. Influenced and conditioned in a general way, imbued in particular with a sense of their own superiority and racial kinship as well as Jewish inferiority and otherness, many of them undoubtedly were; explicitly prepared for the task of killing Jews they most certainly were not.

Along with ideological indoctrination, a vital factor touched upon but not fully explored in Milgram's experiments was conformity to the group. The battalion had orders to kill Jews, but each individual did not. Yet 80 to 90 percent of the men proceeded to kill, though almost all of them—at least initially—were horrified and disgusted by what they were doing. To break ranks and step out, to adopt overtly nonconformist behavior, was simply beyond most of the men. It was easier for them to shoot.

Why? First of all, by breaking ranks, nonshooters were leaving the "dirty work" to their comrades. Since the battalion had to shoot even if individuals did not, refusing to shoot constituted refusing one's share of an unpleasant collective obligation. It was in effect an asocial act vis-à-vis one's comrades. Those who did not shoot risked isolation, rejection, and ostracism—a very uncomfortable prospect within the framework of a tight-knit unit stationed abroad among a hostile population, so that the individual had virtually nowhere else to turn for support and social contact.

This threat of isolation was intensified by the fact that stepping out could also have been seen as a form of moral reproach of one's comrades: the nonshooter was potentially indicating that he was "too good" to do such things. Most, though not all, nonshooters intuitively tried to diffuse the criticism of their comrades that was inherent in their actions. They pleaded not that they were "too good" but rather that they were "too weak" to kill.

Such a stance presented no challenge to the esteem of one's comrades; on the contrary, it legitimized and upheld "toughness" as a superior quality. For the anxious individual, it had the added advantage of posing no moral challenge to the murderous policies of the regime, though it did pose another problem, since the difference between being "weak" and being a "coward" was not great. Hence the distinction made by one policeman who did not dare to step out at Józefów for fear of being considered a coward, but who subsequently dropped out of his firing squad. It was one thing to be too cowardly even to try to kill; it was another, after resolutely trying to do one's share, to be too weak to continue.

Insidiously, therefore, most of those who did not shoot only reaffirmed the "macho" values of the majority—according to which it was a positive quality to be "tough" enough to kill unarmed, noncombatant men, women, and children—and tried not to rupture the bonds of comradeship that constituted their social world. Coping with the contradictions imposed by the demands of conscience on the one hand and the norms of the battalion on the other led to many tortured attempts at compromise: not shooting infants on the spot but taking them to the assembly point; not shooting on patrol if no "go-getter" was along who might report such squeamishness; bringing Jews to the shooting site and firing but intentionally missing. Only the very exceptional remained indifferent to taunts of "weakling" from their comrades and could live with the fact that they were considered to be "no man."

Here we come full circle to the mutually intensifying effects of war and racism noted by John Dower, in conjunction with the insidious effects of constant propaganda and indoctrination. Pervasive racism and the resulting exclusion of the Jewish victims from any common ground with the perpetrators made it all the easier for the majority of the policemen to conform to the norms of their immediate community (the battalion) and their society at large (Nazi Germany). Here the years of anti-Semitic propaganda (and prior to the Nazi dictatorship, decades of shrill German nationalism) dovetailed with the polarizing effects of war. The dichotomy of racially superior Germans and racially inferior Jews, central to Nazi ideology, could easily merge with the image of a beleaguered Germany surrounded by warring enemies. If it is doubtful that most of the policemen understood or embraced the theoretical aspects of Nazi ideology as contained in SS indoctrination pamphlets, it is also doubtful that they were immune to "the influence of the times" (to use Lieutenant Drucker's phrase once again), to the incessant proclamation of German superiority and incitement of contempt and hatred for the Jewish enemy. Nothing helped the Nazis to wage a race war so much as the war itself.

In wartime, when it was all too usual to exclude the enemy from the community of human obligation, it was also all too easy to subsume the Jews into the "image of the enemy," or *Feindbild.*

In his last book, *The Drowned and the Saved,* Primo Levi included an essay entitled "The Gray Zone," perhaps his most profound and deeply disturbing reflection on the Holocaust. He maintained that in spite of our natural desire for clear-cut distinctions, the history of the camps "could not be reduced to the two blocs of victims and persecutors." He argued passionately, "It is naive, absurd, and historically false to believe that an infernal system such as National Socialism sanctifies its victims; on the contrary, it degrades them, it makes them resemble itself." The time had come to examine the inhabitants of the "gray zone" between the simplified Manichean images of perpetrator and victim. Levi concentrated on the "gray zone of *protekcya* [corruption] and collaboration" that flourished in the camps among a spectrum of victims: from the "picturesque fauna" of low-ranking functionaries husbanding their miniscule advantages over other prisoners; through the truly privileged network of Kapos, who were free "to commit the worst atrocities" at whim; to the terrible fate of the Sonderkommandos, who prolonged their lives by manning the gas chambers and crematoria. (Conceiving and organizing the Sonderkommandos was in Levi's opinion National Socialism's "most demonic crime.")

While Levi focused on the spectrum of victim behavior within the gray zone, he dared to suggest that this zone encompassed perpetrators as well. Even the SS man Muhsfeld of the Birkenau crematoria—whose "daily ration of slaughter was studded with arbitrary and capricious acts, marked by his inventions of cruelty"—was not a "monolith." Faced with the miraculous survival of a sixteen-year-old girl discovered while the gas chambers were being cleared, the disconcerted Muhsfeld briefly hesitated. In the end he ordered the girl's death but quickly left before his orders were carried out. One "instant of pity" was not enough to "absolve" Muhsfeld, who was deservedly hanged in 1947. Yet it did "place him too, although at its extreme boundary, within the gray band, that zone of ambiguity which radiates out from regimes based on terror and obsequiousness."

Levi's notion of the gray zone encompassing both perpetrators and victims must be approached with a cautious qualification. The perpetrators and victims in the gray zone were not mirror images of one another. Perpetrators did not become fellow victims (as many of them later claimed to be) in the way some victims became accomplices of the perpetrators. The relationship between perpetrator and victim was not symmetrical. The range of choice each faced was totally different.

Nonetheless, the spectrum of Levi's gray zone seems quite applicable to Reserve Police Battalion 101. The battalion certainly had its quota of men who neared the "extreme boundary" of the gray zone. Lieutenant Gnade, who initially rushed his men back from Minsk to avoid being involved in killing but who later learned to enjoy it, leaps to mind. So do the many reserve policemen who were horrified in the woods outside Józefów but subsequently became casual volunteers for numerous firing squads and "Jew hunts." They, like Muhsfeld, seem to have experienced the brief "instant of pity" but cannot be absolved by it. At the other boundary of the gray zone, even Lieutenant Buchmann, the most conspicuous and outspoken critic of the battalion's murderous actions, faltered at least once. Absent his protector, Major Trapp, and facing orders from the local Security Police in Luków, he too led his men to the killing fields shortly before his transfer back to Hamburg. And at the very center of the perpetrators' gray zone stood the pathetic figure of Trapp himself, who sent his men to slaughter Jews "weeping like a child," and the bedridden Captain Hoffmann, whose body rebelled against the terrible deeds his mind willed.

The behavior of any human being is, of course, a very complex phenomenon, and the historian who attempts to "explain" it is indulging in a certain arrogance. When nearly 500 men are involved, to undertake any general explanation of their collective behavior is even more hazardous. What, then, is one to conclude? Most of all, one comes away from the story of Reserve Police Battalion 101 with great unease. This story of ordinary men is not the story of all men. The reserve policemen faced choices, and most of them committed terrible deeds. But those who killed cannot be absolved by the notion that anyone in the same situation would have done as they did. For even among them, some refused to kill and others stopped killing. Human responsibility is ultimately an individual matter.

At the same time, however, the collective behavior of Reserve Police Battalion 101 has deeply disturbing implications. There are many societies afflicted by traditions of racism and caught in the siege mentality of war or threat of war. Everywhere society conditions people to respect and defer to authority, and indeed could scarcely function otherwise. Everywhere people seek career advancement. In every modern society, the complexity of life and the resulting bureaucratization and specialization attenuate the sense of personal responsibility of those implementing official policy. Within virtually every social collective, the peer group exerts tremendous pressures on behavior and sets moral norms. If the men of Reserve Police Battalion 101 could become killers under such circumstances, what group of men cannot?

Women prisoners at a German labor camp, ca. 1944. Photograph by Ullstein Bild / The Granger Collection, New York

III The Victims' Experiences

Variety of Opinion

> *The prisoners developed types of behavior which are characteristic of infancy or early youth. . . . When a prisoner had reached the final stage of adjustment to the camp situation, he had changed his personality so as to accept various values of the SS as his own.*
>
> Bruno Bettelheim

> *The assumption that there was no moral or social order in the concentration camps is wrong. . . . Through innumerable small acts of humanness, most of them covert but everywhere in evidence, survivors were able to maintain societal structures workable enough to keep themselves alive and morally sane.*
>
> Terrence Des Pres

> *[T]he hybrid class of the prisoner-functionary constitutes . . . a gray zone, poorly defined, where the two camps of masters and servants both diverge and converge . . . [T]he network of human relationships inside the Lagers . . . could not be reduced to the two blocs of victims and persecutors.*
>
> Primo Levi

Assumptions about women's behavior obscure the diversity of their Holocaust experiences . . . [M]any people shy away from confronting the full horrors of the Holocaust, yet this will continue as long as testimonies are projected as "epics of love and courage."

Zoë Vania Waxman

What it was like to be swept up in the Nazi whirlwind of violence and misery has been told in the memoirs of hundreds of survivors. Although each one presents only a small piece of the puzzle, together they give us a sense of the variety of what were, after all, many millions of Holocaust experiences. How were the victims treated, and how did they react in the camps? Was there anything they could do to enhance the chances of living through this terror? This section contrasts two conflicting views on these issues and then explores the experiences of prisoner-functionaries and women in the Holocaust.

Bruno Bettelheim, for many decades until his death in 1990 one of the world's leading child psychologists, was himself an inmate of Nazi concentration camps for about a year in the late 1930s. Although he escaped the Holocaust itself, he called on his own experiences and those of others to formulate an influential view of the experience. The systematic dehumanization of the victims in Nazi camps, Bettelheim argues, crippled inmates psychologically and caused them to regress to childlike behavior. The conclusion implied by this line of reasoning seems inescapable: utterly at the mercy of a pitiless totalitarian leviathan, the victims could do little to influence their fate one way or another. Those who survived until they could be liberated by outside forces were, above all, incredibly lucky.

Terrence Des Pres, an American professor of literature, has drawn on accounts by survivors in an effort to refute Bettelheim's claims. Rejecting the psychological method, Des Pres attributes the inmates' behavior to raw necessity rather than regression. Moreover, he observes that many acts of mutual kindness and aid were decisive in determining whether individuals lived or died. Survival was to some degree in the victims' own hands. It was more a matter of being determined to outlast one's tormentors, and of helping and being helped, than it was of luck.

Primo Levi examines the complicated position of camp inmates who tried to enhance their chances of survival by assisting the Germans as prisoner-functionaries: kapos, barracks chiefs, clerks, and the like. Although Levi recognizes the human need to stress opposites (good/bad, victims/oppressors), he locates these prisoners in a gray zone of moral ambiguity and compromise, refusing to pass judgment on them. In this view the "Lager" (Levi uses the German word for "camp") was a place where the Nazis debased and destroyed the human personality by enticing some prisoners to become oppressors of their fellow inmates. They were rewarded with more and better food, more comfortable living conditions, and exemptions from beatings and deportations. Levi pays particular attention to the Auschwitz *Sonderkommando*, the "Special Squads" of prisoners who assisted in the gassings, searched the bodies for valuables, and disposed of the corpses. Himself an Auschwitz survivor, Levi gives a clear picture of the impact of privileged prisoners on the rest of the camp population. His description invites comparison with the differing views about survival advanced by Bettelheim and Des Pres.

Zoë Vania Waxman ponders the ways in which women experienced the Holocaust differently from men. Earlier explorations of this subject argued that women in ghettos and camps possessed superior survival skills related to personal hygiene and the capacity to bond with others for mutual aid. Waxman argues that this is not the whole story. In this view, preconceptions about gender roles lead to an emphasis on women as mothers and caregivers, obscuring the diversity of women's Holocaust experiences. Those experiences were sometimes very different for men and women, but not always. Waxman's essay invites us to consider the ways in which gender expectations can distort both survivors' memories and historians' reconstructions of the Holocaust.

These essays should lead us to reflect on the fate of victims in ghettos and camps and the qualities that preserved life in the Holocaust. Was survival largely fortuitous or did it depend in great part on the attitudes and actions of the prisoners? Survivors' memoirs help answer the question, but we need to remember that their accounts are not necessarily typical. Most members of the targeted groups who fell into Nazi hands did not live to tell their stories, and no one can be certain how much their experiences differed from those of the survivors. It is also well to keep in mind that the Holocaust was a vast and complex process that involved millions of people. It can never be neatly encompassed in the accounts of a few, or even a few hundred, survivors.

Bruno Bettelheim

Helpless Victims

The prisoners developed types of behavior which are characteristic of infancy or early youth. Some of these behaviors developed slowly, others were immediately imposed on the prisoners and grew only in intensity as time went on. Some of these more-or-less infantile behaviors have already been discussed, such as ambivalence toward one's family, despondency, finding satisfaction in daydreaming rather than in action.

Whether some of these behavior patterns were deliberately produced by the gestapo is hard to ascertain. Others were definitely produced by it, but again we do not know whether this was consciously done. It has been mentioned that even during the transportation the prisoners were tortured in the way in which a cruel and domineering father might torture a helpless child; here it should be added that the prisoners were also debased by techniques which went much further into childhood situations. They were forced to soil themselves. In the camp defecation was strictly regulated; it was one of the most important daily events, discussed in great detail. During the day, prisoners who wanted to defecate had to obtain the permission of a guard. It seemed as if education to cleanliness would be once more repeated. It also seemed to give pleasure to the guards to hold the power of granting or withholding permission to visit the latrines. (Toilets were mostly not available.) The pleasure of the guards found its counterpart in the pleasure the prisoners derived from visiting the latrines, because there they usually could rest for a moment, secure from the whips of the overseers and guards. However, they were not always so secure, because sometimes enterprising young guards enjoyed interfering with the prisoners even at these moments. . . .

In speaking to each other, the prisoners were forced to employ the familiar *du* ("thou") — a form which in Germany is indiscriminately used only among small children; they were not permitted to address one another with the many titles to which middle- and upper-class

Germans are accustomed. On the other hand, they had to address the guards in the most deferential manner, giving them all their titles.

The prisoners lived, like children, only in the immediate present; they lost feeling for the sequence of time; they became unable to plan for the future or to give up immediate pleasure satisfactions to gain greater ones in the near future. They were unable to establish durable object-relations. Friendships developed as quickly as they broke up. Prisoners would, like early adolescents, fight one another tooth and nail, declare that they would never again look at one another or speak to one another, and become close friends once more within a few minutes. They were boastful, telling tales about what they had accomplished in their former lives, or how they succeeded in cheating foremen or guards, and how they sabotaged the work. Like children, they felt not at all set back or ashamed when it became known that they had lied about their prowess.

Another factor contributing to the regression into childhood behavior was the work the prisoners were forced to perform. New prisoners particularly were forced to perform nonsensical tasks, such as carrying heavy rocks from one place to another, and after a while back to the place where they had picked them up. On other days they were forced to dig holes in the ground with their bare hands, although tools were available. They resented such nonsensical work, although it ought to have been immaterial to them whether or not their work was useful. They felt debased when forced to perform "childish" and stupid labor, and preferred even harder work when it produced something that might be considered useful. There seems to be no doubt that the tasks they performed, as well as the mistreatment by the gestapo which they had to endure, contributed to their disintegration as adult persons.

The author had a chance to interview several prisoners who before being brought into the camp had spent a few years in prison, some of them in solitary confinement. Although their number was too small to permit valid generalizations, it seems that to spend time in prison does not produce the character changes described in this paper. As far as the regression into childhood behaviors is concerned, the only feature prison and camp seem to have in common is that in both the prisoners are prevented from satisfying their sexual desires in a normal way, which eventually leads them to the fear of losing their virility. In the camp this fear added strength to the other factors detrimental to adult types of behavior and promoted childlike types of behavior.

When a prisoner had reached the final stage of adjustment to the camp situation, he had changed his personality so as to accept various values of the SS as his own. A few examples may illustrate how this acceptance expressed itself.

The SS considered, or pretended to consider, the prisoners to be the scum of the earth. It insisted that none of them was any better than the others. One of the reasons for fostering this attitude was probably to convince the young guards who received their training in the camp that they were superior to even the most outstanding prisoner, and to demonstrate to them that the former foes of the Nazis were now subdued and not worthy of any special attention. If a formerly prominent prisoner had been treated better than the others, the simple guards would have thought that he still had influence; if he had been treated worse, they might have thought that he still was dangerous.

The Nazis wanted to impress on the guards that even a slight degree of opposition to the system led to the complete destruction of the person who dared to oppose, and that the *degree* of opposition made no difference in the punishment. Occasional talks with these guards revealed that they really believed in a Jewish-capitalistic world conspiracy against the German people. Whoever opposed the Nazis was supposed to be participating in it and was therefore to be destroyed, independent of his role in the conspiracy. So it can be understood that the guards' behavior to the prisoners was to treat them as their vilest enemies.

The prisoners found themselves in an impossible situation, due to the steady interference with their privacy on the part of the guards and other prisoners. So a great amount of aggression accumulated. In the new prisoners this aggression vented itself in the way it might have done in the world outside the camp. But slowly prisoners accepted, as the expression of their verbal aggressions, terms which definitely did not originate in their previous vocabularies, but were taken over from the very different vocabulary of the SS. From copying the verbal aggressions of the SS to copying its form of bodily aggressions was one more step, but it took several years to make this step. It was not unusual to find old prisoners, when in charge of others, behaving worse than the SS. In some cases they were trying to win favor with the SS in this way, but more often they considered it the best way to behave toward prisoners in the camp.

Practically all prisoners who had spent a long time in the camp took over the attitude of the SS toward the so-called unfit prisoners. Newcomers presented the old prisoners with difficult problems. Their complaints about the unbearable life in camp added new strain to the life in the barracks, as did their inability to adjust to it. Bad behavior in the labor gang endangered the whole group. So a newcomer who did not stand up well under the strain tended to become a liability for the other prisoners. Moreover, weaklings were those most apt to eventually turn traitor. Weaklings usually died during the first weeks in the camp anyway, so to some it seemed as well to get rid of them sooner. Old prisoners were therefore sometimes instrumental in getting rid of the "unfit"—in this way incorporating Nazi ideology into their own behavior. This was one of many situations in which old prisoners would demonstrate toughness, having molded their treatment of these "unfit" prisoners to the example set by the SS. Self-protection required elimination of the "unfit" prisoners, but the way in which they were sometimes tortured for days by the old prisoners and slowly killed was taken over from the gestapo.

Old prisoners who identified themselves with the SS did so not only in respect to aggressive behavior. They would try to acquire old pieces of SS uniforms. If that was not possible, they tried to sew and mend their uniforms so that they would resemble those of the guards. The length to which prisoners would go in these efforts seemed unbelievable, particularly since the SS punished them for their efforts to copy SS uniforms. When asked why they did it, the old prisoners admitted that they loved to look like the guards. . . .

The satisfaction with which some old prisoners enjoyed the fact that, during the twice-daily counting of the prisoners—which often lasted for hours and always seemed interminable—they had stood really well at attention can be explained only by the fact that they had entirely accepted the values of the SS as their own. These prisoners prided themselves on being as tough as the SS. This identification with their torturers went so far as copying their leisure-time activities. One of the games played by the guards was to find out who could stand to be hit longest without uttering a complaint. This game was copied by some of the old prisoners, as though they had not been hit often and long enough not to need to repeat this experience by inflicting pain on fellow prisoners.

Often the SS would enforce nonsensical rules, originating in the whims of one of the guards. These rules were usually forgotten very quickly, but there were always some old prisoners who would continue to follow the rules and try to enforce them on others long after the gestapo had forgotten about them. Once, for instance, a guard inspecting the prisoners' apparel found that the shoes of some of them were dirty on the inside. He ordered all prisoners to wash their shoes inside and out with water and soap. The heavy shoes, when treated this way, became hard as stone. The order was never repeated, and many prisoners did not even execute it when given. Nevertheless there were some old prisoners who not only continued to wash the inside of their shoes every day but cursed all others who did not do so as negligent and dirty. These prisoners firmly believed that the rules set down by the SS were desirable standards of human behavior, at least within the camp situation. . . .

Among the old prisoners one could observe other developments which indicated their desire to accept the SS along lines which definitely could not originate in propaganda. It seems that once prisoners adopted a childlike attitude toward the SS, they had a desire for at least some of those whom they accepted as all-powerful father-images to be just and kind. They divided their positive and negative feelings—strange as it may be that they should have had positive feelings, they had them—toward the SS in such a way that all positive emotions were concentrated on a few officers who were rather high up in the hierarchy of camp administrators, although hardly ever on the governor of the camp. The old prisoners insisted that these officers hid behind their rough surfaces a feeling of justice and propriety; he, or they, were supposed to be genuinely interested in the prisoners and even trying, in a small way, to help them. Since nothing of these supposed feelings and efforts ever became apparent, it was explained that the officer in question hid them so effectively because otherwise he would not be able to help the prisoners. The eagerness of these prisoners to find support for their claims was pitiful. A whole legend was woven around the fact that of two noncommissioned officers inspecting a barracks, one had cleaned his shoes of mud before entering. He probably did it automatically, but it was interpreted as a rebuff to the other man and a clear demonstration of how he felt about the concentration camp.

After so much has been said about the old prisoners' tendency to conform and to identify with the SS, it ought to be stressed that this was only part of the picture. The author has tried to concentrate on interesting psychological mechanisms in group behavior rather than on reporting types of behavior which are either well known or could reasonably be expected. These same old prisoners who identified with the SS defied it at other moments, demonstrating extraordinary courage in doing so.

Terrence Des Pres

The Will to Survive

With only one exception, so far as I know, psychoanalytic studies of the camp experience maintain that it was characterized by regression to "childlike" or "infantile" levels of behavior. This conclusion is based primarily on the fact that men and women in the concentration camps were "abnormally" preoccupied with food and excretory functions. Infants show similar preoccupations, and the comparison suggests that men and women react to extremity by "regression to, and fixation on, pre-oedipal stages." Here, as in general from the psychoanalytic point of view, context is not considered. The fact that the survivor's situation was itself abnormal is simply ignored. That the preoccupation with food was caused by literal starvation does not count; and the fact that camp inmates were *forced* to live in filth is likewise overlooked.

The case for "infantilism" has been put most forcefully by Bruno Bettelheim. A major thesis of his book *The Informed Heart* is that in extreme situations men are reduced to children; and in a section entitled "Childlike Behavior" he simply equates the prisoners' objective predicament with behavior inherently regressive. Bettelheim observes, for example—and of course this was true—that camp regulations were designed to transform excretory functions into moments of crisis. Prisoners had to ask permission in order to relieve themselves, thereby becoming exposed to the murderous whim of the SS guard to whom they spoke. During the twelve-hour workday, furthermore, prisoners were often not allowed to answer natural needs, or they were forced to do so *while* they worked and on the actual spot *where* they worked. As one survivor says: "If anyone of us, tormented by her stomach, would try to go to a nearby ditch, the guards would release their dogs. Humiliated, goaded, the women did not leave their places—they waded in their own excrement." Worst of all were the days of the death marches, when prisoners who stopped for any reason were instantly shot. To live they simply had to keep going:

> *Urine and excreta poured down the prisoners' legs, and by nightfall the excrement, which had frozen to our limbs, gave off its stench. We were really no longer human beings in the accepted sense. Not even animals, but putrefying corpses moving on two legs.*

Under such conditions, excretion does indeed become, as Bettelheim says, "an important daily event"; but the conclusion does not follow, as he goes on to say, that prisoners were therefore reduced "to the level they were at before toilet training was achieved." Outwardly, yes; men and women were very much concerned with excretory functions, just as infants are, and prisoners were "forced to wet and soil themselves" just as infants do—except that infants are not forced. Bettelheim concludes that for camp inmates the ordeal of excremental crisis "made it impossible to see themselves as fully adult persons any more." He does not distinguish between behavior in extremity and civilized behavior; for of course, if in civilized circumstances an adult worries about the state of his bowels, or sees the trip to the toilet as some sort of ordeal, then neurosis is evident. But in the concentration camps behavior was governed by immediate death-threat; action was not the index of infantile wishes but of response to hideous necessity.

The fact is that prisoners were *systematically* subjected to filth. They were the deliberate target of excremental assault. Defilement was a constant threat, a condition of life from day to day, and at any moment it was liable to take abruptly vicious and sometimes fatal forms. The favorite pastime of one *Kapo* was to stop prisoners just before they reached the latrine. He would force an inmate to stand at attention for questioning; then make him "squat in deep knee-bends until the poor man could no longer control his sphincter and 'exploded'"; then beat him; and only then, "covered with his own excrement, the victim would be allowed to drag himself to the latrine." In another instance prisoners were forced to lie in rows on the ground, and each man, when he was finally allowed to get up, "had to urinate across the heads of the others"; and there was "one night when they refined their treatment by making each man urinate into another's mouth." In Birkenau, soup bowls were periodically taken from the prisoners and thrown into the latrine, from which they had to be retrieved: "When you put it to your lips for the first time, you smell nothing suspicious. Other pairs of hands trembling with impatience wait for it, they seize it the moment you have finished drinking. Only later, much later, does a repelling odor hit your nostrils." And as we have seen, prisoners with dysentery commonly got around camp rules and kept from befouling themselves by using their own eating utensils. . . .

The condition of life-in-death forced a terrible paradox upon survivors. They stayed alive by helping to run the camps, and this fact has led to the belief that prisoners identified not with each other but with their oppressors. Survivors are often accused of imitating SS behavior. Bruno Bettelheim has argued that "old prisoners" developed "a personality structure willing and able to accept SS values and behavior as its own." But that needs clarification, for in order to act like an SS man the prisoner had to occupy a position of real power. A cook could lord it over other prisoners, a locksmith could not. Among *Kapos*, block-leaders and other high camp functionaries, there were indeed prisoners who accepted SS standards as their own—this man for instance:

> *His specialty was strangling prisoners with the heel of his boot, and he would stand erect in the pose of a Roman gladiator, enjoying the approval of the other Kapos, who would speak admiringly of a "good clean job."*

Almost certainly, however, that man had been a killer before he came to the camps. For prisoners like him the camps did not cause brutality so much as simply endorse it. Bettelheim's observations are based on camp conditions in the late 1930's, a time when positions of power were held exclusively by criminals—by men and women who, prior to imprisonment, had been murderers, prostitutes, thieves. The concentration camps had long been a dumping ground for criminals, both in Russia and in Germany, and in the Nazi camps this type was exploited by the SS as the most suitable channel for the delegation of power.

But this is not a case of imitation: such prisoners were like their masters from the start. The Nazis knew their own kind and naturally established an order reflecting SS values. That criminals had so much power was one of the most deadly conditions in the camp world; and only slowly, through years of intrigue, threat, bribery and assassination, were underground resistance groups able to replace the criminal *Kapos* with men of their own. This kind of maneuvering was most successful in Buchenwald, least effective in the Soviet camps. One of the cardinal facts about the camps was that everywhere a battle raged between the "greens" and the "reds"—between those imprisoned for real crimes and those imprisoned for opposition to the regime.

The assumption that survivors imitated SS behavior is misleading because it generalizes a limited phenomenon, but also because it overlooks the duality of behavior in extremity. Eugen Kogon, a member of the Buchenwald underground, points out that "the concentration-camp prisoner knew a whole system of mimicry toward the SS," an "everpresent camouflage" which concealed true feelings and intentions. *Strategic* imitation of the SS was enormously important because thereby political prisoners held positions of power which would otherwise have gone to the criminals. In the following instance, a new prisoner, a baker, is attacked by a passing SS guard:

> *With purely animal rage, he pulled off the baker's upper garments and tore them to shreds, and then whipped his bare back until the blood oozed. . . . Then the overseer, a Czech-German "political," noticed what was going on. He immediately rushed over and began shouting "You goddamned Jewish dog! You'll work for the rest of the day without clothes! I'm sick of the trouble you lousy Jews give me!" He made a threatening gesture, and then roared, "Come with me!"*
> *The SS guard left, confident that the baker was in good hands. Then the overseer took the baker into a tool-shed where it was warm, dressed him, washed his wounds, and gave him permission to stay in the shed until it was time to quit work.*

Or take Franz, the *Kapo* of an SS storeroom in Auschwitz. Every day crates of food were "accidentally" dropped and reported as "shipment damage." The contents were then "organized"—for Franz, for his men and others in need. In the "open," however, there was another Franz:

> *As we walked . . . past other kapos and SS men he began roaring at us. . . . As he shouted, he swung at us with his club. To the passing SS men he looked and sounded a splendid kapo, heartless, brutal, efficient; yet never once did he hit us.*

Imitation of SS behavior was a regular feature of life in the camps, and large numbers of prisoners benefited because positions of power were secretly used in ways which assisted the general struggle for life. Even small jobs—working as a locksmith for instance—dovetailed into the larger fabric of resistance. . . .

Prisoners survived through concrete acts of mutual aid, and over time these many small deeds, like fibers in the shuttle of a clumsy loom, grew into a general fabric of debt and care. At roll-call, for instance, or *Appel*, as it was called in the Nazi camps, prisoners had to form up hours before dawn and stand at attention in thin rags through rain and snow. This occurred again in the evening, and took at least two hours, sometimes three and four, and every survivor remembers roll-calls which lasted all night. Prisoners had to stand there the whole time, caps off, caps on, as SS officers strolled past the ranks. Any irregularity was punished savagely, and irregularities were numerous. Prisoners fainted, collapsed from exhaustion and sickness, simply fell dead on the spot. "Those winter *Appels*," says a survivor of Buchenwald, "were actually a form of extermination. . . . In addition to those who regularly fell dead during *Appel*, there were every day a number who contracted pneumonia and subsequently died."

To fall and be noticed by an SS man was to be beaten or shot, and the universal practice among prisoners was to use their own bodies to prop up inmates no longer able to stand. Almost all reports by survivors include moments at roll-call when an individual either gave, or was given, this kind of support: "I was so weakened that during roll-call I could scarcely stay on my feet. But the others pressed close on either side and supported me with the weight of their bodies."

Help was forbidden, of course, but there was some safety in numbers, for among so many thousands of prisoners packed together, the SS could view any particular rank only briefly. But despite danger, the need to help persisted, often in elaborate ways. It regularly happened that sick prisoners were carried to roll-call by comrades, who then took turns supporting them. Sometimes this went on for days, and care for the sick did not end with roll-call. Many men and women were nursed back to health by friends who "organized" extra food; who shuffled the sick man back and forth from barracks to barracks; who propped him up at roll-call, and kept him out of sight during "selections" and while he was delirious. In one case a prisoner with typhus was smuggled every day into the "Canada" work detail and hidden in the great piles of clothing where he could rest. This particular rescue involved getting the sick man through a gate guarded by a *Kapo* whose job was to spot sick and feeble prisoners and club them to death. Each day, therefore, two prisoners supported the sick man almost to the gate, and then left him to march through on his own. Once past the guard they propped him up again.

Prisoners in the concentration camps helped each other. That in itself is the significant fact. Sometimes it was help individually given, as in the case of a girl in Birkenau who, "at the risk of being severely beaten if her absence in the potato-peeling room was discovered, every evening . . . brought coffee to the sick. The last time she brought it was on the eve of her own death." Sometimes it took the form of one group helping another, as when a work squad had to carry sacks of cement from the storeroom to a building site:

> *I was equal to the job, but working with us were weaker men who grew exhausted after a few trips. The younger of us, myself included, pitched in to help them. We had agreed among our group that we would help one another to whatever extent was possible, rather than surrender to the dog-eat-dog philosophy which poisoned the minds of some prisoners.*

And sometimes help came collectively, unplanned and uncalled for, where and when it was needed:

> *For example, five women are pushing a conveyor car loaded to the brim with gravel . . . the car jumps the track . . . then it gets stuck in the sand. The women stop, completely helpless. Fortunately the chief is not around. All efforts to replace the car on the tracks are fruitless; the heavy-laden car will not budge and the chief may appear at any moment. A clandestine congregating begins. Stealthily, bent figures sneak toward the derailed car from all directions: the women who work on the mound of sand, those who level the gravel, a group just returned from delivering a track. A common exertion of arms and backs raises the car, the spades dig into the sand under the wheels and heave — and the loaded car moves, shivers. Fear gives strength to the workers. With more pushing, one wheel is on the track. A Kapo comes rushing from afar, she has noticed people missing at various points of work. But before she can get there, one more tug, one more push — and the gravel-laden conveyor car proceeds smoothly along the tracks.*

The survivor's experience is evidence that the need *to* help is as basic as the need *for* help, a fact which points to the radically social nature of life in extremity and explains an unexpected but very widespread activity among survivors. In the concentration camps a major form of behavior was gift-giving. Inmates were continually giving and sharing little items with each other, and small acts like these were enormously valuable both as morale boosters and often as real aids in the struggle for life. Sometimes the gift was given outright, with no apparent relation between donor and receiver:

> *One evening we were served a soup made with semolina. I drank this with all the more relish since I often had to forgo the daily cabbage soup because of my bowels. Just then I noticed a woman, one of the prostitutes, who always kept very much to themselves, approaching my bunk, holding her bowl out to me with both hands.*

"Micheline, I think this is a soup you can eat; here, take mine too."
She emptied her bowl into mine and went without food that day.

The assumption that there was no moral or social order in the concentration camps is wrong. Except peripherally and for brief periods similar to the "initial collapse" of individuals, the general condition we call chaos or anomie—what philosophers designate as the "state of nature"—did not exist. Certainly it did not prevail. Through innumerable small acts of humanness, most of them covert but everywhere in evidence, survivors were able to maintain societal structures workable enough to keep themselves alive and morally sane. The "state of nature," it turns out, is not natural. A war of all against all must be imposed by force, and no sooner has it started than those who suffer it begin, spontaneously and without plan, to transcend it. . . .

The survivor is the figure who emerges from all those who fought for life in the concentration camps, and the most significant fact about their struggle is that it depended on fixed activities: on forms of social bonding and interchange, on collective resistance, on keeping dignity and moral sense active. That such thoroughly *human* kinds of behavior were typical in places like Buchenwald and Auschwitz amounts to a revelation reaching to the foundation of what man is.

Primo Levi

The Gray Zone

[T]he network of human relationships inside the Lagers was not simple: it could not be reduced to the two blocs of victims and persecutors. Anyone who today reads (or writes) the history of the Lager reveals the tendency, indeed the need, to separate evil from good, to be able to take sides, to emulate Christ's gesture on Judgment Day: here the righteous, over there the reprobates. The young above all demand clarity, a sharp cut; their experience of the world being meager, they do not like ambiguity. In any case, their expectation reproduces exactly that of the newcomers to the Lagers, whether young or not; all of them, with the exception of those who had already gone through an analogous experience, expected to find a terrible but decipherable world, in conformity with that simple model which we atavistically carry within us—"we" inside and the enemy outside, separated by a sharply defined geographic frontier.

Instead, the arrival in the Lager was indeed a shock because of the surprise it entailed. The world into which one was precipitated was terrible, yes, but also indecipherable: it did not conform to any model; the enemy was all around but also inside, the "we" lost its limits, the contenders were not two, one could not discern a single frontier but rather many confused, perhaps innumerable frontiers, which stretched between each of us. One entered hoping at least for the solidarity of one's companions in misfortune, but the hoped for allies, except in special cases, were not there; there were instead a thousand sealed off monads, and between them a desperate covert and continuous struggle. This brusque revelation, which became manifest from the very first hours of imprisonment, often in the instant form of a concentric aggression on the part of those in whom one hoped to find future allies, was so harsh as to cause the immediate collapse of one's capacity to resist. For many it was lethal, indirectly or even directly: it is difficult to defend oneself against a blow for which one is not prepared.

Various aspects can be identified in this aggression. Remember that the concentration camp system even from its origins (which coincide with the rise to power of Nazism in Germany) had as its primary purpose shattering the adversaries' capacity to resist: for the camp management the new arrival was by definition an adversary, whatever the label attached to him might be, and he must immediately be demolished to make sure that he did not become an example or a germ of organized resistance. On this point the SS had very clear ideas, and it is from this viewpoint that the entire sinister ritual must be interpreted—varying from Lager to Lager, but basically similar—which accompanied the arrival: kicks and punches right away, often in the face; an orgy of orders screamed with true or simulated rage; complete nakedness after being stripped; the shaving off of all one's hair; the outfitting in rags. It is difficult to say whether all these details were devised by some expert or methodically perfected on the basis of experience, but they certainly were willed and not casual: it was all staged, as was quite obvious.

Nevertheless, the entry ritual, and the moral collapse it promoted, was abetted more or less consciously by the other components of the concentration camp world: the simple prisoners and the privileged ones. Rarely was a newcomer received, I won't say as a friend but at least as a companion-in-misfortune; in the majority of cases, those with seniority (and seniority was acquired in three or four months; the changeover was swift!) showed irritation or even hostility. The "newcomer" (*Zugang:* one should note that in German this is an abstract, administrative term, meaning "access," "entry") was envied because he still seemed to have on him the smell of home, and it was an absurd envy, because in fact one suffered much more during the first days of imprisonment than later on, when habituation on one hand and experience on the other made it possible to construct oneself a shelter. He was derided and subjected to cruel pranks, as happens in all communities with "conscripts" and "rookies," as well as in the initiation ceremonies of primitive peoples: and there is no doubt that life in the Lager involved a regression, leading back precisely to primitive behavior.

It is probable that the hostility toward the *Zugang* was in substance motivated like all other forms of intolerance, that is, it consisted in an unconscious attempt to consolidate the "we" at the expense of the "they," to create, in short, that solidarity among the oppressed whose absence was the source of additional suffering, even though not perceived openly. Vying for prestige also came into play, a seemingly irrepressible need in our civilization: the despised crowd of seniors was prone to recognize in the new arrival a target on which to vent its humiliation, to find compensation at his expense, to build for itself and at his expense a figure of a lower rank on whom to discharge the burden of the offenses received from above.

As for the privileged prisoners, the situation was more complex, and also more important: in my opinion, it is in fact fundamental. It is naive, absurd, and historically false to believe that an infernal system such as National Socialism sanctifies its victims: on the contrary, it degrades them, it makes them resemble itself, and this all the more when they are available, blank, and lacking a political or moral armature. . . . Privileged prisoners were a minority within the Lager population; nevertheless they represent a potent majority among survivors. In fact, even apart from the hard labor, the beatings, the cold, and the illnesses, the food ration was decisively insufficient for even the most frugal prisoner: the physiological reserves of the organism were consumed in two or three months, and death by hunger, or by diseases induced by hunger, was the prisoner's normal destiny, avoidable only with additional food. Obtaining that extra nourishment required a privilege—large or small, granted or conquered, astute or violent, licit or illicit—whatever it took to lift oneself above the norm.

Now, one mustn't forget that the greater part of the memories, spoken or written, of those who came back begin with the collision with the concentrationary reality and, simultaneously, the unforeseen and uncomprehended aggression on the part of a new and strange enemy, the functionary-prisoner, who instead of taking you by the hand, reassuring you, teaching you the way, throws himself at you, screaming in a language you do not understand, and strikes you in the face. He wants to tame you, extinguish any spark of dignity that he has lost and you perhaps still preserve. But trouble is in store for you if this dignity drives you to react. . . . I was told the story of an Italian "newcomer," a Partisan, flung into a work Lager with the label "political prisoner" when he still had his full strength. He had been beaten when the soup was being distributed and he had dared to shove the distributor-functionary: the latter's colleagues rushed to his aid, and the culprit was made an example of by being drowned, his head held down in the soup tub.

The ascent of the privileged, not only in the Lager but in all human coexistence, is an anguishing but unfailing phenomenon: only in utopias is it absent. It is the duty of righteous men to make war on all undeserved privilege, but one must not forget that this is a war without end. Where power is exercised by few or only one against the many, privilege is born and proliferates, even against the will of the power itself. On the other hand, it is normal for power to tolerate and encourage privilege. Let us confine ourselves to the Lager, which (even in its Soviet version) can be considered an excellent "laboratory": the hybrid class of the prisoner-functionary constitutes its armature and at the same time its most disquieting feature. It is a gray zone, poorly defined, where the two camps of masters and servants both diverge and converge. This gray zone possesses an incredibly complicated internal structure and contains within itself enough to confuse our need to judge.

The gray zone of privilege and collaboration springs from multiple roots. In the first place, the more the sphere of power is restricted, the more it needs external auxiliaries. The Nazism of the final years could not do without these external auxiliaries, determined as it was to maintain its order within subjugated Europe and feed the front lines of the war, bled white by their opponents' growing military resistance. The occupied countries had to provide not only labor but also forces of order, delegates and administrators of the German power, which was by now committed elsewhere to the point of exhaustion. Within this category fall, albeit to varying degrees, Quisling in Norway, the Vichy government in France, the Judenrat in Warsaw, the Saló Republic in Italy, right down to the Ukrainian and Baltic mercenaries employed elsewhere for the filthiest tasks (never in combat) and the *Sonderkommandos*, about which we will have more to say.

But collaborators who originate in the adversary camp, ex-enemies, are untrustworthy by definition: they betrayed once and they can betray again. It is not enough to relegate them to marginal tasks; the best way to bind them is to burden them with guilt, cover them with blood, compromise them as much as possible, thus establishing a bond of complicity so that they can no longer turn back. This way of proceeding has been well known to criminal associations of all times and places. The Mafia has always practiced it. It is also the only way to explain the otherwise indecipherable excesses of Italian terrorism in the 1970s.

In the second place, and in contrast to a certain hagiographic and rhetorical stylization, the harsher the oppression, the more widespread among the oppressed is the willingness, with all its infinite nuances and motivations, to collaborate: terror, ideological seduction, servile imitation of the victor, myopic desire for any power whatsoever, even though ridiculously circumscribed in space and time, cowardice, and, finally, lucid calculation aimed at eluding the imposed orders and order. All these motives, singly or combined, have come into play in the creation of this gray zone, whose components are bonded together by the wish to preserve and consolidate established privilege vis-à-vis those without privilege.

Before discussing separately the motives that impelled some prisoners to collaborate to some extent with the Lager authorities, however, it is necessary to declare the imprudence of issuing hasty moral judgment on such human cases. Certainly, the greatest responsibility lies with the system, the very structure of the totalitarian state. . . . If it were up to me, if I were forced to judge, I would lightheartedly absolve all those whose concurrence in the guilt was minimal and for whom coercion was of the highest degree. Around us, prisoners without rank, swarmed low-ranking functionaries, a picturesque fauna: sweepers, kettle washers, night watchmen, bed smoothers (who exploited to their minuscule advantage the German fixation about bunks made up flat and square), checkers of lice and scabies, messengers, interpreters, assistants' assistants. In general, they were poor devils like ourselves, who worked full time like everyone else but who for an extra half-liter of soup were willing to carry out these and other "tertiary" functions: innocuous, sometimes useful, often invented out of the whole cloth. They were rarely violent, but they tended to develop a typically corporate mentality and energetically defended their "job" against anyone from below or above who might covet it. Their privilege, which at any rate entailed supplementary hardships and efforts, gained them very little and did not spare them from the discipline and suffering of everyone else; their hope for life was substantially the same as that of the unprivileged. They were coarse and arrogant, but they were not regarded as enemies.

Judgment becomes more tentative and varied for those who occupied commanding positions: the chiefs (*Kapos*) . . . of the labor squads, the barracks chiefs, the clerks, all the way to the world (whose existence at that time I did not even suspect) of the prisoners who performed diverse, at times most delicate duties in the camps' administrative offices, the Political Section (actually a section of the Gestapo), the Labor Service, and the punishment cells. Some of these . . . were not at all, or were only apparently, collaborators, but on the contrary camouflaged opponents. Not so the greater part of the other persons with positions of command, human specimens who ranged from the mediocre to the execrable. Rather than wearing one down, power corrupts; all the more intensely did their power corrupt, since it had a peculiar nature.

Power exists in all the varieties of the human social organization, more or less controlled, usurped, conferred from above or recognized from below, assigned by merit, corporate solidarity, blood, or position. Probably a certain degree of man's domination over man is inscribed in our genetic patrimony as gregarious animals. There is no proof that power is intrinsically harmful to the collectivity. But the power of which the functionaries of whom we are speaking disposed, even if they were low-ranking, such as the *Kapos* of the work squads, was, in substance, unlimited; or, more accurately put, a lower limit was imposed on their violence, in the sense that they were punished or deposed if they did not prove to be sufficiently harsh, but there was no upper limit. In other words, they were free to commit the worst atrocities on their subjects as punishment for any transgressions, or even without any motive whatsoever: until the end of 1943 it was not unusual for a prisoner to be beaten to death by a *Kapo* without the latter having to fear any sanctions. Only later on, when the need for labor became more acute, were a number of limitations introduced: the mistreatment the *Kapos* were allowed to inflict on the prisoners could not permanently diminish their working ability. But by then the malpractice was established and the regulation was not always respected.

Thus the Lager, on a smaller scale but with amplified characteristics, reproduced the hierarchical structure of the totalitarian state, in which all power is invested from above and control from below is almost impossible. But this "almost" is important: never has there existed a state that was really "totalitarian" from this point of view. Never has some form of reaction, a corrective of the total tyranny, been lacking, not even in the Third Reich or Stalin's Soviet Union: in both cases public opinion, the magistrature, the foreign press, the churches, the feeling for justice and humanity that ten or twenty years of tyranny were not enough to eradicate, have to a greater or lesser extent acted as a brake. Only in the Lager was the restraint from below nonexistent and the power of these small satraps absolute. It is understandable that power of such magnitude overwhelmingly attracted the human type who is greedy for power, that even individuals with moderate instincts aspired to it, seduced by the many material advantages of the position, and that the latter became fatally intoxicated by the power at their disposal.

Who became a *Kapo*? It is once again necessary to distinguish. The first to be offered this possibility, that is, those individuals in whom the Lager commander or his delegates (who were often good psychologists) discerned a potential collaborator, were the common criminals, taken from prisons, to whom a career as a torturer offered an excellent alternative to detention. Then came political prisoners broken by five or ten years of sufferings, or in any case morally debilitated. Later on it was Jews who saw in the particle of authority being offered them the only possible escape from the "final solution." But many, as we mentioned, spontaneously aspired to power, sadists, for example, certainly not numerous but very much feared, because for them the position of privilege coincided with the possibility of inflicting suffering and humiliation on those below them. The frustrated sought power as well, and this too is a feature in which the microcosm of the Lager reproduced the macrocosm of totalitarian society: in both, without regard to ability and merit, power was generously granted to those willing to pay homage to hierarchic authority, thus attaining an otherwise unattainable social elevation. Finally, power was sought by the many among the oppressed who had been contaminated by their oppressors and unconsciously strove to identify with them. . . .

It remains true that in the Lager, and outside, there exist gray, ambiguous persons, ready to compromise. The extreme pressure of the Lager tends to increase their ranks; they are the rightful owners of a quota of guilt (which grows apace with their freedom of choice), and besides this they are the vectors and instruments of the system's guilt. It remains true that the majority of the oppressors, during or (more often) after their deeds, realized that what they were doing or had done was iniquitous, or perhaps experienced doubts or discomfort, or were even punished, but this suffering is not enough to enroll them among the victims. By the same token, the prisoners' errors and weaknesses are not enough to rank them with their custodians: the prisoners of the Lagers, hundreds of thousands of persons of all social classes, from almost all the countries of Europe, represented an average, unselected sample of humanity. Even if one did not want to take into account the infernal environment into which they had been abruptly flung, it is illogical to demand—and rhetorical and false to maintain—that they all and always followed the behavior expected of saints and stoic philosophers. In reality, in the vast majority of cases, their behavior was rigidly preordained. In the space of a few weeks or months the deprivations to which they were subjected led them to a condition of pure survival, a daily struggle against hunger, cold, fatigue, and blows in which the room for choices (especially moral choices) was reduced to zero. Among these, very few survived the test, and this thanks to the conjunction of many improbable events. In short, they were saved by luck, and there is not much sense in trying to find something common to all their destinies, beyond perhaps their initial good health.

An extreme case of collaboration is represented by the *Sonderkommandos* of Auschwitz and the other extermination camps. Here one hesitates to speak of privilege: whoever belonged to this group was privileged only to the extent that—but at what cost!—he had enough to eat for a few months, certainly not because he could be envied. With this duly vague definition, "Special Squad," the SS referred to the group of prisoners entrusted with running the crematoria. It was their task to maintain order among the new arrivals (often completely unaware of the destiny awaiting them) who were to be sent into the gas chambers, to extract the corpses from the chambers, to pull gold teeth from jaws, to cut women's hair, to sort and classify clothes, shoes, and the contents of the luggage, to transport the bodies to the crematoria and oversee the operation of the ovens, to extract and eliminate the ashes. The Special Squad in Auschwitz numbered, depending on the moment, from seven hundred to one thousand active members.

These Special Squads did not escape everyone else's fate. On the contrary, the SS exerted the greatest diligence to prevent any man who had been part of it from surviving and telling. Twelve squads succeeded each other in Auschwitz, each remaining operative for a few months, whereupon it was suppressed, each time with a different trick to head off possible resistance. As its initiation, the next squad burnt the corpses of its predecessors. In October 1944 the last squad rebelled against the SS, blew up one of the crematoria, and was exterminated in an unequal battle that I will discuss later on. The survivors of the Special Squad were therefore very few, having escaped death because of some unforeseeable whim of fate. . . .

At first, the SS chose them from among the prisoners already registered in the Lager, and it has been testified that the choice was made not only on the basis of physical strength but also by a deep study of physiognomies. In a few rare cases enrollment took place as a punishment. Later on it was considered preferable to pick out the candidates directly at the railroad platform, on the arrival of each convoy: the SS "psychologists" noticed that recruitment was easier if one drew them from among those desperate, disoriented people, exhausted from the journey, bereft of resistance, at the crucial moment of stepping off the train, when every new arrival truly felt on the threshold of the darkness and terror of an unearthly space.

The Special Squads were made up largely of Jews. In a certain sense this is not surprising since the Lager's main purpose was to destroy Jews, and, beginning in 1943, the Auschwitz population was 90–95 percent Jews. From another point of view, one is stunned by this paroxysm of perfidy and hatred: it must be the Jews who put the Jews into the ovens; it must be shown that the Jews, the subrace, the submen, bow to any and all humiliation, even to destroying themselves. On the other hand, we know that not all the SS gladly accepted massacre as a daily task; delegating part of the work—and indeed the filthiest part—to the victims themselves was meant to (and probably did) ease a few consciences here and there.

Obviously it would be iniquitous to attribute such acquiescence to some specifically Jewish peculiarity: members of the Special Squads were also non-Jewish, German and Polish prisoners, although with the "more dignified" duties of *Kapos*, and also Russian prisoners of war, whom the Nazis considered only one degree superior to the Jews. They were few, because the Russians in Auschwitz were few (for the greater part having been exterminated before, immediately after capture, machine-gunned at the edge of enormous common graves): but they did not behave any differently from the Jews.

The Special Squads, being bearers of a horrendous secret, were kept rigorously apart from the other prisoners and the outside world. Nevertheless, as anyone who has gone through similar experiences knows, no barrier is ever without a flaw: information, possibly incomplete or distorted, has a tremendous power of penetration, and some of it always does filter through. Concerning these squads, vague and mangled rumors already circulated among us during our imprisonment and were confirmed afterward by the other sources mentioned before. But the intrinsic horror of this human condition has imposed a sort of reserve on all the testimony, so that even today it is difficult to conjure up an image of "what it meant" to be forced to exercise this trade for months. It has been testified that a large amount of alcohol was put at the disposal of those wretches and that they were in a permanent state of complete debasement and prostration. One of them declared: "Doing this work, one either goes crazy the first day or gets accustomed to it." Another, though: "Certainly, I could have killed myself or got myself killed; but I wanted to survive, to avenge myself and bear witness. You mustn't think that we are monsters; we are the same as you, only much more unhappy." . . .

Conceiving and organizing the squads was National Socialism's most demonic crime. Behind the pragmatic aspect (to economize on able men, to impose on others the most atrocious tasks) other more subtle aspects can be perceived. This institution represented an attempt to shift onto others—specifically, the victims—the burden of guilt, so that they were deprived of even the solace of innocence. It is neither easy nor agreeable to dredge this abyss of viciousness, and yet I think it must be done, because what could be perpetrated yesterday could be attempted again tomorrow, could overwhelm us and our children. One is tempted to turn away with a grimace and close one's mind: this is a temptation one must resist. In fact, the existence of the squads had a meaning, a message: "We, the master race, are your destroyers, but you are no better than we are; if we so wish, and we do so wish, we can destroy not only your bodies but also your souls, just as we have destroyed ours."

Miklos Nyiszli, a Hungarian physician, was one of the very few survivors of the last Special Squad in Auschwitz. . . . Nyiszli was also the attending physician of the squad, with which he lived in close contact. Well, he recounts an episode that seems significant to me.

The SS, as I already said, carefully chose, from the Lagers or the arriving convoys, the candidates for the squads, and did not hesitate to eliminate on the spot anyone who refused or seemed unsuitable for those duties. The SS treated the newly engaged members with the same contempt and detachment that they were accustomed to show toward all prisoners and Jews in particular. It had been inculcated in them that these were despicable beings, enemies of Germany, and therefore not entitled to life; in the most favorable instance, they should be compelled to work until they died of exhaustion. But this is not how they behaved with the veterans of the squad: in them, they recognized to some extent colleagues, by now as inhuman as themselves, hitched to the same cart, bound together by the foul link of imposed complicity. So, Nyiszli tells how during a "work" pause he attended a soccer game between the SS and the SK (*Sonderkommando*), that is to say, between a group representing the SS on guard at the crematorium and a group representing the Special Squad. Other men of the SS and the rest of the squad are present at the game; they take sides, bet, applaud, urge the players on as if, rather than at the gates of hell, the game were taking place on the village green.

Nothing of this kind ever took place, nor would it have been conceivable, with other categories of prisoners; but with them, with the "crematorium ravens," the SS could enter the field on an equal footing, or almost. Behind this armistice one hears satanic laughter: it is consummated, we have succeeded, you no longer are the other race, the anti-race, the prime enemy of the millennial Reich; you are no longer the people who reject idols. We have embraced you, corrupted you, dragged you to the bottom with us. You are like us, you proud people: dirtied with your own blood, as we are. You too, like us and like Cain, have killed the brother. Come, we can play together.

Nyiszli describes another episode that deserves consideration. In the gas chamber have been jammed together and murdered the components of a recently arrived convoy, and the squad is performing its horrendous everyday work, sorting out the tangle of corpses, washing them with hoses, and transporting them to the crematorium, but on the floor they find a young woman who is still alive. The event is exceptional, unique; perhaps the human bodies formed a barrier around her, sequestered a pocket of air that remained breathable. The men are perplexed. Death is their trade at all hours, death is a habit because, precisely, "one either goes mad on the first day or becomes accustomed to it," but this woman is alive. They hide her, warm her, bring her beef broth, question her: the girl is sixteen years old, she cannot orient herself in space or time, does not know where she is, has gone through without understanding it the sequence of the sealed train, the brutal preliminary selection, the stripping, the entry into the chamber from which no one had ever come out alive. She has not understood, but she has seen; therefore she must die, and the men of the squad know it just as they know that they too must die for the same reason. But these slaves debased by alcohol and the daily slaughter are transformed; they no longer have before them the anonymous mass, the flood of frightened, stunned people coming off the boxcars: they have a person. . . .

A doctor is called, and he revives the girl with an injection: yes, the gas has not had its effect, she will survive, but where and how? Just then Muhsfeld, one of the SS men attached to the death installations, arrives. The doctor calls him to one side and presents the case to him. Muhsfeld hesitates, then he decides: No, the girl must die. If she were older, it would be a different matter, she would have more sense, perhaps she could be convinced to keep quiet about what has happened to her. But she's only sixteen: she can't be trusted. And yet, he does not kill her with his own hands. He calls one of his underlings to eliminate her with a blow to the nape of the neck. Now, this man Muhsfeld was not a compassionate person; his daily ration of slaughter was studded with arbitrary and capricious acts, marked by his inventions of refined cruelty. He was tried in 1947, sentenced to death and hung in Krakow and this was right, but not even he was a monolith. Had he lived in a different environment and epoch, he probably would have behaved like any other common man. . . . That single, immediately erased instant of pity is certainly not enough to absolve Muhsfeld. It is enough, however, to place him too, although at its extreme boundary, within the gray band, that zone of ambiguity which radiates out from regimes based on terror and obsequiousness.

It is not difficult to judge Muhsfeld, and I do not believe that the tribunal which sentenced him had any doubts. On the other hand, in contrast to this, our need and our ability to judge falters when confronted by the Special Squad. Questions immediately arise, convulsed questions for which one would be hard-pressed to find an answer that reassures us about man's nature. Why did they accept that task? Why didn't they rebel? Why didn't they prefer death?

To a certain extent, the facts available to us permit us to attempt an answer. Not all did accept; some did rebel, knowing they would die. Concerning at least one case we have precise information: a group of four hundred Jews from Corfu, who in July 1944 had been included in the squad, refused without exception to do the work and were immediately gassed to death. We have learned of various individual mutinies, all immediately punished by an atrocious death (Filip Müller, one of the squads' very few survivors, tells of a companion whom the SS pushed into the oven alive), and many cases of suicide at the moment of recruitment, or immediately after. Finally, it must be remembered that it was the Special Squad which in October 1944 organized the only desperate attempt at revolt in the history of the Auschwitz Lager.

The information about this exploit that has come down to us is neither complete nor without contradictions. It is known that the insurgents (the personnel of two of the five Auschwitz-Birkenau crematoria), poorly armed and without contacts with the Polish Partisans outside the Lager or the clandestine defense organization inside the Lager, blew up Crematorium no. 3 and engaged the SS in battle. The battle was soon over, and a number of the insurgents managed to cut the barbed wire and escape to the outside but were captured soon afterward. Not one of them survived: approximately four hundred and fifty were immediately killed by the SS; among the latter, three were killed and twelve wounded.

Those whom we know about, the miserable manual laborers of the slaughter, are therefore the others, those who from one shift to the next preferred a few more weeks of life (what a life) to immediate death, but who in no instance induced themselves, or were induced, to kill with their own hands. I repeat: I believe that no one is authorized to judge them, not those who lived through the experience of the Lager and even less those who did not. I would invite anyone who dares pass judgment to carry out upon himself, with sincerity, a conceptual experiment: Let him imagine, if he can, that he has lived for months or years in a ghetto, tormented by chronic hunger, fatigue, promiscuity, and humiliation; that he has seen die around him, one by one, his beloved; that he is cut off from the world, unable to receive or transmit news; that, finally, he is loaded onto a train, eighty or a hundred persons to a boxcar; that he travels into the unknown, blindly, for sleepless days and nights; and that he is at last flung inside the walls of an indecipherable inferno. . . . Now nobody can know for how long and under what trials his soul can resist before yielding or breaking. Every human being possesses a reserve of strength whose extent is unknown to him, be it large, small, or nonexistent, and only through extreme adversity can we evaluate it. Even apart from the extreme case of the Special Squads, often those of us who have returned, when we describe our vicissitudes, hear in response: "In your place I would not have lasted for a single day." This statement does not have a precise meaning: one is never in another's place. Each individual is so complex that there is no point in trying to foresee his behavior, all the more so in extreme situations; nor is it possible to foresee one's own behavior. Therefore I ask that we meditate on the story of "the crematorium ravens" with pity and rigor, but that judgment of them be suspended.

Zoë Vania Waxman

Women and the Holocaust

Studies of women in the Holocaust often project their own concerns, which set the agenda for future testimony. They tend to emerge from preconceived ideas regarding women's abilities to act in moral, heroic, or noble ways. However, the Holocaust was not discriminatory towards its victims. No moral test was required for the gas chamber, only a test of race. Of course, there were people who performed 'heroic' acts, but there were also many who merely did what they had to do in order to survive. To show that people are fallible and act just as human beings is not to demonize them, but to attempt to present a more rounded picture of responses to extreme suffering.

Studies of women and the Holocaust tend to portray female witnesses in much the same way as child witnesses, as unproblematic victims. Little reference is made to the Jewish women who, as a result of intolerable circumstances, acted contrary to traditional expectations of female behaviour, such as the women who placed their own survival above that of their children, and the few female Jewish *Kapos* who came to mimic the behaviour of the SS captors. Fania Fénelon, a member of the women's orchestra at Auschwitz-Birkenau, deported in January 1944 for her participation in the French Resistance Movement, describes what happened when her former friend, half-Jewish Clara, was appointed *Kapo*: 'Clara rose up before us, arm band in place, club in hand. . . . Everything that was left of the timid, bashful young girl had just disappeared, destroyed once and for all by the environment of the camp.' Fénelon tried to reason with Clara by pointing out that her actions would make her life difficult after Auschwitz:

> '*Clara, look at yourself! You've become a monster. If you lash out at your friends, you'll never dare to go back home. Remember your childhood, your girlhood, your parents. . . . Clara, look at yourself!*'
> *Her eyes shone with a positively mineral brightness. . . . 'Be quiet and listen to me . . . it's me who's the stronger, it's me who's in charge. I've heard enough, now get away!*'

Responses such as Clara's might well have been the exception rather than the norm; it is hard to give figures, since women like her are precisely the ones who are least likely to record their testimonies. They are the ones who most want to forget the past, either because the pain of remembering is too great, or because of fears of retribution or condemnation. While Fénelon's memoir has been the subject of much controversy, her description of Clara should provoke further research into the complexities of women's responses to the Holocaust. . . .

To avoid 'preempting' the Holocaust, testimonies must not be taken as exhaustive of all Holocaust experiences. Not only are experiences of hiding different from those of living in the concentration camps, but also from those of life within the confines of the ghettos. Dalia Ofer and Lenore Weitzman highlight Emmanuel Ringelblum's[1] observation that women's coping strategies and nurturing roles continued under

---

[1]Ringelblum was the historian and chronicler of life in the Warsaw ghetto at the time he lived there, 1940–1943. — Ed.

wartime conditions, although they acknowledge that this might derive in part from the middle-class bias of Ringelblum's subjects, whom they still present as typical 'women . . . fac[ing] overwhelming forces with incredible resourcefulness, courage, and persistence'. In particular, they highlight Ringelblum's praise of the Jewish woman for her valiant attempts to care for her family. . . . But what about the unfortunate women who could not resist eating their paltry bread ration or the men too exhausted to even consider volunteering for such hard work? Their responses are just as human. The shame at not being able to control one's hunger can produce a terrible self-hatred. It is possible too that some did not even attempt to control their hunger. The phenomena of starvation and frustration in the ghettos were not just the preserve of the good. Furthermore, the valorizing of sacrifice often means that the struggles surrounding temptation are glossed over, although they could traumatize both those who gave in to temptation and those who fought desperately to overcome it. . . .

In pointing out that women's particular skills and knowledge provided them with tools for survival, Lenore Weitzman rightly draws attention to women's ability to hide by disguising their Jewishness. Her research . . . shows . . . that there are important differences in the wartime experiences of men and women. This is not surprising considering that women's lives in Eastern and Western Europe, during the 1920s and 1930s, revolved around specific gender roles. Paula Hyman explains that while Jewish women in more affluent Western Europe tended not to participate in business, higher education, and politics, and were therefore denied access to knowledge of the Gentile world and the possibility of assimilation, in Poland and other countries in Eastern Europe, where the majority of Jews were far less affluent and women needed to help out financially, women were likely to have a considerable knowledge of local languages and customs.

When it came to passing as Aryan, women had certain advantages over men, in particular a physical one: in Eastern Europe it was very rare for any man not Jewish to be circumcised. If a man was suspected of being Jewish, he was ordered to undress. Piotr Rawicz, describes his constant fear that his circumcision would betray his Jewishness. Women at least knew they could not be discovered by physical examination, although having stereotypically Jewish features such as dark hair and eyes, the markings of emotional and physical suffering, as well as a lack of financial resources, similarly prohibited the ability to pass. They hid either with forged documents, moving from place to place in both cities and small villages, in convents, in factories, and sometimes in forced-labour camps, or without documents by physically concealing themselves in fields, forests, attics, and stables. In Warsaw it is estimated that about two-thirds of Jews in hiding on the Aryan side were women. In towns and cities, women had to learn to enter any place with the placard 'No Jews Allowed' without showing any signs of fear. . . .

Although the Nazi policy of *Rassenschande* (race defilement) firmly prohibited sexual relations between Aryan men and Jewish women, and the incidence of rape and sexual assault seems to have been relatively rare in the concentration camps—although, as will be seen shortly, there are reported cases of rapes perpetrated by other prisoners, in particular by low-level functionaries—numerous acts of sexual violence were committed against 'non-Aryan' women throughout Eastern Europe. Women were particularly sexually vulnerable when in hiding. Fanya Gottesfeld Heller tells the story of a Gestapo raid which resulted in the rape of her aunt:

> *Unable to find me, Gottschalk and his henchman left and went looking for me at the home of one of my aunts. When they didn't find me there, they raped her and forced her husband to watch. The rape had to be kept secret because if the Gestapo [presumably she is referring to the higher ranks of the Gestapo] found out about it they would have killed her immediately, since Germans were forbidden to 'fraternise' with 'subhuman' Jews. My aunt told a few members of the family but they didn't believe her—they didn't want to hear or know about it. She never told her children, and for that reason, I have not disclosed her name.*

Gottesfeld Heller herself waited fifty years before telling the story. She also describes what she terms as a consensual sexual relationship between herself as a teenager and the Ukranian militia man who rescued and protected her family. Clearly, whether or not a sexual relationship based on such an extreme power imbalance can be understood as consensual makes for a contentious discussion. The feminist researcher Joan Ringelheim gives a further example of a Jewish survivor called 'Pauline' who was molested by male relatives of the people hiding her. Pauline was told that if she complained they would denounce her. The effects of this on her life are enduring. In an interview she told Ringelheim: 'I can still feel the fear. . . . Sometimes I think it was equally as frightening as the Germans. It became within me a tremendous . . . I (didn't) know how (to deal with it) . . . what to do with it. I had nobody to talk (to) about it. Nobody to turn to.' It is an experience which, as Pauline herself realizes, is not easily reconciled with traditional Holocaust narratives. She states: 'In respect of what happened, (what we) suffered and saw—the humiliation in the ghetto, seeing people jumping out and burned—is this (molestation) important?' In the words of Ringelheim: 'Her memory was split between traditional versions of Holocaust history and her own experience.' In other words, traditional Holocaust narratives can make it difficult to discuss anything considered to be outside the range of accepted Holocaust experiences as outlined by existing testimony. Witnesses may feel obliged to stay silent about certain aspects of their experiences for fear that they do not belong to the history of the Holocaust, or that the experiences will not be easily understood. This can prevent us from challenging traditional narratives, or adding to them by acquiring further information about the diversity of experiences during the Holocaust. . . .

While the observation that rape and sexual assault were relatively rare in the concentration camps is based upon the absence of descriptions of sexual abuse in testimonies, it is possible that such an absence inhibits other witnesses who did experience abuse from including descriptions of it in their testimonies. Ringelheim presents the case of 'Susan', who was deported to Auschwitz when she was 21 years old and quickly became a 'privileged prisoner'. A male Polish prisoner came to Susan one day and offered her some sardines. He told her when and where to meet him, and not realizing his motives, she did. Then, as Susan confessed to Ringelheim, 'he grabbed and raped me'. While it is significant that Susan is careful to point out that it was not a Jewish prisoner, but a Polish prisoner who raped her—thereby connecting herself to classic narratives by talking of Polish anti-Semitism—Ringelheim is correct to observe: 'I believe that we avoid listening to stories we do not want to hear. Sometimes we avoid listening because we don't understand the importance of what is being said. Without a place for a particular memory, without a conceptual framework, a possibly significant piece of information will not be pursued.'

As the examples of both Pauline and Susan indicate, Holocaust survivors may feel that traditional versions of Holocaust history prohibit them from telling their stories. Perhaps it is only because Susan's assailant was Polish rather than Jewish that she is able to speak of the assault at all. But, although Ringelheim is right to suggest that women were vulnerable to rape or sexual abuse, she fails to acknowledge that men were also at risk from such attacks. Although they occurred, these incidents have almost never been published. One of the very few testimonies to testify to the experience of rape comes from a male survivor. Roman Frister's testimony *The Cap or the Price of a Life,* which, like Gottesfeld Heller's memoir, was written a long time after the events it describes, tells the story of a young Jewish boy born in Poland and his rape in Auschwitz at the age of 15 by a fellow inmate who then stole his uniform cap. Inmates who appeared at morning roll-call without it would be shot on the spot. Presumably this was the rapist's intention. In order to survive, Frister promptly stole another cap from a sleeping prisoner. Three hours later, at roll-call, the prisoner was shot dead. In contrast to many survivors who tend to supply their experiences with a positive moral or emotional subtext, Frister states quite bluntly that at the time he had no qualms. Today, however, he does feel guilt, but suggests that it is probably irrational; believing morality to be a relative rather than a universal concept, he asks: 'Does anyone have the right to judge me against the standards of our civilised society for acts I committed in the darkness of the human jungle? Survival is the law of the jungle, and yes, I willingly submitted to that law.' It is noticeable that Frister focuses on the morality, or lack of morality, of stealing the cap, rather than on the trauma of the rape, thereby turning the story into a further opportunity to explore the more familiar territory of the nature of morality in the concentration camps. It will not be until comprehension of the Holocaust is broadened to acknowledge types of experience that stand outside traditional narratives that stories such as Frister's will be understood and explored. . . .

Research on the particularity of women's Holocaust experiences is right to draw attention to the role of mother, but this must be put in the context of the difficulty in fulfilling that role under a Nazi regime ruthlessly committed to destroying the Jewish family. In November 1941, Ringelblum recorded: 'Jews have been prohibited from marrying and having children. Women pregnant up to three months have to have an abortion.' While Avraham Tory wrote in his diary in the Kovno ghetto, 'From September on, giving birth is strictly forbidden. Pregnant women will be put to death', he went on to write on 4 February 1943: 'It was terrible to watch the women getting on the truck; they held in their arms their babies of different ages and wrapped in more and more sweaters so that they would not catch cold on the way (to their death).' Also in the Theresienstadt ghetto a decree for compulsory abortion was issued in July 1943, and afterwards any woman who refused to comply with this order, or who gave birth, was placed on the next transport to the concentration camps in the East. Women's responses to this climate of anti-mothering are complex and varied.

In March 1943, when the Germans began liquidating the Polish city of Lwów, forcing the Jews from the ghetto and murdering thousands, a small group, including several small children, managed to escape into the sewers. They lived in a confined space among the city's waste for 14 months. One of the members of the group, Genia Weinberg, gave birth to a baby boy, assisted only by her comrades with a pair of rusty scissors and a towel. Needless to say, it would be almost impossible to care for a baby under such conditions. The dilemma was whether to attempt to raise the child at all costs, or to sacrifice its life for the sake of the group, since its cries could attract attention. Due to the appalling nature of such a choice, it is not surprising that there are differing versions of what happened. The mother herself provides the following version of events: 'The group quickly realized the hopelessness of trying to care for a baby. . . . The baby's cries would alert people in the street of their presence and so it was agreed, unanimously, that the baby be terminated. It was taken away, killed, and disposed of.' In this account Mrs Weinberg seems to be trying to distance herself both from her baby and from a personal decision to end its life. However, an alternative version of events is provided by a family called Chiger and confirmed by a woman named Klara Margulies. They recall:

> She [Mrs Weinberg] began to hug the baby closer and closer to herself, covering its face with a towel or rag, supposedly to quiet the sound of his whimpering. But my wife realized that she was in fact trying to suffocate the baby and she tried to pull the cloth away.
> The struggle continued for some time until the two women were just too exhausted to continue. . . . In the morning, the little corpse was lying beside his mother, who had fallen into a sullen trance. . . .

If Mrs Weinberg did suffocate her own baby, her testimony of events can be read either as a coping strategy to avoid facing the full horror of what had happened, or as a partial suppression of a painful truth. She can be understood not just as a mother . . . but as a woman who had perhaps not yet relinquished her hope for a future.

On arrival at the concentration camps, men and women were separated before being murdered in the gas chambers or sent to separate camps or barracks. At Auschwitz-Birkenau, women who refused to be separated from children under the age of 14 were sent to the gas chambers with them. Mothers were faced with what Lawrence Langer calls 'a choiceless choice': they could attempt to dissociate themselves from their children in the uncertain hope of survival or accompany them to a certain death. Some women did not realize that they were going with their children to their deaths, as the Nazis took pains to conceal the reality of the gas chambers until it was too late. Experienced prisoners, who did know the truth, sometimes tried to tell the mothers to hand the children over to the elderly, for the elderly were already condemned to death on account of their age. However, studies of women and the Holocaust continue the theme of the dutiful mother by suggesting, for example, that on arrival at Auschwitz 'most women clung to their children (and many young girls to their mothers) and were sent to the gas chambers with them'. This statement . . . may indeed be true of most women, but there are exceptions.

In his semi-autobiographical work *This Way for the Gas, Ladies and Gentlemen,* which recalls events he is known to have experienced but are filtered through the voice of 'Tadek', Tadeusz Borowski tells the story of a young woman's attempt to distance herself from her crying child by pretending no knowledge of it, although she in fact fails and is forced to share the child's fate:

> *Here is a woman—she walks quickly, but tries to appear calm. A small child with a pink cherub's face runs after her and, unable to keep up, stretches out his little arms and cries: Mama! Mama!*
> *'Pick up your child, woman!'*
> *'It's not mine, sir, not mine!', she shouts hysterically and runs on, covering her face with her hands. She wants to hide, she wants to reach those who will not ride the trucks, those who will go on foot, those who will stay alive. She is young, healthy, good-looking, she wants to live. But the child runs after her, wailing loudly: 'Mama, mama, don't leave me!'*
> *'It's not mine, not mine, no!'*
> *Andrei, a sailor from Sevastopol, grabs hold of her. His eyes are glassy from vodka and the heat. With one powerful blow he knocks her off her feet, then, as she falls, takes her by the hair and pulls her up again. His face twitches with rage.*
> *'Ah, you bloody Jewess! So you're running from your own child! I'll show you, you whore!' His huge hand chokes her, he lifts her in the air and heaves her on the truck like a heavy sack of grain.*
> *'Here! And take this with you, bitch!' and he throws the child at her feet.*

'Gut gemacht, *good work. That's the way to deal with degener-ate mothers,' says the S.S. man standing at the foot of the truck.* 'Gut, gut, Russki.'

It is not easy to make sense of this young mother's response within frameworks of interpretation based on the notion of the dutiful mother. If this mother had lived, and had possibly become a mother to other children, she would need to find some way of binding her memories. She would have to assign a boundary to her suffering if she were to be able to function in a new life. If she did give voice to her story, the woman might find a less self-incriminating framework in which to tell of the loss of her child. However, this does not mean that she would not continue to suffer silently the trauma and guilt of what she had done.

Pregnant woman were occasionally admitted to the camps, either because they were married to Gentile husbands, or because their preg-nancy was not yet noticeable. Some would undergo induced miscar-riages, often as late as the fourth or fifth month. The 'choiceless choice' finds particular expression when women gave birth in the camps. Ilona Karmel explores pregnancy in the slave labour camps, to understand the moral dilemmas of survival. Karmel, who survived such camps herself, points out that there were many responses to motherhood. For exam-ple, she contrasts one woman's 'longing for a child' with another's sense of her unborn baby as 'a tormentor who sucked her strength, snatched every crumb away'. Significantly, newborn children were not allowed to survive: if discovered, it meant certain death for both mother and child. Therefore, many of the inmate doctors decided that such chil-dren must die so that the mother might live. They saved poison for this purpose, but in its absence were forced to smother the babies. Some-times they managed to kill the baby without the mother's knowledge, in the expectation that this would spare her some measure of pain; but on other occasions she was aware of the situation. . . .

Ilona Karmel tells us what happened when women did try to save a newborn baby, when Nazi doctors had ordered that the child be placed in cotton wool but not fed anything, including water. The women involved risked their own lives to feed the baby sugar water, but the baby died anyway, its suffering prolonged. . . .

Studies of women in the concentration camps pay a great deal of at-tention to stories of mutual support, primarily women who survived with close relatives—daughters, mothers, sisters, cousins. Some realized that they could only survive the camps by being caring to one another. In her memoir *Rena's Promise: A Story of Sisters in Auschwitz*, Rena Kornreich Gelissen recalls . . . that the presence of her sister in Auschwitz allowed her to maintain a connection with the past and hope for the future. Her need to be a good sister and daughter is illustrative not only of a desire to help another, but also of a very important survival strategy that provides Rena with a sense of purpose and a means to survival. . . .

Accounts of mutual care and concern become problematic when used to obscure the horrors of the concentration camps by introducing a redemptive message into the Holocaust. Testimonies document the sharp and often violent divisions among prisoners within the concentration camps based on factors like position in the camp hierarchy, political affiliation, religious observance, or geographical origin. Helen Lewis describes the deep sense of division in Auschwitz between the Yiddish-speaking *Ostjuden* (Eastern European Jews) and the more assimilated Western European Jews:

> There were three hundred of us newcomers who had previously been in Terezin and in the family camp at Birkenau. We came from Czechoslovakia, Germany and Austria and we shared a fairly similar background and outlook. . . . The five hundred prisoners who had arrived some weeks earlier came from Poland and the Baltics, as well as Hungary and Romania. Most of them had had a strict religious upbringing, which gave them a strong sense of identity, but sadly manifested itself in their hostility towards us and their rejection of our group. They could speak the languages of their home countries, but preferred to talk to each other in Yiddish, a language which I and the rest of my group didn't understand. They bitterly resented our lack of religious ardour; we thought them uneducated, uncivilised even.

The brutality and deprivation of the concentration camps dictated that both on a group and an individual level any sense of solidarity, friendship, or familial feeling would have its dark side. The scope for action was so constrained that caring for someone invariably meant doing so at somebody else's expense. When Rena manages to get her sister a place on her bunk, she acknowledges: 'I do not ask what will happen to the girl who is sleeping next to me. . . . This is a selfish act, perhaps, but I have a sister who I have to keep alive and she is all that matters.' . . .

Women's testimonies in particular also highlight the trauma of losing a sense of one's physical self. For example, for many women, and particularly religious women, it was the first experience of the showers that eroded their sense of self and will to live. A comparative study of women's and men's testimonies suggests that more women describe the trauma of their initiation into the concentration camp world. Women write of the agony of having to stand naked in front of men, of being searched for hidden valuables, of being subjected to obscene remarks, of being shorn of all their hair, and of being tattooed. Rena Kornreich Gelissen remembers: 'I try to prevent tears from falling down my disinfected cheeks. Only married women shave their heads [orthodox Jewish women shave their heads after marriage]. Our traditions, our beliefs, are scorned and ridiculed by the acts they commit.'

Many women found the experience so traumatic that they went to their deaths soon after. A further step in the erosion of the self was the stopping of menstruation shortly after arrival at the concentration camps. (While this might have been the result of shock or starvation, it was also rumoured that the food the women ate was laced with bromide as part of an experiment in mass sterilization.) This made some women fearful that they would be infertile forever. Livia Bitton-Jackson writes: 'Married women keep wondering about the bromide in their food again and again. Will they bear children again? What will their husbands say when they find out?' Some even tried to eat less food in the hope that it would cause less damage. However, hunger generally made this a short-lived strategy.

Assumptions about women's behaviour obscure the diversity of their Holocaust experiences. The Holocaust was indiscriminate in its targeting of the Jews—every Jew, male and female, was condemned to death. The religious, the secular, the educated, the ignorant, the good, and the corrupt were all sentenced to the same fate. For those who survived, feelings of guilt can exist regardless of whether or not they are justified. The identities of women are constructed on the basis of roles such as 'mother', 'caregiver', 'daughter', and testimonies are often selected to reinforce these pre-existing ideals. Many testimonies do focus on the desire to fulfil traditional gendered expectations. While in Auschwitz, Rena was determined to prove herself a caring sister. Since she and her sister both survived, she was able to maintain this self-image. Other testimonies describe the split between the desire to meet particular expectations and the realization that they could not be attained. Ilona Karmel tells us that when women did try to save a baby by secretly feeding it, very often they were merely prolonging the child's suffering. Other women such as Clara abandoned all ideals of female (or human) decency and became vicious *Kapos*. They refused to acknowledge who they had been or might be expected to be. Women such as Clara show that under extreme circumstances people can act in unexpected ways. Before arriving at Auschwitz, the young mother described by Tadeusz Borowski might have fulfilled all the criteria demanded of 'mother', but realizing that her child was sentenced to die, tried to abandon him in order to live. She, like the majority of those who experienced the Holocaust, did not survive to write her testimony.

Survivors who write testimony can feel compelled to make their experiences compatible with pre-existing narratives of survival. Part of the process of writing a testimony may be to record a story of survival in a way that helps the survivor to carry on with his or her own life within a culture in which gender norms are strong. For example, Genia Weinberg might need to deny suffocating her child in order to go on living. For most survivors, Holocaust testimony is rooted in traumatic experiences, and the act of writing a testimony involves the rediscovering of an identity—be it witness, survivor, Jew, loving mother, or dutiful daughter, to name but a few. For many, the desire to be a witness was present at the time of the Holocaust. The post-war adoption of the role of the witness can provide survivors with a sense of purpose, or identity, but their testimony is mediated by the myriad of factors which play a part in a survivor's narrative, especially the accepted Holocaust narratives, studies, and testimonies. . . . [T]he function of collective memory is not to focus on the past in order to find out more about the Holocaust, but to use the past to inform and meet present concerns. In the case of women, the purpose is to say something universal about women, not about their particular Holocaust experiences. Unfortunately, the distressing stories of people who acted desperately, under appalling circumstances, in order to survive, are often overlooked. It is, of course, understandable that many people shy away from confronting the full horrors of the Holocaust, yet this will continue as long as testimonies are projected as 'epics of love and courage'.

Jewish prisoners taken during the Warsaw Ghetto uprising, April 1943. Photograph by AFP / Getty Images

The Problem of Jewish Resistance

Variety of Opinion

[O]ver a period of centuries the Jews had learned that in order to survive they had to refrain from resistance. . . . A 2,000-year-old lesson could not be unlearned; the Jews could not make the switch. They were helpless.

Raul Hilberg

Jewish armed resistance was considerably more widespread than has been assumed. . . . The range of Jewish resistance was broad . . . : armed, unarmed but organized, semi-organized or semi-spontaneous.

Yehuda Bauer

The situation into which the Jewish councils were forced . . . draws us into a profound crisis for a moral consciousness based . . . on behavior perceived as rational [and] faith in the enemy's ultimate interest in self-preservation.

Dan Diner

With few exceptions, Jews in Eastern European ghettos, labor camps, and extermination centers yielded to their fate with minimal resistance. Modern scholars are divided about how to explain the virtual absence of armed Jewish opposition. Was it because the Jews lacked the will or the opportunity to meet violence with violence?

Raul Hilberg, the dean of American Holocaust scholars, argued in his pioneering 1961 history of the Holocaust that the European Jews lacked the will to resist. Steeped in a culture that put a premium on accommodating Gentiles and looking to political authorities for protection against outbreaks of popular antisemitism, they could not, or would not, adjust to vastly changed circumstances. Now persecution came from the authorities themselves, but the Jews did not draw the only logical conclusion from this state of affairs: they could fight back, die with honor, and have perhaps a chance at surviving; or they could perish like the "cattle" that Franz Stangl recalled from his days as commandant at Treblinka. Hilberg has been criticized for allegedly lacking sensitivity to the Jews' impossible situation, but he remains convinced of his position, restating it in the recent revision of his book. In his view the Jews could have resisted more than they did, and their failure to do so helped to seal the fate of European Jewry.

Yehuda Bauer denies that Jews missed opportunities for armed revolt. They took up arms when they could, he states, noting cases of militant Jewish resistance. But for most the opportunity never came. They lacked arms and outside support, and they were crushed by the brutal Nazi policy of collective responsibility. Moreover, Bauer suggests a far broader definition of resistance, one that places nonviolent group action to save Jewish lives on the same level as armed resistance. Presenting a highly nuanced appreciation of the conditions of life for Jews during the war, he denies that they could have known that the only alternative to death was militant resistance. Bauer is one of several, mainly Jewish, historians who have sought to rehabilitate the reputation of Jewish leaders and argued for a more understanding view of the dilemma of the Jewish masses under Hitler.

Dan Diner responds to accusations by Hilberg (and others) that the Jewish Councils that ran the ghettos during the Holocaust were guilty of groveling compliance in the destruction process. The Jewish Council (Diner uses the German name *Judenrat*), created by the Germans but made up of authentic Jewish leaders, typically organized the production of vital military products for the Wehrmacht, delivered Jews for "resettlement," and restrained ghetto inhabitants from armed resistance. It did so, Diner argues, in the belief that the Germans were motivated by self-interest in making use of ghetto labor. The Councils could not by any reasonable standard have been expected to understand that extermination ultimately triumphed over economic considerations. Diner concludes that Nazi policies were fundamentally "counterrational" (i.e., inaccessible to the thought processes and values of rational individuals). Trapped in a "borderline situation" between self-preservation and self-destruction, the Jewish Councils occupied another Holocaust "gray zone."

Evaluating Jewish resistance during the Holocaust poses overlapping questions of definition and opportunity. As we have seen, some scholars concentrate on armed resistance, whereas others adopt broader definitions that include nonviolent measures. Were nonviolent measures reasonable at the time, or did they play into Nazi hands and merely delay the final day of doom? Should Jews in Eastern European ghettos have refused to serve on Jewish Councils, thereby forcing the Germans to rule them directly? Historians are also divided over the chances of Jews carrying out effective armed resistance to the Germans in Eastern Europe. Should we lament failures to fight back on a broader front, or marvel that there was as much armed resistance as there was? To answer these questions with absolute certainty, we would have to know whether and how the Nazis would have coped with more extensive and militant Jewish opposition. That, of course, is impossible. History is no laboratory science in which one can run the experiment over and change the variables. Answers will suggest themselves only through informed and sensitive appreciation of the situation confronting the victims at the time.

Raul Hilberg

Two Thousand Years of Jewish Appeasement

In a destruction process the perpetrators do not play the only role; the process is shaped by the victims too. It is the *interaction* of perpetrators and victims that is "fate." We must therefore discuss the reactions of the Jewish community and analyze the role of the Jews in their own destruction.

When confronted by force, a group can react in five ways: by resistance, by an attempt to alleviate or nullify the threat (the undoing reaction), by evasion, by paralysis, or by compliance. Let us consider each in turn.

The reaction pattern of the Jews is characterized by almost complete lack of resistance. In marked contrast to German propaganda, the documentary evidence of Jewish resistance, overt or submerged, is very slight. On a Europeanwide scale the Jews had no resistance organization, no blueprint for armed action, no plan even for psychological warfare. They were completely unprepared. In the words of Anti-Partisan Chief and Higher SS and Police Leader Russia Center von dem Bach, who observed Jews and killed them from 1941 to the end:

> *Thus the misfortune came about. . . . I am the only living witness but I must say the truth. Contrary to the opinion of the National Socialists that the Jews were a highly organized group, the appalling fact was that they had no organization whatsoever. The mass of the Jewish people were taken completely by surprise. They did not know at all what to do; they had no directives or slogans as to how they should act. That is the greatest lie of anti-Semitism because it gives the lie to the slogan that the Jews are conspiring to dominate the world and that they are so highly organized. In reality they had no organization of their own at all, not even an information service. If they had had some sort of organization, these people could have been saved by the millions; but instead they were taken completely by surprise. Never before has a people gone as unsuspectingly to*

its disaster. Nothing was prepared. Absolutely nothing. It was not so, as the anti-Semites say, that they were friendly to the Soviets. That is the most appalling misconception of all. The Jews in the old Poland, who were never communistic in their sympathies, were, throughout the area of the Bug eastward, more afraid of Bolshevism than of the Nazis. This was insanity. They could have been saved. There were people among them who had much to lose, business people; they didn't want to leave. In addition there was love of home and their experience with pogroms in Russia. After the first anti-Jewish actions of the Germans, they thought now the wave was over and so they walked back to their undoing.

The Jews were not oriented toward resistance. Even those who contemplated a resort to arms were given pause by the thought that for a limited success of a handful, the multitude would suffer the consequences. Outbreaks of resistance were consequently infrequent, and almost always they were local occurrences that transpired at the last moment. Measured in German casualties, Jewish armed opposition shrinks into insignificance. The most important engagement was fought in the Warsaw ghetto (sixteen dead and eighty-five wounded on the German side, including collaborators). Following the breakout from the Sobibór camp, there was a count of nine SS men killed, one missing, one wounded, and two collaborators killed. In Galicia sporadic resistance resulted in losses also to SS and Police Leader Katzmann (eight dead, twelve wounded). In addition, there were clashes between Jewish partisans and German forces in other parts of the east, and occasional acts of resistance by small groups and individuals in ghettos and killing centers. It is doubtful that the Germans and their collaborators lost more than a few hundred men, dead and wounded, in the course of the destruction process. The number of men who dropped out because of disease, nervous breakdowns, or court martial proceedings was probably greater. The Jewish resistance effort could not seriously impede or retard the progress of destructive operations. The Germans brushed that resistance aside as a minor obstacle, and in the totality of the destruction process it was of no consequence.

The second reaction was an attempt to avert the full force of German measures. The most common means of pursuing this aim were written and oral appeals. By pleading with the oppressor, the Jews sought to transfer the struggle from a physical to an intellectual and moral plane. If only the fate of the Jews could be resolved with arguments rather than with physical resources and physical combat—so Jewry reasoned—there would be nothing to fear. . . .

There was yet another way in which the Jews tried to avoid disaster. They anticipated German wishes, or divined German orders, or attempted to be useful in serving German needs. A Jewish council in Kislovodsk (Caucasus), acting with full awareness of the German threat, confiscated all Jewish valuables, including gold, silver, carpets, and clothing, and handed the property to the German Commander. The council in Šiauliai (Lithuania) had been asked three times whether any births had occurred in the ghetto and, each time it had replied in the negative. At one point, however, the council was confronted with twenty pregnancies. It decided to use persuasion and, if need be, threats on the women to submit to abortions. One woman was in her eighth month. The council decided that in this case a doctor would induce premature birth and that a nurse would kill the child. The nurse would be told to proceed in such a way that she would not know the nature of her act.

The most important mode of anticipatory action was the widespread effort, particularly in Eastern Europe, to seek salvation through labor. Indeed, the records of several ghettos reveal an upward curve of employment and output. The zeal with which the Jews applied themselves to the German war effort accentuated the differences of interests that paired industry and armament inspectorates against the SS and Police, but the Germans were resolving their conflicts to the detriment of the Jews. Generally, Jewish production did not rise fast enough or high enough to support the entire community. In the balance of payments of many an East European ghetto, the gap between income and subsistence living could not be bridged with limited outside relief or finite sales of personal belongings. Starvation was increasing, and the death rate began to rise. The clock was winding down even as German deportation experts were appearing at the ghetto gates. Ultimately, "productivization" did not save the ghettos. The Germans deported the unemployed, the sick, the old, the children. Then they made distinctions between less essential and more essential labor. In the final reckoning, all of Jewish labor was still Jewish.

The Jewish dedication to work was based on a calculation that liberation might come in time. To hold on was the essential consideration also of appeals and the many forms of Jewish "self-help," from the elaborate social services in the ghetto communities to the primitive "organization" in the killing centers. The Jews could not hold on; they could not survive by appealing.

The basic reactions to force are fundamentally different from each other. Resistance is opposition to the perpetrator. Nullification or alleviation is opposition to the administrative enactment. In the third reaction, evasion, the victim tries to remove himself from the effects of force by fleeing or hiding. The phenomenon of flight is more difficult to analyze. . . .

We know that only a few thousand Jews escaped from the ghettos of Poland and Russia; that only a few hundred Jews hid out in the large cities of Berlin, Vienna, and Warsaw; that only a handful of Jews escaped from camps. Von dem Bach mentions that in Russia there was an unguarded escape route to the Pripet Marshes, but few Jews availed themselves of the opportunity. In the main, the Jews looked upon flight with a sense of futility. The great majority of those who did not escape early did not escape at all.

There were instances when in the mind of the victim the difficulties of resistance, undoing, or evasion were just as great as the problem of automatic compliance. In such instances the futility of all alternatives became utterly clear, and the victim was paralyzed. Paralysis occurred only in moments of crisis. During ghetto-clearing operations, many Jewish families were unable to fight, unable to petition, unable to flee, and also unable to move to the concentration point to get it over with. They waited for the raiding parties in their homes, frozen and helpless. Sometimes the same paralytic reaction struck Jews who walked up to a killing site and for the first time gazed into a mass grave half-filled with the bodies of those who had preceded them.

The fifth reaction was automatic compliance. To assess the administrative significance of that cooperation, one must view the destruction process as a composite of two kinds of German measures: those that perpetrated something upon the Jews and involved only action by Germans, such as the drafting of decrees, the running of deportation trains, shooting, or gassing, and those that required the Jews to do something, for instance, the decrees or orders requiring them to register their property, obtain identification papers, report at a designated place for labor or deportation or shooting, submit lists of persons, pay fines, deliver up property, publish German instructions, dig their own graves, and so on. A large component of the entire process depended on Jewish participation—the simple acts of individuals as well as organized activity in councils. . . .

Not all Jewish cooperation was purely reflexive observance of German instructions, nor was all of it the last act of emaciated, forsaken people. There was also an institutional compliance by Jewish councils employing assistants and clerks, experts and specialists. During the concentration stage the councils conveyed German demands to the Jewish population and placed Jewish resources into German hands, thereby increasing the leverage of the perpetrator in significant ways. The German administration did not have a special budget for destruction, and in the occupied countries it was not abundantly staffed. By and large, it did not finance ghetto walls, did not keep order in ghetto streets, and did not make up deportation lists. German supervisors turned to Jewish councils for information, money, labor, or police, and the councils provided them with these means every day of the week. The importance of this Jewish role was not overlooked by German control organs. On one occasion a German official emphatically urged that "the authority of the Jewish council be upheld and strengthened under all circumstances."

Members of the Jewish councils were genuine if not always representative Jewish leaders who strove to protect the Jewish community from the most severe exactions and impositions and who tried to normalize Jewish life under the most adverse conditions. Paradoxically, these very attributes were being exploited by the Germans against the Jewish victims.

The fact that so many of the council members had roots in the Jewish community or had been identified from prewar days with its concerns gave them a dual status. They were officiating with the authority conferred upon them by the Germans but also with the authenticity they derived from Jewry. Day by day they were reliable agents in the eyes of the German perpetrators while still retaining the trust of Jews. The contradiction became sharper and sharper even as they kept on appealing, to the Germans for relief, to the Jews for acquiescence.

Similarly, when the councils endeavored to obtain concessions they made a subtle payment. Placing themselves into a situation of having to wait for German decisions, they increased not only their own subservience but also that of the entire community, which perforce was waiting as well.

The councils could not subvert the continuing process of constriction and annihilation. The ghetto as a whole was a German creation. Everything that was designed to maintain its viability was simultaneously promoting a German goal. The Germans were consequently aided not only by Jewish enforcement agencies but also by the community's factories, dispensaries, and soup kitchens. Jewish efficiency in allocating space or in distributing rations was an extension of German effectiveness, Jewish rigor in taxation or labor utilization was a reinforcement of German stringency, even Jewish incorruptibility could be a tool of German administration. In short, the Jewish councils were assisting the Germans with their good qualities as well as their bad, and the very best accomplishments of a Jewish bureaucracy were ultimately appropriated by the Germans for the all-consuming destruction process.

If we should now review the Jewish reaction pattern, we would see its two salient features as a posture of appeals alternating with compliance. What accounts for this combination? What factors gave rise to it? The Jews attempted to tame the Germans as one would attempt to tame a wild beast. They avoided "provocations" and complied instantly with decrees and orders. They hoped that somehow the German drive would spend itself. This hope was founded in a 2,000-year-old experience. In exile the Jews had always been a minority, always in danger, but they had learned that they could avert or survive destruction by placating and appeasing their enemies. Even in ancient Persia an appeal by Queen Esther was more effective than the mobilization of an army. Armed resistance in the face of overwhelming force could end only in disaster.

Thus over a period of centuries the Jews had learned that in order to survive they had to refrain from resistance. Time and again they were attacked. They endured the Crusades, the Cossack uprisings, and the czarist persecution. There were many casualties in these times of stress, but always the Jewish community emerged once again like a rock from a receding tidal wave. The Jews had never really been annihilated. After surveying the damage, the survivors had always proclaimed in affirmation of their strategy the triumphant slogan, "The Jewish people lives [*Am Israel Chai*]." This experience was so ingrained in the Jewish consciousness as to achieve the force of law. The Jewish people could not be annihilated.

Only in 1942, 1943, and 1944 did the Jewish leadership realize that, unlike the pogroms of past centuries, the modern machinelike destruction process would engulf European Jewry. But the realization came too late. A 2,000-year-old lesson could not be unlearned; the Jews could not make the switch. They were helpless.

Yehuda Bauer

Forms of Jewish Resistance

We have already seen that the basic situation of Jews during the Hitler period was one of political powerlessness. Negotiations to save them, if conducted at all, would have to have been supported by one or more of the major powers; without that there would be little chance of success. Jews could appeal to the powers, they could try to impress public opinion in the Western democracies, but in the end they were perilously dependent upon the mercy of others. In the free world, Jews could appeal or beg for help; behind the barbed wire of Hitler's hell they could cry out in the hope that muted echoes would reach the outside. Was there anything more that the trapped Jews of Europe could do? If so, did they do it? What was the reaction of the victims to the most terrible terror any regime had yet exercised?

Jewish reaction to Nazi rule is of tremendous importance to Jews and non-Jews alike. The Jew wants to know the tradition to which he is heir. How did that tradition, that whole range of historically developed values, stand up to the supreme test of Hitler's death sentence on the Jewish people? Did Jewish civilization, demoralized under the blows of the brutal enemy, surrounded in the East by largely indifferent or hostile populations, simply collapse?

These questions are equally significant for non-Jews. Nothing like the Holocaust had happened before, but there are no guarantees against its recurrence. Jews are not the only possible victims of genocide. It is urgent to know how people react in such extreme circumstances; to find out how people, who were Jews, reacted when it happened to them.

What do we mean by resistance? What, more specifically, do we mean by that term in the context of World War II? What, when we apply it to Jews? Henri Michel, perhaps the most important contemporary historian of anti-Nazi resistance, defines the term negatively: resistance was the maintenance of self-respect. He writes that "acceptance of defeat whilst still capable of fighting, was to lose one's self-respect; self-respect dictated that one should not yield to the blandishments of collaboration." But it is practically useless to analyse Jewish resistance with such categories—the Nazis certainly did not use the blandishments of collaboration on the Jews.

Professor Raul Hilberg, on the other hand, seems to regard armed resistance as the only, or nearly only, legitimate form of real resistance. In his monumental book, *The Destruction of the European Jews* (Chicago, 1961), he stated categorically and, to my mind, mistakenly, that the lack of Jewish armed resistance to the Holocaust was a consequence of the fact that Jews during their long diaspora had not had occasion to learn the art of self-defence.

Let me start off with a definition of my own and we shall then subject it to the test of known facts. I would define Jewish resistance during the Holocaust as any *group* action consciously taken in opposition to known or surmised laws, actions, or intentions directed against the Jews by the Germans and their supporters. I cannot accept Michel's definition because there were in fact very few Jews who consciously collaborated with the Germans, or who were willing to help Germany achieve victory in the hope that they would help themselves or the Jewish people. There were, of course, paid Jewish Gestapo agents and others who helped the Germans having been promised their lives—quite a number of these. But I know of only one clear and one marginal case of collaboration as defined here: I am referring to the group known as the 13 (*Dos Dreizentl*) of Avraham Gancwajch, in Warsaw, and to Moshe Mietek Merin's Judenrat in Zaglębie.

I cannot accept Hilberg's definition or description for two reasons. In the first place, I do not think he is being historically accurate. Jews did defend themselves throughout the ages by force of arms when this was feasible or when they had no other choice—in Polish towns against Chmielnicki's hordes in 1648; in Palestine against the Crusaders; in medieval York. One could cite many such instances. In pre-1939 Poland, moreover, the socialist Bund party had special defence groups that fought street battles with antisemitic hooligans. Early in this century, Jewish students in Prague, Vienna, and Berlin established fraternities that fought duels against antisemites, and so on.

The second and more important point is surely that armed resistance during the Holocaust was possible only under conditions that most Jews did not enjoy. You either have arms or you do not; for the most part, the Jews did not. Still, the nature of Jewish armed resistance was more complicated than one might expect.

In the Generalgouvernement (the central area of Poland ruled by the Nazis) there were, according to exhaustive historical accounts, about 5,000 Jewish fighters. Of these about 1,000 fought in the Warsaw ghetto rebellion, 1,000 in the Warsaw Polish uprising in 1944, and the rest as partisans in forests and in a number of ghetto and camp uprisings. There were some 1.5 million Jews in the area in 1939, so one gets a ratio of resisters of 0.33 per cent—not a very high figure—and concludes that Jewish armed resistance was marginal at best. In eastern Poland, where there were about one million Jews before the war, 15,000 armed Jews came out of the forests at liberation—a ratio of 1.5 per cent—which will still not cause one to change the verdict. But during the time Jews were organizing to fight, that is in 1942 and 1943, they accounted for one half of all the partisans in the Polish forests. The other half, about 2,500, were Poles. There were more than 20 million Poles in the General-gouvernement, so one arrives at a resistance ratio of 0.0125 per cent. The same game can be played regarding other nations in Nazi Europe. One begins to appreciate Mark Twain's adage that there are lies, damned lies, and statistics.

Let us then disregard such futile exercises and examine the real facts concerning Jewish armed resistance in Poland and, subsequently, elsewhere. It is generally accepted that large-scale operations were mainly dependent on two ingredients: the availability of weapons, and the support of a civilian population capable of aiding underground fighters. Neither of these preconditions existed for the Jews. Jews did not have access to the arms buried by the collapsing Polish army in 1939. There were very few Jewish officers in that army, fewer of them holding high ranks (e.g., one general), and the secrets of the buried arms were kept by right-wing officers who went into hiding.

The Polish government underground, the Armia Krajowa (AK), did not buy any arms from deserting German soldiers until very late in the war. No partisan detachments of any importance were established by it before 1943, and, anyway, not only were Jews not accepted in AK ranks, but a number of AK detachments were actively engaged in hunting down and murdering them. Thus when the Jews realized that they were being threatened with mass murder in 1942, there were no AK detach-ments for them to join. When these did come into existence, most Jews had already been murdered, and the detachments, in any case, would still not accept the survivors.

The Communist Gwardia Ludowa, later the Armia Ludowa (AL), was founded in the spring of 1942. It was then very weak, had very few arms, and about half its partisan forces were in fact the Jewish detachments in the forests of the Lublin area and elsewhere. By the time the AL grew stronger (in 1943) large numbers of Jews were no longer alive, but survivors did join the AL. Its weapons were bought or captured from peasants or, in most cases, parachuted by Soviet aircraft.

Jews locked in ghettos generally had no way to procure arms. The AK would not provide them; the Communists still did not have them. Controls at the gates were so strict that it was virtually impossible to bring any arms that could be obtained into the ghetto. The best known exception to the rule was in Vilna where Jews worked in German armouries. There, despite very stringent security measures, arms were smuggled into the ghetto from the city. The same general conditions applied in Czestochowa, which explains why the underground there had secured arms despite the obstacles.

Let us now turn to the three basic scenes of armed resistance in the east—the ghettos, the forests, and the camps. In the ghettos, the Jewish population was starved and decimated by disease and forced labour. They were, moreover, surrounded by a gentile population whose reaction to Jewish suffering varied between indifference, mostly hostile, and open enmity toward the victims. As applied to the ghettos Hilberg's thesis seems correct, that so long as the Jews thought they would survive the Nazi rule and the war they could see an incentive to re-enact the modes of passive conduct that in the past had tended to ensure the survival of the community, and they were accordingly reluctant to engage in armed resistance.

Resistance would have met with the disapproval, not only of the Polish population, but even of the Polish underground, the AK. Stefan Rowecki, commander in chief of the AK, issued an order (No. 71) as late as 10 November 1942 which bluntly stated that "the time of our uprising has not come." He mentioned the fact that the "occupant is exterminating the Jews," and warned his people not to be drawn into a "premature" (!) action against the Germans.

An examination of ghetto armed underground organizations shows quite clearly that, indeed, the Jews entered into the phase of practical preparations for armed action only *after* the first so-called *Aktion*, i.e., mass murder operation by the Nazis. Ghetto rebellions never took place when a hope of survival could be entertained—only when the realization finally struck that all Jews were going to be killed anyway. All other armed rebellions during World War II were predicated on the assumption that there was some chance of success. In the ghettos, no such success could be contemplated; the only result of ghetto rebellion would be the annihilation of all Jewish residents and the subsequent plundering of the empty Jewish houses by the surrounding population—that is, when the Germans did not plunder the houses themselves. This plunder, by the way, ensured the cooperation of the local population in the murder of the Jews and also prevented the escape of survivors: the local population had a strong incentive to ensure that no witnesses survived.

By the time of the first major waves of Nazi murder in 1942, only a small remnant (some 15 to 20 per cent) of the Jewish population still lived in the ghettos. This remnant then had to form an organization which might either be opposed by the Judenrat or, if the Judenrat supported a rebellion, would have to coordinate its plans with the latter in some way, and would have to secure arms in the face of supreme difficulties. In the western and central part of Poland, moreover, there were no forests where partisans could hide, so that escape was impossible. During the summer of 1942 the Warsaw underground did send Jewish groups into forests some distance from the capital, but the hostility of the Poles, the murderous actions of the AK, and German patrols quickly put an end to these attempts.

The situation was different in the eastern parts of Poland, western Byelorussia, and the eastern parts of Lithuania. Here the forests were thick, but in 1942 and early 1943 very few Soviet partisan groups were operating. In Minsk, where there was a ghetto of 84,000 Jews, the Judenrat led by Eliahu Mishkin was part of an underground movement which tried to smuggle Jews out to the forests. Some arms were obtained, luckily, for the few Soviet partisans in the area would not accept Jews without them. But only a small number of persons could be suitably equipped from among the many who were sent out. In the city itself no effective non-Jewish underground was organized for a long time and no help was obtained from the Byelorussians; on the contrary, the ghetto had to hide anti-Nazis who could not hold out in the city. We do not yet know how many Jews were smuggled out to the forests from Minsk; we are working on a list, and it will take a long time yet before the job is finished. But I would guess the number to be between 6,000 and 10,000.

About 5,000 survived the war in the forests—which shielded only those bent on escape and capable of bearing arms.

I should now like to address another problem: collective responsibility. The Nazis murdered a great many persons in retribution for the rebellious acts or suspected sedition of the few. In Dolhynov, near Vilna, for instance, two young men who were about to leave the ghetto for the forest were caught, but managed to escape and hide. The Germans told the Judenrat that if these men did not return and surrender, the ghetto would be annihilated immediately. The two men refused to return, knowing that they were endangering the lives of hundreds of others. On the morrow the inhabitants of the ghetto were shot. What would we have done in the place of the youngsters?

Yet the main internal problem for the Jews was not that of the collective responsibility imposed upon them by Nazi reprisals so much as the more fundamental problem of family responsibility. To belong to a resistance group one had to abandon one's family to death—not just leave it at some risk, as with the non-Jewish resister. The young Jewish man had to make the clear-cut decision to leave his parents, brothers, sisters, relatives, and sweethearts, and watch them being transported to death while he stood helpless, albeit wearing the mantle of the resistance fighter. Abba Kovner, the great Israeli poet and former head of the FPO (*Farainikte Partisaner Organizacje*), the resistance movement in the Vilna ghetto, has told how he gave the order to his people to assemble at an appointed hour: they were to leave the ghetto through the sewers in order to continue the battle in the forests. When the time came, and he stood at the entrance to the sewer, his old mother appeared and asked him for guidance. He had to answer her that he did not know. And, said Kovner, from that time on he did not know whether he deserved the prestige of a partisan fighting the Nazis or the stigma of a faithless son.

Let us then recount, in the face of these facts, what the armed resistance of Jews in the East amounted to. In the Généralgouvernement there were three armed rebellions, at Warsaw, Czestochowa, and Tarnów; four attempted rebellions, at Kielce, Opatów, Pilica, and Tomaszów Lubelski; and seventeen places from which armed groups left for the forests, Chmielnik, Cracow, Iwanska, Józefów, Kalwaria, Markuszew, Miedzyrzec Podlaski, Opoczno, Radom, Radzyn, Rzeszów, Sokolów Podlaski, Sosnowiec, Tomaszów Lubelski, Tarnów, Wlodawa, and Zelechów.

There were moreover rebellions in six concentration and death camps—Kruszyna, Krychów, Minsk Mazowiecki ('Kopernik'), Sobibor, and Treblinka, together with the famous Jewish rebellion in the gas chambers at Auschwitz in late 1944. These were the only rebellions that ever did take place in any Nazi camps, except for that of Soviet prisoners of war at Ebensee at the end of the war. There were armed international undergrounds, in Buchenwald and Auschwitz for instance, but they never acted. (In Buchenwald they took over the camp after the SS withdrew.)

We know also of 30 Jewish partisan detachments in the General-gouvernement, and a further list of 21 detachments where Jews formed over 30 per cent of the partisans. These latter groups were all part of the AL, because, as I have explained, the AK wouldn't accept them. Individual Jews fulfilled important functions in the AK, but they had to hide their Jewishness and appear under assumed names. A further 1,000 Jews participated in the Polish Warsaw uprising of August 1944. The total number of these fighters was about 5,000, of whom over 4,000 were killed.

The situation in Lithuania, eastern Poland, and Byelorussia is much more complicated, and I cannot render a complete picture. At least sixty ghettos had armed rebellions (such as those in Tuczyn, Lachwa, and Mir), attempted rebellions (as in Vilna), or armed underground movements which sent people to the forests (as in Kovno, Zetl, and so on). In some ghettos resistance took more than one form, as in Nieswiez, where an armed rebellion was followed by an escape to the forests. An estimate of Jewish partisans in this area is most difficult to make, though, again, we are currently working on a list. We know that there were some 15,000 Jewish partisans in the area towards the end of the war, and many more must have died before that. Some 2,000 Jewish partisans in the Tatra mountains of Slovakia must be added to any account dealing with eastern Europe.

Two further points. First, the problem of defining a "Jewish partisan" is no simple matter. Do we include in that category only Jews who fought in Jewish groups? Or may we include Jews who fought as individuals in non-Jewish groups, such as Soviet partisan units? Moreover, what about Jews who denied their Jewishness and fought as Poles, or Russians? There were, after all, a number of communists (such as Yurgis-Zimanas, the commander of the Lithuanian partisans) who emphatically defined themselves as Soviet or Polish citizens, specifically denying their Jewish backgrounds. This is also true of a few Jews in the AK, and of some of the central figures in the AL command. But these cases were generally few and far between, for Jews were required to identify as such, irrespective of their particular political ideology. Indeed, the attitude toward Jews who refused to identify as anything but Poles or Soviets was often negative in character, so that one is left to wonder whether there is any justification for excluding even communist leaders and assimilationists from an analysis of Jewish resistance. Were not their individual idiosyncrasies overwhelmed by the intruding fate of the Jewish community to which they perceived themselves to belong only by birth?

Second, we cannot ignore antisemitism even in the Soviet partisan detachments, especially those in which Ukrainian partisans had great influence. A large number of such cases have been documented, as have the fatal consequences for a number of Jewish fighters. This hatred was directed not only against Jewish units—which the Soviet partisan command disbanded—but also against individual Jews in general units. Where there were large numbers of Jews in some unit[s], a struggle against antisemitism was likely; but in smaller detachments with relatively few Jews, defiance was much more difficult.

Let us also deal, albeit summarily, with western Europe. Here the story is less dramatic, first, because the total number of Jews in France, Belgium, and Holland was less than one-sixth of the Jewish population of prewar Poland and, second, because armed resistance movements of a serious kind did not become active until well into 1943. By that time there were not many Jews left to fight. In the west, of course, the same hostility towards the Jews did not exist as in the east, but there were notable exceptions. In France, for instance, the French police effected most of the anti-Jewish measures.

There were Jewish armed groups in the OJC (*Organisation juive de combat*) and the MOI (a communist group) in France, two groups in Belgium, and two communist groups of Jews in Germany. By and large, however, Jews participated as individuals in non-Jewish organizations because no ghettos were set up in western Europe. Should we consider them as Jewish resisters, or as Belgian and French resisters?

I think the answer depends on the way these Jews acted. Was their behaviour more likely the result of specifically Jewish concerns or not? The answer is important because it would help us to measure the depths of Jewish identification among western Jews. It would also help to reveal the extent of integration among Jews and non-Jews. We are still in the middle of these researches, but I would venture the general conclusion that these Jews were usually fighting for "Jewish" reasons.

How many Jews fought? In France there were thousands rather than hundreds and there were probably close to a thousand in Belgium. Moreover, the Jews were usually the first to act—for example, the first urban guerrillas fighting against the Nazis in Paris during the spring of 1942 were members of a Jewish unit of the pro-communist MOI. The Guttfreund group in Belgium took up arms as early as September 1941, killing a Jewish Gestapo agent, robbing a factory producing for the Germans, and later burning a card index of Jews at the Judenrat offices in Brussels. Finally, thousands of Jews fought in northern Italy in 1943–4, and thousands more fought with Tito's army in Jugoslavia.

Let me summarize: Jewish armed resistance was considerably more widespread than has been subsequently assumed. In eastern Europe, a high proportion of those who survived the first wave of murders participated in armed activities. Jewish rebellions in Warsaw and elsewhere were the first urban struggles against the Germans anywhere in Europe, and the Jewish rebellions in the camps were the only ones of their kind. Michel's conclusion that Jewish armed resistance was proportionately higher than that of other people, with few exceptions, is probably true. This is remarkable in light of the greater difficulties Jews encountered and of their lack of modern military tradition. Surely the radical nature of the Nazi threat to Jewish communities is pertinent here. But persecution does not explain resistance, especially when the former is attended by elaborate forms of control and coercion. At any rate, it seems easier to explore the ways Jews in Palestine and then Israel met their military challenges in the light of the above analysis than to believe, with Hilberg, that there was little struggle in Europe and then a sudden inexplicable upsurge of martial skills that enabled the Jews of Israel to fight for their existence.

I have dealt with armed resistance first because unarmed active resistance is best explained against the background of armed struggle. Let us now therefore consider the problem of resistance without weapons.

Unarmed struggle took place largely before the murder actions began. In such situations, when Jews were unaware of any Nazi intentions to murder them, Jewish behaviour was at least in some measure comparable to the behaviour of non-Jewish populations under Nazi rule. Such comparisons are important as measuring-rods for the behaviour of populations subject to the rule of terror. On the other hand, differences between Jewish and non-Jewish situations will stand out clearly as time moves on, and we cannot avoid approaching both comparable and noncomparable situations with the knowledge that the Jews were later subjected to Holocaust, whereas other nationalities were not.

What, then, did these other subject nationalities in Europe do? Did they obey German law, even those laws forbidding education in Poland and Russia? Yes, they did. Did they resist the shipment of slave labour to Germany? No, they did not.

By and large the Jews, on the other hand, proved recalcitrant. History had taught them the art of evasion, and they showed themselves to be highly skilled practitioners. In the first place, contrary to conventional wisdom, most German and Austrian Jews, some 410,000 out of 700,000, did manage to leave the Third Reich. (Some of these, tragically, were caught again as the German armies advanced.)

In Poland, after the war had begun, German rules were so brutal that, had the Jews passively acquiesced—even though every infringement of Nazi law was punishable by death—they would have died out in no time at all. Let me give a few examples. Official German food allocations distributed by the Warsaw Judenrat came to 336 calories daily in 1941. It is unlikely that the Warsaw Jews could have survived longer than a few months on such rations. But smuggling, illicit production on a considerable scale, and great inventiveness produced an average of 1,125 calories daily. Unfortunately, a large population of unemployed Jewish refugees who had been expelled by the Germans from their homes in the provinces into Warsaw slowly died because their food supplies fell below that average. Many others managed to survive on these rations nevertheless. I would consider this stubbornness, this determination to survive in defiance of Nazi authority, to be an act of resistance under the definition I offered at the beginning of this essay. In Kovno, similar smuggling was organized by groups that were controlled by the Judenrat and the Jewish police—the police here were the very heart of the armed resistance organization. It was thus an organized act, under public supervision of sorts, and the aim was very definitely to subvert German laws.

Consider the question of education. Until the late autumn of 1941, education of any kind was forbidden in Jewish Warsaw. But it took place clandestinely, in so-called *complets* where small groups of pupils would meet either in the soup kitchen or in the home of the teacher. We find evidence for this, in fact, in a large number of places in Poland. There were also clandestine high schools in Warsaw which received some funds from illegal JDC (American Jewish Joint Distribution Committee) sources. The activities of such schools are documented. Their older students passed official matriculation exams under conditions which were, to put it mildly, unusual.

Also, according to Ringelblum, there were in Warsaw alone some 600 illegal *minyanim*, groups of Jews praying together throughout the period when all public religious observance was forbidden. Political parties were of course proscribed, as were newspapers or printing of any description. But we now know of more than fifty titles of underground newspapers in Warsaw alone, and most of the political parties continued their clandestine existence.

There is, one is inclined to think, something typically Jewish or— more profoundly—*traditionally* Jewish, in the importance that cultural institutions achieved in such a time. There was, for instance, YIVO, the Yiddish Scientific Institute in Vilna, where Kovner and the poet Abraham Sutzkever were active in preserving materials, establishing a library system, and encouraging literary output in a conscious effort to maintain morale. It was no accident that the YIVO group was a recruiting ground for FPO, the resistance movement in Vilna. The most famous of these cultural institutions was the Oneg Shabbat group in Warsaw. Founded and headed by Dr Emmanuel Ringelblum, the historian and public figure, it methodically assembled reports and diaries and initiated research in order to preserve documentary evidence of the life of the Jews in the Warsaw ghetto. Among its studies were the famous medical investigations into the effects of hunger on the human body under the direction of Dr Milejkowski, which were published after the war in 1946 in Poland.

Oneg Shabbat did not know of the speech in Poznan in 1943 in which Himmler boasted that nothing would ever become known of the Final Solution. But the basic idea of Oneg Shabbat was that knowledge and documentation were forms of defiance of Nazi intent. In this the group succeeded. Despite the fact that only two-thirds of the Oneg Shabbat archives were found after the war, they are our main source of knowledge regarding Jewish life in Poland during the Holocaust.

Of all active unarmed resistance, most intriguing, I believe, were the activities of the "Joint" (the Joint Distribution Committee), the American-based social welfare agency. The Joint was actually just an office which, in Poland, distributed American funds to local Jewish agencies such as TOZ, a health agency, Centos, a society for the care of orphans, Cekabe, a network of free-loan banks, and Toporol, a society for agricultural vocational training. On the face of it, nothing more tame could be devised. But when war came the Joint offices in Warsaw happened to be headed by a group of men with leftist political convictions, among whom Dr Ringelblum is perhaps the best known today. They very early on realized that it would be their job to fight against Nazi-imposed starvation, humiliation, and gratuitous cruelty.

Until the end of 1941, certain sums still arrived from America through a complicated transfer system; although no dollars were actually sent to Nazi-controlled territory, German marks left behind by Jewish emigrants were sent to Warsaw from Berlin and Vienna. This stopped in December 1941, and the Joint became an illegal institution. But even before this, additional funds were being obtained by illegal means. In 1941, the Joint fed 260,000 Jews in the Generalgouvernement, including some 42,000 children. Centos and TOZ, which had themselves been declared illegal, still maintained their operations under the cover of an official welfare organization. Kitchens and children's homes became the centres of illegal political activities, including party meetings, clandestine presses, and illegal schooling. All this was consciously activated by the Joint.

Parallel to this was Joint support for so-called house committees, of which over 1,000 existed in the ghetto of Warsaw. Residences in eastern Europe were usually built around a courtyard, so that in each instance the "house" included four apartment buildings, about 200 or 300 families. These groups of people organized spontaneously, outside any Judenrat groupings, to institute mutual aid, schooling for children, cultural activities, and so on. (Unfortunately these groups included Warsaw Jews only; the refugees, crammed in their shelters, were dependent on the woefully insufficient feeding of Joint soup kitchens which were meant to provide only supplementary nourishment.) The house committees sprang up from below, but the Joint quickly realized their potential and Ringelblum set up a roof organization called Zetos. This body tried to create a central fund through which more affluent house committees would help the poorer ones, and encouraged activity essentially opposed to the Judenrat. The steering committee of Zetos became the political base for the resistance movement. The Joint was also behind the preparations for the Warsaw ghetto rebellion, and financed the uprising to a large degree. Giterman, the Joint's chief director, also helped to finance resistance movements in Bialystok and elsewhere by sending them money explicitly for this purpose.

The Joint's was a mass activity which embraced hundreds of thousands of Jews. Still, it obviously could not stand up to the forces of mass murder. Giterman was killed on 19 January 1943 in Warsaw, and Ringelblum was murdered in March 1944 when the Germans finally found his hiding place. They shared the fate of the millions whom they had tried to feed, encourage, and lead. But we cannot be concerned here with their ultimate fate; we are concerned rather with their behaviour prior to their murder. We want to know how widespread was unarmed active opposition to Nazi rule among the Jews; and we discover that owing to the work of men like Ringelblum and Giterman the range of such resistance was considerable. . . .

I have dealt with eastern Europe; but it would be wrong to disregard the 500,000 Jews of western Europe, or indeed the Jews of Germany, Austria, and Czechoslovakia. The Joint, Zetos, and various cultural institutions could be classified as self-governing institutions interposed between the Judenrat and the Jewish masses. Similar groups and organizations existed in western and central Europe as well.

Take for example the OSE. This was a general Jewish health organization which had a rather modest branch in prewar France. During the Holocaust, OSE became the main child-care organization in the Jewish sector. In France, of course, the gentile population had a much more positive attitude toward Jews than that which prevailed in Poland. German rule was comparatively less oppressive; Nazi police and SS were less numerous, while German Army interests, which did not always parallel those of the SS, were more important. In this climate OSE and some other groups managed to hide about 7,000 Jewish children, some in Catholic and Protestant institutions but mostly among peasants, and we do not know of one single case where children were betrayed by those undertaking to hide them. OSE, the Jewish Scout movement, and some other groups managed to smuggle some 2,000 people into Switzerland and a smaller number into Spain. In Belgium, the Comité de défense des juifs, headed by a Jewish member of the Belgian underground, hid thousands of Jews as well.

Let us now turn, very briefly, to what is probably the most important, but also the most diffuse, form of resistance: that of popular, mass reaction. Here we are on uncertain ground, because this form barely comes within our own definition. Can one speak of an unorganized, spontaneous action of Jews as expressing true resistance to Nazi enactments?

Well, up to a point it seems one can. Let us cite a few examples. In Holland, which had a Judenrat of the Lodz type, the Jewish proletariat of Amsterdam reacted forcefully in February 1941 to provocations by Dutch Nazis. A Dutch Nazi died in the scuffle, and Jewish and non-Jewish inhabitants of the Jewish quarter chased the Nazis out. This was the immediate cause for the famous strike of Dutch workers in support of the Jews. It failed, largely because of the intervention of the Jewish leaders who were told by the Nazis that, if the strike did not stop, large numbers of Jews would be taken to concentration camps and killed. The Dutch desisted, and the same Jewish leaders became the nucleus of the Dutch Judenrat. But what should concern us here is the popular Jewish reaction, especially since the story of the anti-Nazi acts in Amsterdam had further installments.

Nazi documents record that after the first deportations from Holland in July 1942, the Jews ceased to appear at the appointed time and place when called. From the summer of 1942 on the Nazi and the Dutch police had to ferret the Jews out. This was popular unarmed resistance. We know, of course, that this tactic did not succeed; but the measure of resistance is not its success but its incidence. Was the moral backbone of the Dutch-Jewish population broken? It appears, rather, that their desire to live as free human beings was maintained.

Turning to the east, let us inspect another example. The so-called Slovak National Uprising broke out in the hills of Slovakia in August 1944. The Jews from some Slovak towns and camps fled there in large numbers. Those who could, fought; those who could not tried to hide. As the German troops advanced into the Slovak mountains suppressing the uprising, the Jews refused to obey Nazi orders and certainly avoided concentrating in places where they could be picked up by the Germans. This was typical unarmed resistance.

Some of the popular mood of this kind of resistance is captured in diaries which have survived: the young boy who believes that his father is being taken away and will not come back but writes that he believes his own place is with his father; the young man who jumps out the window of the deportation train only when he is already separated from his mother, whom he had not dreamed of leaving to face her fate alone; Chaim A. Kaplan, in Warsaw, who is sorry he will not see the Nazis' downfall which he is sure will come. Such acts and sentiments are beyond our definition of resistance, to be sure; but they form the background to those acts of unarmed circumspect defiance which I have tried to relate.

Let us not exaggerate. There were communities that collapsed. One cannot even find the dignity of quiet defiance in some Jewish responses. In Copenhagen, for example, the whole Jewish community was saved without its lifting a finger to help itself; in Vienna, but for a few hundred people in hiding, nothing but abject submission was the rule. Unfortunately it is impossible to explore here the reasons behind this apparent lethargy.

The range of Jewish resistance was broad, as I have shown: armed, unarmed but organized, semi-organized or semi-spontaneous. Let me conclude with a form of resistance which I have saved to the last because it is the most poignant. My example is from Auschwitz, and I am relating it on the authority of the late Yossel Rosensaft, head of the Bergen-Belsen Survivors' Association. Yossel was also a "graduate" of Auschwitz, and he testified that in December 1944 he and a group of inmates calculated when Hanukka would occur. They went out of their block and found a piece of wood lying in the snow. With their spoons, they carved out eight holes and put pieces of carton in them. Then they lit these and sang the Hanukka song, "Ma Oz Tsur Yeshuati."

None of the people who did this were religious. But on the threshold of death, and in the hell of Auschwitz, they demonstrated. They asserted several principles: that contrary to Nazi lore, they were human; that Jewish tradition, history, and values had a meaning for them in the face of Auschwitz; and that they wanted to assert their humanity in a Jewish way. We find a large number of such instances in concentration and death camps. Of course, there were uncounted instances of dehumanization in a stark fight for survival: bread was stolen from starving inmates by their comrades, violent struggles broke out over soup, over blankets, over work details—struggles which only too often ended with death. In the conditions of the camps, incidents of this kind are not surprising or unusual, but examples such as the one mentioned are. The few Jews who did survive could not have done so without the companionship and cooperation of friends. And friendship under such conditions is itself a remarkable achievement.

I think the story of Kosów is also appropriate. It exemplifies most vividly the refusal of so many Jewish victims to yield their humanity in the face of impending murder. Kosów is a small town in eastern Galicia, and it had a Judenrat which was not very different from others. On Passover 1942, the Gestapo announced it would come into the ghetto.

The Judenrat believed that this was the signal for the liquidation of the ghetto, and told all the Jews to hide or flee. Of the twenty-four Judenrat members, four decided to meet the Germans and offer themselves as sacrificial victims—to deflect the wrath of the enemy. With the ghetto empty and silent, the four men sat and waited for their executioners. While they were waiting one of them faltered. The others told him to go and hide. The three men of Kosów prepared to meet the Nazis on Passover of 1942. Was their act less than firing a gun?

Dan Diner

Why the Jewish Councils Cooperated

If we are to base our definition of the Judenrat on the impossible position in which representatives of the Jewish community in German-occupied Poland found themselves, it would seem appropriate to include other Central and Western European institutions of "Jewish self government" within the definition's purview. For all these institutions found themselves in the same situation of compulsory, incriminatory cooperation with Nazi rule—this even when working toward the still-tenable goal of emigration. In fact, Jewish institutions already in existence before the inception of the mass-murder process became deeply entangled in its unfolding: Vienna's Central Bureau for Jewish Emigration, for instance, established in August 1938 on Jewish initiative for the sake of Jewish welfare, saw the emigration lists it had painstakingly assembled transformed, covertly, into death-camp deportation lists. This slippage from steps meant to preserve life to those facilitating its destruction, scarcely perceptible to the Jewish authorities at the start, marks the tragic situation of the Jewish councils throughout occupied Europe.

As with the Viennese example, the Jewish councils in German-occupied Poland did not at first confront exterminatory measures that, once put in motion, they would try their best to delay, and that would finally lead to forced self-selection. Starting in the autumn and winter of 1939, the newly established councils concerned themselves above all with Jewish social welfare in the widest sense—a thoroughly sensible response, it seemed, to the Nazi concentration of Jews into demarcated, soon to be sealed-off areas, and to the ensuing loss of sources of normal sustenance (that is, work and property). The subsequent outbreak of disease and death throughout the ghettos—the result of malnourishment and disastrous hygienic conditions—pointed, already, toward the Nazi campaign of mass extermination; the Jewish councils' decision to ask the German authorities for work, the Germans being their only remaining source, should be thus reconsidered in light of the terrible circumstances of seclusion. It was an effort to cope with the plight facing those for whom they bore responsibility: to slow down, at least, the steady worsening of their circumstances. But above all—as with the Warsaw Judenrat's proviso in its offer of labor at the end of 1939—it was an effort to end the brutally executed and unpredictable seizure of Jews by the Germans for the sake of forced labor, to render the German actions relatively predictable instead. Such an approach by the councils must be distinguished from their later strategy of "rescue through labor" in the face of extermination. Nevertheless, it is evident that the earlier procedure facilitated the later one to a considerable degree. Blinded by anti-Semitic contempt, the Nazis decided to systematically use Jewish artisanal and industrial workers only in the middle of 1940. What followed had its precedent in the shift of organized Jewish emigration in prewar Central Europe to eventual enforced cooperation with the Nazis: in Eastern Europe, the representatives of the Jewish ghettos ended up, by way of their approach to labor, in a relation of dependency that would turn against themselves.

The horrible form taken by this turn involved a constant exchange of the lives of those capable of work for the death of those no longer "useful": an exchange that, in its steady decimation of the Jewish population, reveals the drastic hopelessness of the Jewish situation. Different responses to the situation were possible, ranging from clear-cut gestures of resistance to undertaking something like a Faustian contest with the Nazis: an effort to salvage the life of some through a controlled and limited fulfillment of the Nazi need for Jewish deaths, always in the hope of the behemoth's imminent military defeat. In face of the variety of individual responses, generalization is difficult. To a considerable degree responses depended on the identity and personality of the different Jewish elders, as well as on specificities of location, as was the case with the Lodz ghetto: lying in the Warthegau region annexed to the Reich, it owed its relatively long survival to conflicts of responsibility between Gauleiter Greiser and the SS. At the same time, the degree of community organization was an important factor. In Poland, the Jewish communities to a large extent remained intact corporate entities; as prolonged instances of Nazi will, they were thus subject to instrumentalization via the Jewish councils. The circumstances were very different in conquered areas of the Soviet Union, where the authorities had dissolved Jewish communal structures more than twenty years before. The Jews here were also put in ghettos, unless they were not immediately seized by the mobile firing squads of the various *Einsatzgruppen*. But in the absence of such traditional structures, the selections imposed by the Germans on the Jewish councils in these areas were far more arbitrary in nature.

Once burdened with knowledge of the deportations' end goal, and confronted with the demand for self-selection, the Jewish councils displayed a range of defiant responses, described in detail by the Israeli historian Aharon Weiss in his work on the councils in eastern Galicia and eastern Upper Silesia. Such responses ranged from open refusal to deliver up Jews entrusted to the councils—a decision promptly punished by the Nazis with death for those responsible—to suicides like that of Adam Czerniaków[1]—he declared the delivery of children to their murder a border he could not cross—to the decision to join the resistance (as far as this was possible). There were also the many elders who gave up their functions: the stand taken by the Jewish elder Weiler from Vladzimierz, who abstained from a selection with the words "I am not God and will not pass judgment over who shall live and who shall die" was far from an exception. In view of the historical evidence, the generally over-sharp line of demarcation—particularly in the collective Jewish memory—between Judenrat and resistance is scarcely tenable. Tensions and conflicts between the two only emerged, in any event,

---

[1]Chairman of the Warsaw Jewish Council, 1939–1942.—Ed.

with the onset of deportations in the autumn of 1941. Cooperation between the councils and the armed resistance, including supplying the latter with money, material, and information, was commonplace.

In the Bialystok ghetto, for instance, contacts and arrangements between the Judenrat led by Efraim Barasz and the resistance were routine. Until the rebellion broke out in August 1943, the resistance saw itself compelled—just like the Jewish council—to wait for a moment judged propitious, that is, to play for time, meanwhile complying with the draconian principle of sacrificing *some* for the sake of those who remained. It is important to recognize that because of the partisan activity in the Soviet territory captured by the Germans in 1941, effective armed Jewish resistance such as that in Bialystok—forming a sharp contrast to the hopeless Warsaw revolt, with its essential motive of salvaging historical honor—was far more likely, across the board, than in the Generalgouvernement established in Poland in 1939. To be sure, not all partisan groups were ready to accept Jews into their ranks. Hostility to the Germans did not necessarily translate into friendly feelings for the Jews, and many who managed to escape from the enforced community of camp or ghetto found their death at the hands of anti-Semitic partisans.

In a comparison of the strategy of reluctant compliance for which the Judenrat generally stands with that of armed Jewish struggle, the latter emerges more ambivalently than is commonly assumed. For a start, the imperatives of military organization undermined the family structure—hence survival in the ghetto. Whoever managed to reach the partisans left behind old people, children, the weak, in circumstances making death very likely. For most people, the factor of family loyalty thus constituted an unassailable barrier—or in the words of a contemporary witness: "the feelings for one's own family were far stronger than fear of death." Those most firmly opposing flight from the ghetto to the armed bands were Jewish elders who had now set upon the clearly demarcated and terrible path they termed "rescue through labor," its reverse side being constant self-selection for destruction. In Vilna, for instance, Jakob Gens spoke up against youths who joined the partisans by pointing to the ghetto's loss of productive workers and subsequent reduced chances for survival. The feeling was that such resisters threatened the ghetto with reprisals; and as suggested, although standing up for themselves, by the very nature of armed resistance, they were abandoning those left behind to their fates. In contrast to those joining the partisans, the Judenrat—such was the feeling—had a sense of responsibility for the collective. The only tenable strategy involved becoming indispensable to the Germans—through labor.

In Poland, as mentioned above, the Jews offered labor to the Germans in the early phase of the ghetto's formation (the fall and winter of 1939), the offer having, however a different character than "rescue through labor." The latter procedure came into force only with the onset of the Nazis' organized, industrial mass-murder project. And let us note the low likelihood—then or later, during the mass murder—that the Jewish elders who had decided to embark on "rescue through labor" (in particular Chaim Rumkowski in Lodz, Jakob Gens in Vilna, Mosche Merin in Upper Silesia, and Efraim Barasz in Bialystok), along with the Jewish councils they headed, would recognize something more than a local or regional phenomenon behind the murder operations. The various German agencies offered ample grounds for such a limited perspective. Not all of them, for example, adhered to the instructions handed down from the Reich's ministry for the conquered eastern territories to the Reich commissioner for what was termed Ostland—comprising Lithuania, Latvia, Estonia, and the greater part of White Russia—upon the latter's query (November 15, 1941): to exterminate all the Jews in the region, regardless of economic priorities. This drive toward total extinction ran into countervailing policies on a local level in December. We thus find Karl Jäger, the head of Einsatzkommando 3, responsible for murder operations in the Baltic region, complaining of being forced by the Wehrmacht and civil authorities to refrain from exterminating 15 percent of Lithuania's Jews, since they were needed for labor.

By means of their strategy of "rescue through labor," the Jewish councils did their best to exploit this tension within the Nazi administration between a will toward absolute extinction and the war-determined interest in exploiting Jewish labor capacity. In however limited a sense, the councils would thus maintain an ability to act, for the sake of gaining time: time worth struggling for in the expectation of a turn in the war's course and—most concretely—the arrival of the Soviet army. The possibility of gaining time was hence made available, paradoxically, by the requirements of the German war effort. Crucially, underlying the councils' apparently compliant adaptation to such requirements—that is, underlying their postponement of total extinction by means of labor and the self-selection of those really or supposedly incapable of labor—were presumptions of purpose-oriented rationality on the part of the enemy: of an overriding interest by the Nazis in their own self-preservation. In this respect, it is striking that such presumptions were frequently confirmed by information gleaned on emerging conflicts between the different Nazi agencies, and on their real divergent interests. In his monumental study of the Jewish councils, Isaiah Trunk indicates that Barasz, Gens, and Rumkowski, in particular, were informed about policy conflicts by "good" Germans in the administration—a favor, by the way, that often had a steep price.

In essence, there was a built-in conflict between organs of the SS and police, who took their orders from Berlin, and agencies of the Wehrmacht and civil administration, located on site. In his diary of February 14 and 18, 1943, Mordechai Tenenbaum-Tamaroff—one of the central figures in the Bialystok resistance—notes the surfacing of heated differences in the office of Königsberg's armament inspector regarding the planned murder operation in Bialystok, causing its postponement: "Our fate is supposed to be settled on Friday, when General Constantin Canaris [commander of East Prussia's security police and security services] will be back. . . . Klein [administrative director for the head of the civil administration], our generous protector, has become lord of the ghetto. We see in this a victory for moderate circles in the Gestapo. He maintains that 'there'll always be time to exterminate the Bialystok Jews, even at the end—meantime they can slave for us.'"

Indeed, behind the admonishment of Jakob Gens in Vilna, "Jewish woman, remember: labor spares blood!" lay the assumption that the Germans desired above all else to win the war. In that case, its material requirements, hence the war economy, would necessarily have absolute priority. It is this basic assumption of the Jewish councils, grounded in sound common sense, that Raul Hilberg sees as the first step into the trap laid by the Nazis: for Hilberg, such work amounted to cognitive bait, meant to keep the Jews calm so the extermination could proceed as planned. And yet no remotely plausible alternative seemed available to the exchange of labor for time and life. For this reason, it became a principle around which all generally accepted norms and values centered. It is manifest in Efraim Barasz's criticism, in October 1942, of the Bialystok ghetto doctors for maintaining an ethos befitting normal circumstances, trying to free patients with TB from work: "the doctors don't understand that today people are not dying from tuberculosis, but because they do not work."

The strategy of "rescue through labor" hardly ever succeeded. But in many places Jews would certainly not have survived without such a strategy—for instance in Czestochowa, where several thousand Jewish workers, including many from Lodz, made it through the war in the Hasag factory complex. The same can be said for Radom, where 4,700 out of 30,000 Jews survived—one of the highest Jewish survival rates in Poland, as Yehuda Bauer stresses—and for the ghettos of Bialystok and Siauliai. But the most controversial and remarkable example certainly remains the Lodz ghetto under Rumkowski's leadership. In many respects it was a special case, but it defines, better than any other historical example, what the Judenrat truly signified as a situation. Granted the self-aggrandizing, autocratic nature of the elder Rumkowski's policies: under the stewardship of his Jewish council, the Lodz ghetto could survive until July 1944, not only the largest, but also the last of the Polish Jewish ghettos. Had the Soviets not stopped their advance that very month, had they begun it again earlier than January 1945, the 70,000 Jews remaining in the ghetto would certainly have remained alive thanks to "rescue through labor" and the accompanying self-selections. And yet if the ghetto had chosen a strategy of direct armed struggle, the Nazis would doubtless have followed through with their deportations in a speedier and more horrible manner. Adam Czerniaków has in fact been criticized for not mobilizing the Warsaw ghetto's work potential at an early point, as Rumkowski was doing in Lodz. To be sure, it would be sheer speculation to suggest that a total deportation could then have been avoided. Nevertheless, many survivors of the Lodz ghetto asserted that they owed their lives precisely to the absence of an armed revolt in the city.

Whereas work was the sole available key to winning time against the German collective death sentence, the self-selections posed an irresolvable ethical dilemma for the Jewish councils. In the context of the ghettos, the phrase *mi lechaim ve mi lamavet* (who receives life and who receives death [referring to God's will]) denoted forced decisions that rarely confront human beings. It is clear that the Jewish elders were well aware of the burden's weight. Even though in the end they lacked free will and were condemned to act as instruments of an executioner, they constantly tried to move, by means of this compulsory function, in a reverse direction. The resulting movement in two directions, along with attacks on the part of the resistance and corrosive self-doubt drove these very ordinary men to a discourse with themselves

and others reflecting well their Faustian dilemma. Jakob Gens laid out
its shattering terms before an assembly of Jewish writers and journalists
who — so, at least, he believed — scorned him as a traitor. Defending
himself with the assertion that he gave life priority over death, he indicated that if ordered by the Nazis to hand over a thousand Jews, he
would do it: otherwise, the Germans would themselves arrive in the
ghetto and seize not a thousand, but many thousands. In sacrificing a
hundred, he saved a thousand; in sacrificing a thousand, he saved ten
thousand: "Should I, Jakob Gens, survive, I will leave the ghetto soiled,
blood on my hands. But I will go before a Jewish court and declare: I
have done everything to save more and more of the ghetto's Jews and
bring them to freedom."

Rudolf Kastner described the situation of the Jewish councils
with penetration: if they fulfilled their functions, they contributed
substantially to the smooth unfolding of the liquidation process.
If they refused, they called down sanctions on the community and
abandoned the possibility of slowing down the mass-murder process.
Almost all of Europe's Jewish councils found themselves caught between
these extremes and incapable of escaping their deadly logic. And yet
the logic's nature was not so clear-cut at the beginning: relatively
"insignificant" demands for precious objects, for money, and apartments.
But finally, what was desired was life; and the Judenrat decided who
went sooner, who later:

> In sacrificing to Moloch, horrible criteria came to prevail, such as age,
> accomplishment, general reputation. Personal considerations pressed to
> the forefront: degree of kinship, predilection, even interests. The way
> taken by the *Judenrat* was tortuous, ending inevitably in an abyss. Every-
> where, the Jews were confronted with the same problem: shall I, who-
> ever I am, become a traitor in order to help or even save others; or shall
> I leave the community to its fate — pass on my wavering responsibility to
> others? But is flight from responsibility not something akin to treachery?

This reproach was in fact leveled at the Warsaw ghetto's Jewish elder
Czerniaków, who ended his life, hence his responsibilities. According to
a report of the underground, he had offered far more support to the
penned-up Jews of Warsaw than his successor, Marek Lichtenbaum.

In respect to the dilemma of the Jewish councils, the words of Leon
Rosenblatt are still terrible to read, despite all we now know concerning
the monstrous nature of the Final Solution. Rosenblatt was head of

the Jewish police in the Lodz ghetto, responsible, on pain of death by shooting, for delivering contingents of Jews to the Nazis—hence presiding over life and death against his will. The words were transmitted by a sympathetic German interlocutor:

> That [=Rosenblatt's own execution] is hence the simplest solution for me. But what happens then? The SS has already explained: then they select. That means the unbroken, the pregnant, the rabbis, the scholars, the professors, the poets, pass first to the ovens. But if I remain, I can take the volunteers. Often they press themselves on me. And sometimes I have the number I need to hand over. Sometimes there are fewer than I need. Then I can take those who are dying, reported to me by the Jewish doctors, and if they don't suffice, then the deathly ill. But if they don't suffice—what then? Then I can take the criminals: but God know—who here is not a criminal? Using our ghetto money, which we have to print according to German exchange rates, a loaf of bread costs three hundred to five hundred marks. I know mothers who inform against their neighbors to procure a piece of bread so their children won't die of hunger. Who can judge that? And yet: if I *still* haven't reached the full number? Often I manage without the criminals. But not always. And sometimes even they aren't sufficient. Then I can take those in advanced old age. But what sort of criterion is that? Herr Hielscher, I'm a poor Jew from Lemberg; I learned my trade and could also lead my battery [Rosenblatt commanded an Austrian motorized mortar battery in World War I]. But I haven't learned what I'm supposed to do here. I've asked the communal elders, the rabbis, the scholars. They've all said to me: you're doing the right thing, stay and select in the way you've arranged it. I've asked the different communal groups into which we've divided the ghetto, I've asked the old people, the condemned, the deathly ill: they've all assented. And still, Herr Hielscher, I'm no longer content with my life. I implore you on the God in whom you believe: if you know of a better way than what I've chosen, please let me know and I'll bless you day and night. And if you know of none, please tell me: shall I remain, or have myself shot?

The German interlocutor gave this answer: "With God's grace, proceed as you have—there is no other path, and when you choose it, you are justified before God. I myself would do nothing different."

Burdened with a demand such as self-selection, enforced at pain of death and challenging the capacities of human reason, religious Jews or those relying on tradition as the basis of their actions often sought out rabbis and scholars for advice. But the extremity of the Jewish councils' situation exceeded even their capacities, sharpened as they were through deep intellectual labor. As found in the codex of Maimonides *(Halikhot yessodai hatora,* chap. 5, par. 5), the basic rule had always been that in situations where Jews are forced by Gentiles to deliver one of their own to death on account of being Jewish, the others thus remaining alive, all should rather opt for self-sacrifice. But what force could such a principle have when the delivery unto death represented, not an exception, but a *universal rule* — one that the Nazis were determined to apply to every living Jew? In Vilna, Jakob Gens was confronted with Maimonides's rule. But the rabbi of Kovno, Abraham Duber Cahan Schapiro, ruled that when the entire community is threatened with physical destruction, and when a chance exists to save a portion of it, the community leaders had a paramount duty to save as many Jews as possible from death, by whatever means at their disposal. . . .

In light of the absolute nature of the Nazis' exterminatory planning, and the accompanying overthrow of all inherited values, the problem of continued Jewish existence could no longer be couched in traditionally conceivable terms: that is, the death of one Jew for the sake of another's survival. The ghetto's leaders understood perfectly the extreme situation they were facing: either total annihilation — or the survival of a fragment.

However varied the councils' circumstances may have been, together they shared the experience of a borderline situation that renders null and void all anticipations of human behavior ordinarily deemed to be universally valid. It is only through the situation of the Jewish councils that we can start to fathom the extent of the civilizational break represented by Nazism: the denial of all commonly valid — hence action-steering — forms of thought based on usefulness and utilitarianism — indeed on the enemy's interest in self-preservation. The heads of the councils made themselves clear: "I act economically, ergo I exist." The Nazis negated this basic assumption when — all ethics and morals long since cast aside — they broke through any abiding scruples, placing the extermination of the Jews above all economic interests and the war's demands.

The Jewish councils' assumption was a response to what they considered a form of *traditional evil:* limitless material egoism and unfettered satisfaction of one's drives. A desire to economically exploit those one has subjugated would fall entirely within the purview of such traditional evil, conforming to basic criteria of rationality. Such criteria had—perhaps they still have today—cultural roots so deep that even when the Nazis had long since revealed as false the belief that work would preserve life, the Jewish councils clung to it, lacking an alternative: in the hope that the enemy's self-interest would help grant work and productivity their civilizational due and place a check on a process of extermination perceived, according to these criteria, as lacking all sense. Such long-trusted, universally internalized forms of thought and action would, however, turn out a trap, since the Nazis transformed them into their opposite. An anticipatory rationality of action, commonly presumed to be life-preserving, ended up as a practical paralysis—extending to cooperation with one's own destruction. The councils did not fall into the trap through attributing to the Nazis a morality that the latter did not acknowledge but because their only choice was a final appeal to socially based behavior: that of furthering one's own, *amoral* interests.

Since the Nazis did not even maintain this final barrier, from a German perspective their behavior may well be considered irrational. From the perspective of the victims, it would appear—far more radically—as *counter-rational*. The situation into which the Jewish councils were forced, without an exit, draws us into those vortexes for which Nazism historically stands: into a profound crisis for a moral consciousness based, necessarily, on the fundamental cognitive building blocks of our ordinary world—that is, on behavior perceived as rational, sustaining, even in the most extreme of cases, faith in the enemy's ultimate interest in self-preservation.

Polish civilians outside the wall of the Warsaw Ghetto, ca. 1940. Photograph by Ewald Gnilka / Bildarchiv Preussischer Kulturbesitz / Art Resource, New York

PART

V Bystander
Reactions

Variety of Opinion

The over-all balance between the acts of crime and acts of help, as described in the available sources, is disproportionately negative. . . . To a significant extent, this negative balance is to be accounted for by the hostility towards the Jews on the part of large segments of the Polish underground, and even more importantly, by the involvement of some armed units of that underground in murders of the Jews.
Yisrael Gutman and Shmuel Krakowski

[N]o reasonable student of World War II can deny that Hitler's policy toward the Poles was also genocidal. . . . If the magnitude of the Polish tragedy were objectively presented, unrealistic and unhistorical judgments about the possibilities and opportunities available to the Poles to render greater aid than they did to the Jews would not be made.
Richard C. Lukas

Collaboration [in occupied western Europe] was never complete, and . . . various officials showed signs of reluctance by the beginning of 1943. . . . But only . . . the defeat of the Reich brought the trains to a halt.
Michael R. Marrus and Robert O. Paxton

177

With the rescuers' view of themselves as independent came the idea that they were propelled by moral values not dependent on the support and approval of others but rather on their own self-approval.

Nechama Tec

At least to some degree, the Jews' chances of survival depended on getting help from their Gentile neighbors. Especially (but not exclusively) in the killing fields of Eastern Europe it was those neighbors who could give or withhold hiding places, food, and even false papers and arms that sometimes made the difference between life and death. Elsewhere the Germans were not in direct control or else lacked sufficient numbers to manage everything, which gave local officials room to take decisive action. That could work for or against the Jews. For example, in Bulgaria, a German ally, local authorities simply refused to give up Jews who were Bulgarian citizens. The same thing happened in Hungary until the Germans took control in March 1944, after which Hungarian officials helped send most of the country's Jews to Auschwitz. In Hungary and other countries that collaborated with Nazi Germany, the rounding up and deportation of Jews to extermination and labor camps could not have been done efficiently without the assistance of local authorities.

This section looks at the attitudes and actions of bystanders, defined here as ordinary people who were neither perpetrators nor victims and who might collaborate with the former, help the latter, or do nothing. These included both neighbors and, in places not completely run by the Germans, local officials. We pay special attention to Poland, where most of the Jewish victims lived and where German rule was harshest.

Yisrael Gutman and Shmuel Krakowski examine the sensitive subject of Polish-Jewish relations during the Holocaust. They acknowledge that the Poles, too, were persecuted by the Nazis and that aiding Jews only increased the dangers to which Poles were exposed. But the authors assert that the two groups were anything but equal victims. The Jews, unlike their Gentile neighbors, were herded into ghettos and camps, and marked for mass extermination. If one group were to aid the other, it would have to be the Poles. Some did, but, the authors conclude, most did not. In the excerpts included, Gutman and Krakowski note the persistence of popular antisemitism in Poland and the failure of the Polish underground to support the

Warsaw ghetto uprising. At the same time they pay tribute to the minority of Poles that helped Jews. In their balancing of acts of kindness against those of hatred, however, the Poles come out wanting. Richard C. Lukas assesses the evidence differently in his book on Poland under Nazi rule. A one-sided emphasis on the Jewish tragedy, he argues, leads to underestimation of the plight of the Poles and to exaggeration of their opportunities to help anyone, even themselves. Antisemitism in Poland, brought on to some degree by the Jews themselves, was qualitatively different from that of the Nazis and did not determine Polish reactions to persecution of the Jews. What did was implacable German pressure on the Poles, which was so intense that documented acts of Polish aid to Jews should be regarded as little short of miraculous. In view of the "forgotten holocaust" against Polish Gentiles, Lukas concludes, the Germans alone must be held responsible for the fate of the Jews.

Michael R. Marrus and Robert O. Paxton are the authors of an important book showing that French acceptance of the anti-Jewish policies of the collaborationist Vichy regime was widespread until late in 1942. Here they survey the situation in all of Nazi-occupied Western Europe. Cautioning against overgeneralizing about the various countries during the Holocaust, they identify the local conditions that determined widely different Jewish losses: from 75 percent in the Netherlands to about 5 percent in Denmark. The authors note that the collaboration of government officials in several of the countries was immensely helpful to the Nazis in the early months of Jewish deportation. On the other hand, increasing resistance to deportation policies slowed the Final Solution to varying degrees in different places. In the end, however, Marrus and Paxton conclude that military defeat alone stopped the German trains from leaving for the East.

Nechama Tec examines the relatively small numbers of Polish bystanders who, voluntarily and with no expectation of external reward, risked their lives to rescue Jews during the Holocaust. These individuals, named "righteous Gentiles" after the war, hid Jews, helped them escape to safety, secured false papers so they could try to "pass" as Gentiles, and assisted in other ways. As a child Tec had survived using false papers and living with Polish families. Later she interviewed hundreds of other Polish survivors and their rescuers in order to discover the latter's motivations. Although some scholars have argued that righteous Gentiles had been socialized to be altruistic, Tec suggests that other influences were also at work.

Essays such as these make it difficult to indulge in facile generalizations about Gentiles during the Holocaust. No one who has read them will easily fall prey to demeaning (or heroic) portrayals of whole nationalities. Rather, our attention should be fixed on issues of will and opportunity. Was bystander behavior determined more by pre-existing values, such as antisemitism or altruism, or by conditions over which bystanders had little or no control, such as the nature of German rule and the availability of hiding places? The answer is not likely to be the same for every part of Nazi-controlled Europe.

Yisrael Gutman and Shmuel Krakowski

The Poles Helped Persecute the Jews

Immediately prior to the Warsaw Ghetto uprising in April 1943, the ZOB[1] had no more than five hundred fighting men at its disposal. Shortage of arms was the principal factor that prevented the organization from increasing its manpower. In fact, there were not enough arms to go around. Even if we accept the figures cited by Pelczynski as accurate, we find that the ghetto fighters had available to them only one pistol for every seven men, one rifle for every fifty men, and one machine gun for more than every hundred and fifty men. The AK's claim about the inadequacy of its own store of arms can be considered from a variety of points of view. The types and quantities of weapons and ammunition available to the AK were certainly inadequate for it to confront the German army in the field. But the claim that the few scores of pistols handed over to

---

Text by Yisrael Gutman and Shmuel Krakowski from *Unequal Victims*, Holocaust Library, 1986. Reprinted by permission of Holocaust Publications.

[1]"Jewish Fighting Organization" in Poland. —Ed.

the ZOB represented a significant sacrifice on the part of the Polish military underground cannot be taken seriously, when we consider that the AK possessed tens of thousands of rifles and approximately one thousand light machine guns. In any event, the unsuitability of the arms made available to the ZOB was patently revealed to the Jews by the time of the ghetto rebellion. So we find Mordecai Anielewicz, commander of the Warsaw Ghetto uprising, writing to Yitzhak Zuckerman, the ZOB representative to the Poles, on April 23, 1943: " . . . and you should know that pistols are absolutely useless, we've almost not used them at all. What we need is: grenades, rifles, machine guns and explosives."

The heads of the Jewish Fighting Organization seem to have been aware of the AK leadership's reservations, even hostility, as expressed by their failure to arm the ZOB adequately during the initial phases of its formations and preparations for battle. In March 1943, as units of the ZOB clashed with the Germans in the ghetto, a letter attributed to Anielewicz was sent to the Jewish underground representative to the Poles. The letter included the following statement: "Please inform the authorities in our name that if massive assistance does not arrive at once, it will look as if the representation and the authorities are indifferent to the fate of the Jews of Warsaw. The allocation of weapons without ammunition seems like a bitter joke and a confirmation of the suspicion that the poison of anti-Semitism still permeates the ruling circles of Poland in full force, despite the tragic and brutal experience of the past three years. We are not about to prove to anyone our readiness and ability to fight. Since January 18 the Jewish community in Warsaw has existed in a state of war with the invader and his noxious henchmen. Whoever denies or doubts this is merely an anti-Semite out of spite."

Most of the weapons the ZOB fought with had to be purchased. The Polish Communists were more magnanimous than the AK in helping the Jewish Fighting Organization; but their resources were so limited as to render their assistance nearly worthless. . . .

Polish attitudes and conduct with respect to the Jewish resistance in Warsaw [were] not as unrelievedly unsympathetic as a dry account of the events makes them appear. There were some Poles who did everything that was in their power to advance the interests of Jewish armed resistance. But the official representatives of the "military authorities in the underground"—the commanders and upper political echelons— tended on the whole to regard the catastrophe of the Jews and Jewish appeals for assistance as something remote from their immediate concerns.

Only when long-range Polish interests became involved, or when the appeals of men and women of conscience became too insistent to be ignored, were they moved to act, though only hesitantly, on a small scope and without conviction. . . .

Thousands of Polish Gentiles became involved in varying degrees in efforts to save Jews. We know that many Poles—hundreds apparently—lost their lives because of their actions on behalf of Jews.

But the gallant record of those Poles who came to the assistance of Jews does not alter the fact that there also existed a malignant element in Polish society that was responsible for creating a hostile climate of opinion among broad sections of the Polish public concerning the rescue of Jews. The *shmaltsovniks* [blackmailers] were a relatively large group in Poland. They operated on an organized basis and made a profession of the betrayal of Jews.

We have already observed that the German invader found it difficult to distinguish between Jews and Gentiles in Poland, and that the fear experienced by Jews hiding out on the "Aryan side" was of being informed on by Poles. Similarly, those who worked to save Jews did so without benefit of support from the great mass of Poles; indeed, they were forced to keep their activities secret from neighbors, friends, and sometimes, even from relatives. The act of concealing or helping a Jew was distinctly unpopular; it was a cause of distress among Poles and often actively opposed by them. One Polish heroine who had taken an abandoned Jewish child under her protection tells of having constantly to change her residence because she was actually driven away by her neighbors, who knew the child was not hers and was Jewish. Many of the accounts of Jewish survivors are replete with expressions of gratitude and esteem for the devotion and courage of the Poles who had helped save them. Most of these stories also tell of the ordeals experienced by Polish benefactors and cite countless instances of Jews being blackmailed or turned over to the German police by Poles. . . .

Just who were these [extortionists and informers] and how large were their numbers? Polish writers are probably correct in claiming that most of them came from the very lowest orders of society and either lived on the fringes of the criminal underworld or were outright criminals themselves. Affiliated with the extortionist gangs, too, were persons with no criminal past but whom wartime conditions freed from all social inhibiting restraints, allowing them to indulge their overriding desire for easy money and their innate taste for debauchery. But such people were at least no more than a by-product of the war, a wild strain produced by circumstances and the times. However, we learn from the reports of many witnesses that these circles were also joined by rabid anti-Semites for whom such contemptible activities provided an opportunity to give vent to their ideological inclinations.

We have no figures concerning the number of street toughs and informers who made up the gangs that victimized Jews. But there were enough of them around to make life a constant nightmare for Jews living as Poles or hiding in the Aryan part of Warsaw. Polish writers argue, not unreasonably, that the entire Polish nation cannot be blamed for crimes committed against the Jews by a mere handful of thugs. They are also correct in observing that under the occupation it was easier for evildoers than for decent men to flourish. Those who blackmailed and informed against Jews acted under the protection of the Polish and Nazi police, or were at least tolerated by them.

Apart from the hunters, their prey and the occupation authorities, there existed another element whose position must be explained—the Polish public, and especially that segment which made up the powerful underground organization, the so-called "underground state," which operated among the populace. The mere reluctance of most Poles to become involved or forcefully to oppose the extortionists cannot in itself account for the extraordinary confidence and freedom with which these gangs were able to carry on their activities. Naturally they were enthusiastically assisted by the anti-Semitic climate of opinion among the Polish people. In that atmosphere the extortionists were given no reason to feel that their activities in any way struck at Polish patriotism. Moreover, as we have observed elsewhere, the underground took no affirmative action against these gangs, as they routinely did in the case of other types of collaborationists. We can assume that the majority in the underground had no sympathy for extortionists and informers who were battening on Jews; but they were also reluctant to declare war against them, since they were aware that such a move would be unpopular among wide sections of the populace. We need only examine the history of the fruitless efforts by members of *Zegota*[2] to convince underground authorities to take effective reprisals against the extortionists for us to

[2] "Council for Aid to Jews," an organization made up of Polish Gentiles.—Ed.

gain a fair idea of the nature of the inhibitions and hesitancies that prevented the Polish underground from taking action.

Ringelblum told in his *Polish-Jewish Relations* about the operations of the *shmaltsovniks* (blackmailers) in Warsaw, and his personal experiences with them:

> *Extortion by* shmaltsovniks *begins the moment a Jew crosses through the gates of the ghetto, or rather while he is still inside the ghetto gates, which are watched by the swarms of* shmaltsovniks . . . *The* shmaltsovniks *walk around in the streets stopping anyone who even looks semitic in appearance. They frequent public squares, especially the square near the central [Railway] station, cafes and restaurants, and the hotels . . . The* shmaltsovniks *operate in organized bands. Bribing one of them does not mean that a second cohort will not appear a moment later, then a third and so on, a whole chain of* shmaltsovniks *who pass the victim on until he has lost his last penny. The* shmaltsovniks *collaborate with police agents, the uniformed police and in general with anyone who is looking for Jews. They are a veritable plague of locusts, descending in large numbers upon the Jews on the Aryan side and stripping them of their money and valuables and often clothing as well. . . .*

It was quite common for the rural populace to take part in raids against the fugitives from liquidated ghettos who hid in the forests. Two major forms of such participation are to be distinguished: (1) Peasant participation in raids organized by the Nazi police and gendarmerie shortly after the deportations from local ghettos, in order to capture the fugitives; (2) the forest campaigns which the larger groups of local peasants organized and carried out on their own initiative, without notifying the Nazi police.

In the raids of the former type, the participating peasants would most typically serve the Nazis in the capacity of guides, pinpointing the possible sites in forest areas with which they were much more thoroughly familiar than the Germans. But it often happened that peasants themselves would murder the encountered Jews with pickaxes or scythes. The usual incentive for their participation in anti-Jewish raids was either German instigation or the hope for an opportunity to loot the belongings, clothes or valuables of captured fugitives. In some instances, the Germans would reward the peasant participants with allotments of sugar or salt. But the most common form of reward was simply the division of spoils.

The self-initiated raids of the second type would usually take place no sooner than several months after the largest mass deportations from local ghettos. Accordingly, such raids tended to be aimed at those Jewish fugitives who had already had some opportunity to establish themselves in well-concealed hiding places in the forests. Unaided by anyone, and long after the meager food rations which they could possibly bring with them to the forest had become exhausted, such fugitives for purposes of self-preservation had no alternative save to supply themselves with food stolen from peasant households or fields. Hence the common purpose of the collective raids of the villagers was to kill the Jews in hiding in forests in order to stave off the recurrent farm thefts.

The peasant participation in the anti-Jewish raids carried out by the Nazis is noted in the diary of S. Zieminski, a Polish teacher from Lukow:

> *On November 5 [1942] I stopped in the village of Siedliska. I entered the cooperative store. The peasants were buying scythes. I heard the saleswoman say: "They will be helpful during the raid today." I asked about the nature of the raid. "Against the Jews." I then asked: "And how much do you get for a captured Jew?" No one answered. I therefore went on: "For Christ they paid thirty pieces of silver; so make sure that you are paid no less." Again no one replied. But the answer came a little later. While crossing the forest, I heard salvos of machine gun fire. The raid was in progress. . . .*

Our file contains the records of participation of the local villagers in raids on the Jews in 172 localities. Here is a sample of pertinent personal accounts by the surviving witnesses of the recorded events:

Ignacy Goldstein recounts that peasants from the village of Iwanisko and its environs (Opatow county, Kielce district) were being rewarded for their participation in raids with a bag of sugar and one liter of refined alcohol. Later, however, it was the clothes of captured Jews which became the sole reward.

Gitla Kopylinska recounts that in Zambrow region there were a number of Jews hiding in the forest. The peasants were aware of this, but at the beginning showed no interest. Once the Germans announced the reward of one kilogram of sugar for every captured Jew, the local populace began raiding them. . . .

No less common were the murders of Jews usually perpetrated by rural groups of relatives or neighbors, whose general purpose was plunder.

Here is a sample of cases of this category of anti-Jewish crimes from our records:

A group of villagers [from] Lukowa, Bilgoraj county, tracked down, robbed and shot Abraham Gutherc who was sheltered by the murderer's neighbor, a farmer by the name of Machen.

In the village of Markowa near Lancut, Przeworsk county, a group of Poles led by Antoni Cyran murdered twenty-eight Jews and looted their belongings.

In the village of Dolmatowszczyzna near Wilno, Janek Achron, twenty-five, organized five persons into a gang which on November 18, 1942, murdered a hiding physician, Dr. Jehuda Barzak, his wife, mother, and son. . . .

Single-handed murders were no less common than the collective ones. The murderers who acted alone were in most cases peasants whom the Jewish fugitives approached for shelter. As in collective murders, the usual motive of the crime was the intent to ransack whatever money, valuables or clothes could be found on the bodies of the victims. Here is a sample of pertinent cases from our files:

A farmer by the name of Sienkiewicz from a village in the vicinity of Nowe Miasto murdered the parents of Nachman Segal. Sienkiewicz had previously provided the couple with shelter: he murdered them only when they ran out of money and could no longer pay him.

A farmer by the name of Kumin from the village of Smoryn near Frampol murdered and looted the body of a Jew by the name of Yitzhak, a cousin of Aharon Kislowicz.

Kapczuk from Komorowka Podlaska murdered the three-year-old daughter of Estera Rybak, after extorting a considerable amount of money which he had received for sheltering the child. . . .

Tracking down the Jews in hiding, capturing them, and handing them over to German police or gendarmerie, to Polish "blue" police or to Ukrainian auxiliary police was another very common form of anti-Jewish crime. As a rule, the police would in such cases shoot the Jews delivered into their hands in this way on the spot. Here is a sample of cases from our records:

A Jewish woman by the name of Maurer, with two children, completely exhausted after several months of hiding in the woods, returned to their former home in the village of Kurzyna near Ulanow, Nisko county. Maurer's Polish neighbors apprehended and escorted them to the German police post in Ulanow. All three were shot at once.

In the town of Frampol a certain Poteranski captured two children of Yakov Mordechaj Lichtfeld, and handed them over to the Germans.

On the landed estate of Starzyna near Horodlo, Hrubieszow county, Stanislaw Siemicki captured Mirela Pipler and handed her over to the Germans.

The inhabitants of the village of Potok, Bilgoraj county, captured Moshe Knoch with two children, and delivered all three to the Germans. . . .

Organized murders of Jews committed by various underground formations began toward the end of 1942, and occurred quite frequently thereafter. They did not stop entirely at the moment of termination of the Nazi occupation, but continued for some time afterwards. The largest number of such murders were perpetrated by the units of National Armed Forces; but some groups of the Home Army also shared this guilt. Obviously most of these units may have belonged to that part of the National Armed Forces which joined the Home Army.

Beginning with December 1942, some Polish underground formations undertook searches for the Jews in hiding. Whenever they discovered any, they would kill them on the spot. Beginning with the summer of 1943, crimes of this type reached a high frequency, due to the simple fact that the first major armed Polish underground formations appeared in the forests at that time. From then on, we can distinguish between the searches for the Jews hiding in village households, and the murders of accidentally encountered Jews, whatever their place of hiding. Many murders were also committed in the first days after the withdrawal of the German troops, when the Jewish survivors, finally feeling secure, were resurfacing from their places of hiding.

Our file contains cases of murder of Jewish fugitives by Polish underground groups from 120 different localities or forest ranges. Here is a sample:

Eight Jews found a hiding place in a forest bunker near the village of Kamieniec near Polaniec, Sandomierz county. After several weeks their bunker was surrounded by a local unit said to belong to the Home Army. The Jews were ordered to get out of the bunker, and then fired upon. Seven, including Moshe Gladstein, were killed; one, David Sznyper, managed to escape.

In the village of Zarki near Janow, Zawiercie county, a detachment of Jedrusie units encountered a Jewish woman disguised as a peasant girl. After checking her identity, they notified the police station in Zarki.

Several days later the "Jedrusie" members learned that the girl avoided capture and was still alive. Thereupon they murdered her on their own, afterwards notifying the gendarmerie in Zarki. . . .

Of all crimes committed against the Jews, the most common and probably the most lethal was informing. It assumed epidemic proportions, and it affected as well the Poles who provided the Jews with any help. Informing incurred no risks. Ordinarily, it was sufficient to mail an unsigned postcard to the Gestapo. But many informers acted openly, appearing in person at a station of either the German or Polish auxiliary ("blue") police. This was especially true, when an informer hoped to receive a reward for a Jewish fugitive whom he delivered into German hands. Our records seldom make it possible to identify informers. In most cases they merely ascertain the fact and the identity of the informer's victims. Here is an extensive sampling of cases of informing:

Josef Zajwel and Icek Szer were hiding in an abandoned house in Lezajsk. They were aided by Tosiek Krasinski and Zygmunt Przybylski who supplied them with food. But some of the neighbors notified the Germans. The Germans came, surrounded the house, captured Zajwel and Szer, and shot them.

Ten Jews were hiding on farmland adjacent to the forest near Okrzeja, Lukow county. In the summer of 1943, they were betrayed by the farm owner's son. The Germans murdered them all.

In the town of Gorlice, Cracow district, a Polish woman turned the Meinhardt family over to the Germans: the parents and two children. All four were shot by a single SS man, whose name was Otto. As a result of her guilty feeling the informer went insane. . . .

Plunder of Jewish property and blackmail of Jews for the purpose of extortioning ransom were also quite common occurrences. Here is a sample of typical cases of such crimes:

Wicek Mincenty from the village of Zwada near Czestochowa sheltered Gabriel Horowicz's family for some time, then looted their belongings and evicted them from his premises.

The director of the KKO savings bank in Staszow, Rzadkobulski, accepted deposits of money and valuables from the Jews, then later refused to return anything.

In the vicinity of Jadow, Warsaw district, Chana Dzbanowicz left her hiding place in the forest in order to visit the Kalinski family whom she had known from before the war. Mrs. Kalinski fed her and hid her in her garret. But when Mr. Kalinski returned home, he began to scream and told Dzbanowicz to go away. On her way back to her hiding place in the forest she was assaulted by a group of Poles who stripped her of her shoes and sweater. In the same locality, Meir Dzbanowicz was stripped of his jacket during a similar assault. . . .

Obviously, we have succeeded in authenticating merely a fraction—perhaps only an infinitesimal fraction—of the crimes actually perpetrated against Jewish fugitives in hiding. Crimes such as murders, or informing, or turning Jews over to the Germans, were as a rule committed underhandedly. Seldom did the perpetrators want to have any witnesses. In very rare cases would a Jew who accidentally witnessed a crime committed against other Jews be allowed to survive. Also, the Polish witnesses of crimes against the Jews were later seldom willing to testify, if their statements would have implicated their friends or neighbors. As for the perpetrators themselves, they obviously wouldn't reveal their own crimes either. To compound matters, those directly implicated in crimes can usually rely on the solidarity of the people from within the social environment in which they operate. Actually, it is the latter who are often most helpful in covering up the traces.

The instances of participation by Poles in raids on Jewish fugitives have been authenticated as having occurred in 172 localities and the murders committed by Polish underground formations (National Armed Forces and a part of the Home Army) as having occurred in 120 localities. Beyond any doubt these figures are incomplete: there certainly were other localities in which collective crimes against the Jews were committed, either by groups of local populace or by underground units. Unfortunately, there is absolutely no way of estimating the total number of victims of these crimes in even the roughest general terms. Some Jewish survivors recount that tens and even hundreds of Jews could be either murdered on the spot or turned over to the Germans as a result of one raid in a single locality. The accounts of Icchak Golabek and Icchak Szumowicz which describe the raids in the forests surrounding the town of Zambrow are cases in point. Golabek tells of hundreds of Jews captured by Poles and turned over to the Germans during one single raid of no more than one day's duration. Szumowicz estimates that about 150 Jews who escaped the deportation from Zambrow on January 15, 1943, were subsequently tracked down by the local villagers in a nearby forest and turned over to the Germans.

Similar facts are reported by the survivors from dozens of other localities. The existing evidence does not make it possible, however, to corroborate reliably the raid casualty estimates as given by the authors of the accounts. When totaled, these estimates would reach many thousands who fell prey to raids which Poles either organized or were involved in. Of this, the figure of over 3,000 Jews whom Poles (under varying circumstances) either murdered or turned over to the Germans can be considered reliably authenticated on the basis of the existing sources. . . .

We have studied the files concerning 2,652 Jews rescued by help obtained from the Poles. Likewise, we have identified 965 Polish individuals and families outside Warsaw who under many differing circumstances and for specific considerations sheltered Jews or helped them otherwise to hide. We have found that of the 965, eighty persons paid for their deeds with their lives. But again, the existing documentation has undoubtedly failed to record all the acts of help which the Jews received from the Poles. As in the case of the crimes, the actual number of Jews saved by the Poles and the actual number of their Polish benefactors (and of those from among them who made the ultimate sacrifice of their lives) are certainly much higher than the figures presented here. Yet there are reliable reasons to presume that the figures concerning the help to the Jews deviated from the actual realities comparatively less often than the figures concerning the crimes against the Jews. Simply put, the dead can no longer produce information, and the perpetrators of crimes prefer to remain silent. In contrast, the survivors can speak, and they have indeed recounted numerous instances of help received from the Poles. Furthermore, the Poles who did extend such help have had no reasons to be ashamed of their deeds either.

This is applicable in cases where the Poles paid for their help to the Jews with their lives. As noted, the actual number of such cases is certainly higher than the figure cited above. It is well documented that the Polish population was subjected by the Germans to brutal terror. Within the framework of that terror, particularly atrocious reprisals were meted out even for minor breaches of all conceivable rulings of the Nazi authorities. Adding the general balance sheet of anti-Polish repression, however, the reprisals for helping the Jews rank rather low in frequency. . . .

In summation, documents reviewed in our study point to a negative balance, in which instances of help to the Jews are outnumbered by instances of crimes against the Jews. To a considerable extent, this negative balance can be accounted for by the policies of the German conquest, which consciously aimed at spreading corruption within as large a fraction of the Polish society as possible. Severe penalties for even the slightest relief offered to a Jew, coupled with rewards for committing crimes against them, did exert a negative influence upon the Polish society's attitudes. Recurrently posted announcements warning of the death penalty for helping the Jews were visible at all the locations in the Government General beginning with September 1942. They were followed by the promulgation of executive ordinances in each of its counties. At the same time, the occupation authorities did everything possible to encourage the Poles to participate in raids on the Jewish fugitives in hiding, and to loot their property. . . .

The overall balance between the acts of crime and acts of help, as described in the available sources, is disproportionately negative. The acts of crime outnumbered the acts of help. To a significant extent, this negative balance is to be accounted for by the hostility towards the Jews on the part of large segments of the Polish underground, and, even more importantly, by the involvement of some armed units of that underground in murders of the Jews. Still, several thousand Jews from our files succeeded in finding shelter and in being rescued because of Polish help. Yet for a Jewish fugitive, the chance of obtaining any help was slight under the conditions of the raging Nazi terror, of the death penalty for anyone extending such help, and of widespread hostility towards the Jews in both the Polish society and its underground organizations. Of the many who sought help, only a few found it. The overwhelming majority of Jews who approached Poles for help fell prey either to Nazi police or gendarmerie, or to rabid anti-Semites in the Polish society and in the Polish underground.

Thousands who sought help but failed to obtain it, unable to cope any longer with all the constant dangers lurking about, were returning to the ghettos already reduced after the mass deportations, or to the newly formed secondary ghettos. It meant that they would be killed eventually, during a later deportation to death camps.

Still more tragic were the instances when Jewish fugitives would come to a German police station to seek death by turning themselves in, after they lost all hope of survival in the forest or elsewhere, or of ever obtaining shelter or any other help from the Poles.

Richard C. Lukas

The Poles Were Fellow Victims

One of the most controversial aspects of the history of wartime Poland is the subject of Polish-Jewish relations. Much that has been written on this subject is badly flawed: Jewish historians tend to make sweeping claims that label most Poles anti-Semites who did little to help the Jews against the Nazis; Polish writers tend to minimize Polish anti-Semitism and sometimes exaggerate the amount of assistance Poles gave the Jews. Anti-Semitism was less a factor in Polish-Jewish wartime relations than the reality of the Nazi terror, which was so overwhelming that the opportunities to assist the Jews were more limited in Poland than anywhere else in occupied Europe. When one considers the fact that most of the three million Jews who lived in Poland were unassimilated, the task of saving Jews was even more formidable.

Anti-Semitism did exist in wartime Poland, but it did not meet with a sympathetic response among the majority of people, who were preoccupied with their own survival during the German occupation. Further, a minority of Poles from various social classes, including former anti-Semites, risked their lives to aid Jews. . . .

It is impossible to generalize about Polish attitudes toward the Jews during the German occupation, because there was no uniformity. Despite German persecution of the Polish people, a small minority of Poles openly approved of German policies toward the Jews, and some actively aided the Nazis in their grim mission. But even the anti-Semitic National Democrats in Poland altered some of their traditional views toward the Jews as the bizarre logic of German racial policy became apparent in the extermination campaign; and some National Democrats personally aided Jews. Other Poles showed no outward pleasure at the removal of Jews from Polish offices, professions, and businesses but were not opposed to the economic expropriation involved. These people had anti-Semitic views which were economic, not racial in character; if we can hazard any generalization at all, it is that to the extent there was anti-Semitism among some Poles, it reflected this *economic* anti-Semitic attitude. Still others quietly felt compassion for the Jewish people; they might be described, in Philip Friedman's words as "passive humanitarians." These people either feared becoming actively involved in aiding Jews because of the risk of the death penalty the Germans automatically imposed on Poles who helped Jews—Poland was the only occupied country where this was done—or were so pauperized by the war they simply could not afford to aid anyone without jeopardizing the survival of their own families. Then there was a very active group of Poles who were openly sympathetic toward the Jews, and many of these risked their lives to help Jews.

Several factors had a negative impact on Polish attitudes toward Jews. Until at least the latter part of 1941, when the Germans began to exterminate the Jews, Poles felt that their situation was far worse than the Jews who lived in ghettos. They saw a big difference in Nazi aims toward the two groups; the Germans wanted to destroy the Poles politically, while they seemed to want only to cripple the Jews economically. After all, Jews as a group were not deported or executed as the Poles were in these early years. On the other hand, Jews in the ghettos tended to see only advantages that the Poles enjoyed on the Aryan side of the walls, while they alone experienced difficulties. Before the resistance efforts of the Jews developed later in the occupation, Poles perceived the Jews as being craven in their behavior toward the Germans, accepting without defiance the restrictions and persecutions imposed on them, collaborating with the Germans, and even denouncing Poles who hid them when the Germans discovered their hiding places outside the ghettos. By contrast, the Poles saw themselves as bearing their ordeal with pride and defiance. Poles were outraged by the active business the Jews conducted with the Germans, accused them of buying food which kept prices high, and saw many Jews preferring to have the Germans confiscate their goods rather than share them with Poles. On the other hand, those Poles who had economically benefitted from the move of the Jews to the ghettos by acquiring homes and businesses opposed the Polish government-in-exile's decree declaring all such actions under German occupation as illegal. "We will not return the shops and factories" was an all-too-familiar Polish cry.

"We shall never forget their [Jewish] behavior toward the Bolsheviks" was a familiar statement heard in Poland during the war, underscoring the negative behavior of many Jews during the Soviet occupation of eastern Poland beginning in September 1939. Some of these Jews were influenced by Soviet propaganda which promised them improvement in their social and economic status. Others were known to be sympathizers with the Soviet system and welcomed the opportunity that presented itself. No doubt there were also Jews who, unhappy with some of the discrimination that had existed in prewar Poland, believed their condition would improve under new landlords, a hope that soon proved illusory.

Jews in cities and towns displayed Red flags to welcome Soviet troops, helped to disarm Polish soldiers, and filled administrative positions in Soviet-occupied Poland. . . .

Jewish collaboration with the Soviets, more than any other factor, was responsible for increasing anti-Semitism in Poland during the war. In these circumstances, many Poles did not understand and were even critical of the pro-Jewish declarations during these early years of the Polish government-in-exile. When the Germans invaded the Soviet Union in June 1941, the Polish government was understandably alarmed that once the Germans reoccupied eastern Poland, the Poles there would try to revenge themselves on the Jews.

In the midst of the mutual antagonisms shared by Poles and Jews during the German occupation, the Germans launched a massive program of anti-Semitic propaganda through the media. They installed loudspeakers on street corners and in public places and published newspapers in Polish and German which continually spewed forth anti-Semitic themes. . . .

[T]he most overt examples of anti-Semitism came during the early months of the occupation when the Germans encouraged gangs of young Polish hoodlums to attack Jews. Sometimes these criminals even attacked Poles. The pogroms against the Jews were not spontaneous; they usually were well-orchestrated by the Germans, who even conducted a course for members of anti-Semitic groups. The youngsters, often intoxicated, were paid by the Germans for their activity. One Jewish eyewitness described the scene in Warsaw during the Passover pogrom in 1940:

> *The Passover pogrom continued about eight days. It began suddenly and stopped as suddenly. The pogrom was carried out by a crowd of youth, about 1,000 of them, who arrived suddenly in the Warsaw streets. Such*

types have never been seen in the Warsaw streets. Clearly these were young ruffians specially brought from the suburbs. From the characteristic scenes of the pogrom I mention here a few: On the second day of Passover, at the corner of Wspólna and Marszalkowska Streets about 30 to 40 broke into and looted Jewish hat shops. German soldiers stood in the streets and filmed the scenes. . . .

The Polish youngsters acted alone, but there have been instances when such bands attacked the Jews with the assistance of German military. The attitude of the Polish intellectuals toward the Jews was clearly a friendly one, and against the pogrom. It is a known fact that at the corner of Nowogrodzka Street and Marszalkowska a Catholic priest attacked the youngsters participating in the pogrom, beat them and disappeared. These youngsters received two zlotys daily from the Germans.

Of course, anti-Semitic groups rejoiced at these attacks, but moderate and socialist opinion in Poland condemned them. The Socialists joined the government press in decrying the criminal behavior of some Poles. The Socialists went so far as to label any Pole a collaborator who was involved in the least anti-Semitic incident and thus an "enemy who should be exterminated with complete ruthlessness." Even Emmanuel Ringelblum, who was often a severe critic of Polish behavior toward the Jews, admitted that the pogroms in Warsaw were limited to a small number of Poles: "No one will accuse the Polish nation of committing these constant pogroms and excesses against the Jewish population. The significant majority of the nation, its enlightened working-class, and the working intelligentsia, undoubtedly condemned these excesses, seeing in them a German instrument for weakening the unity of the Polish community and a lever to bring about collaboration with the Germans." . . .

It is not known how many Poles actually aided Jews during the German occupation. For that reason, glib generalizations on the subject must be suspect. What is known, however, is that after the Germans ordered the Jews to live in ghettos, and especially after they unleashed the so-called "Final Solution," Poles increasingly responded to the Jewish plight not only as an expression of pity for the Jews but also as an action of resistance against the hated Germans. Poles of all classes gave a variety of assistance to the persecuted Jews; food, shelter, and false documents were some of the more common types of aid. Considering the utter barbarity of German rule in Poland and the continuing persecution of the Poles by the Germans, it is remarkable that so many Poles were involved in the aid efforts. The wonder is not how few but how many Jews were saved in Poland during the German occupation.

Jewish leaders at the time made clear their praise for those Poles who fought against anti-Semitism and extended aid to the Jews. The Jewish Bund, which had especially close ties with the Polish socialists, denied charges of widespread anti-Semitism among the Poles by commenting on how a majority of Polish people—workers and peasants—resisted anti-Semitic propaganda. Szmul Zygielbojm, a respected Jewish member of the Polish National Council in London, gave a speech to the council, during which he read a statement from one of his kinsmen in Poland: "The Polish people showed the Jews much sympathy and gave considerable help in all these events." In the introduction to a pamphlet entitled *Stop Them Now: German Mass-Murders of Jews in Poland*, published in 1942, Zygielbojm wrote: "I must mention here that the Polish population gives all possible help and sympathy to the Jews. . . . The walls of the ghetto have not really separated the Jewish population from the Poles. The Polish and Jewish masses continue to fight together for common aims, just as they have fought for so many years in the past." His colleague in the Polish National Council, Schwarzbart, initiated a motion in the council in 1943 which praised Polish efforts to help save Jews and urged the Poles to continue their efforts. Adolf Berman, who was an important link between the Jewish and Polish underground, eloquently declared later: "Accounts of the martyrdom of Poland's Jews tend to emphasize their suffering at the hands of blackmailers and informers, the 'blue' police and other scum. Less is written, on the other hand, about the thousands of Poles who risked their lives to save the Jews. The flotsam and jetsam on the surface of a turbulent river is more visible than the pure stream running deep underneath, but that stream existed."

Even Emmanuel Ringelblum, who often caustically criticized the Poles for not doing enough to help his kinsmen, said: "There are thousands [of idealists] like these in Warsaw and the whole country. . . . The names of the people who do this, and whom the Poland which shall be established should decorate with the 'Order of Humanitarianism,' will remain in our memory as the names of heroes who saved thousands of human beings from certain death by fighting against the greatest enemy the human race has ever known." His own journal entries at the time confirm how Poles drew closer to the Jews after the September campaign. On September 9, 1940, he recorded how Poles voluntarily taxed themselves for Jewish causes. A month later, he noted "frequent occurrences where Christians take the side of Jews against attacks by hoodlums. That wasn't so before the war." About the same time, he wrote how he "heard many stories" of Polish customers who sent packages to Jewish merchants confined in the Łódź Ghetto. On November 19, 1940, he made this diary entry: "A Christian was killed today . . . for throwing a sack of bread over the wall." In May 1941, he recorded how "Catholics displayed a far-reaching tolerance" and how a Passover program "evoked great respect among the Polish populace." And on July 11, 1941, he wrote: "This was a widespread phenomenon a month ago. Hundreds of beggars, including women and children, smuggled themselves out of the Ghetto to beg on the Other Side, where they were well received, well fed, and often given food to take back to the Ghetto with them. Although universally recognized as Jews from the Ghetto, perhaps they were given alms for that very reason. This was an interesting symptom of a deep transformation in Polish society." In the latter part of 1942, Ringelblum recorded: "Polish organizations combatted and did away with blackmail."

Adam Czerniaków, who headed the Warsaw *Judenrat* until his suicide in 1942, also kept a diary which reflected Polish sympathy for the Jews. On January 29, 1942, he revealed that a Polish Christian had financed repairs on one of the synagogues in the ghetto. On July 18, 1942, he recorded that a young Polish girl had been hiding a Jewish woman in her home. Even extremely critical accounts of Poles by Jews who experienced the German occupation of Poland point up the complexity of Polish-Jewish wartime relations and the difficulty of making generalizations on the subject.

In October, 1942, the *Rzeczpospolita Polska* claimed with some justification that Polish aid to the Jews was so conspicuous and spontaneous that the Germans felt compelled to order the imposition of the death penalty on all Poles who helped Jews, a sentence which was not typical of Nazi policy elsewhere in Europe. And the fact that the Germans continually repeated warnings to the Poles that they would be executed for helping Jews suggests that Polish people ignored the risks and continued to aid them.

Perhaps the best evidence of the response of Poles to the plight of the Jews is revealed by the large number of Polish anti-Semites who, in Ringelblum's words, "grasped that . . . the Poles and Jews had a common enemy and that the Jews were excellent allies who would do all they possibly could to bring destruction on the Jews' greatest enemies."

Even unreconstructed anti-Semites who had Jewish relatives helped them. "Polish anti-Semites did not apply racialism where relatives or friends were concerned," Ringelblum admitted. Many anti-Semitic Poles disliked Jews as abstractions. Once they got to know Jews, they had no personal animosity toward them and even developed genuine affection for them. Thus the truth of the old Polish maxim was confirmed: "Every Pole has his Jew." . . .

Poles who dared aid a Jew assumed risks that were largely unknown to western Europeans. As has been pointed out, the Poles automatically risked death. Since rescuing a Jew usually meant that more than one individual was involved in the effort, apprehension by the Germans often meant the execution of entire families or circles of people. A Polish historian estimated that to hide one Jew the cooperation of about ten people was required. Based on testimonies made to me, I conclude that sometimes the number was even more than that. The Germans, in their zealous efforts to uncover Jews, constantly warned the Poles of retribution for hiding them and held committees responsible in each apartment complex for ferreting them out. It was not unusual for Jews to leave the home of their Polish protectors for fear of jeopardizing their lives; sometimes they chose suicide.

Occasionally, there were Poles who hid a number of Jews and were reluctant for obvious reasons to take in any more but were forced to do so under the threat of blackmail from those who desperately needed shelter. The dangers were so great for the Poles that even the Polish Socialists were reluctant to aid their friends and colleagues in the ghetto. Poles were understandably reluctant to enter the Warsaw Ghetto, because it was not uncommon for them to be mistreated or even shot, even though they had legal passes. Thus to save a Jew in the conditions in Poland at that time represented the highest degree of heroism.

Since the Poles had experienced progressive pauperization during the German occupation and lived in conditions of bare subsistence, most Poles could not offer assistance to Jewish refugees even if they wanted to. Therefore, when Jews gave money to Poles to keep them, it was not out of greed but out of poverty that it was accepted. "There are poor families who base their subsistence on the funds paid daily by the Jews to their Aryan landlords," Ringelblum wrote. "But is there enough money in the world to make up for the constant fear of exposure, fear of the neighbors, the porter and the manager of the block of flats, etc.?"

One of the chief obstacles in rescuing Jews was the fact that the overwhelming majority of them were unassimilated. They did not know the Polish language, had few if any Polish friends, wore distinctive dress, and had been brought up in a pacifist tradition. Wladyslawa Homsowa, who played an active role in saving Jews in the Lwów area, declared, "The greatest difficulty was the passivity of the Jews themselves."

Prewar separation of the Polish and Jewish communities, along with earlier mutual animosities, sometimes got in the way of developing close relationships during the war. As one former Polish underground soldier remarked, "Before the war, they called me *goy, goy*! Now they wanted my help." He added, "Poles helped Jews, but do you realize how difficult it was to save a person who obviously looked Semitic? They had to be hidden all the time, because if they dared to venture out the Germans would pounce on them."

According to one recent sociological study of rescuers throughout occupied Europe, people who knew Jews before the war were more likely to help them than if the Jew was a stranger: "In many cases, perhaps over 75 [percent], the rescued individuals reported that they were saved by some one whom they personally knew or by members of their respective families who knew each other." In the case of Poland, it is important to understand that early in the war much of the Jewish intelligentsia, the most assimilated class of Polish Jews, had been executed along with their Polish counterparts. The Jews who remained came, for the most part, from the lower classes, were unassimilated, and had the fewest contacts with Polish Gentiles.

Finally, there was the enormous number of problems and difficulties involved in hiding a Jew—how to supply food, provide decent sanitary conditions; assure the person's security. It was difficult enough to provide these things for one refugee, let alone twenty-six Jews as Feliks Cywiński did:

> *In a flat where Jews were hiding, suitable hiding places had to be secured. Sometimes, we would set up a new wall in one of the rooms—so that people could hide behind it in case of danger; then I brought bricks home in my briefcase—not more than four at a time lest the neighbours suspect something; in the same way I brought lime and sand; other times we would conceal the last room in a large flat by covering the door with a wardrobe with a movable back wall.*
>
> *The most difficult task was to procure food. Twenty-six people is quite a lot! Food had to be brought in small quantities so that no one*

> should wonder why a single person needed so much food. I carried it in
> my briefcase, in small parcels, in pockets. In one day, I had to bring suc-
> cessive portions many times. The purchase and transport of food consumed
> much of my time.
>
>   Once it turned out that one of the women became ill. Later, the
> others got typhus. I contacted Dr. Ian Mocallo and asked him for
> assistance. The doctor came every day; he brought medicaments.
> Unfortunately, one of the women died. This is hard to understand
> today—but her death made the chances of survival very doubtful for all
> of us: the people under my care and myself who was giving help to Jews.
> We had no other way but to tie up the woman's corpse, put it in a sack
> and thus carry it out as a parcel containing food or, say papers. One of
> my friends drove up with a car; we crammed the body into the car and
> started towards the Jewish cemetery. I feared all the way that we might
> be stopped by a German patrol suspecting that the big parcel contained
> smuggled food. We reached the cemetery without any trouble, though. I
> attached a piece of paper to the sack with the name of the deceased and
> we threw the body over the wall. There was nothing more we could do.

One Polish peasant, who had saved many Jews, remarked candidly that
the penalty for hiding one or ten Jews, was the same: death. He bluntly
added, "The only difference being that it was harder to feed so many
and clean away after them."

As Jewish refugees themselves have observed, it was more difficult to hide Jewish people in the countryside than in towns and cities because everyone knew one another, and any unusual thing—such
as large purchases of food by a Pole—could give away the rescuer to
an informer or to a loquacious friend whose remarks sometimes found
their way back to the police. There were, of course, other major problems that made it difficult to hide a Jew—German house searches for
grain and cattle not delivered by the peasant under the enforced quota
system, frequent pacification operations by German police and regular
troops, periodic roundups of young Poles trying to avoid deportation to
forced labor in Germany.

Although this discussion has dwelt on Poles who provided Jews
with shelter and security, there were thousands of Polish humanitarians who did a plethora of lesser but no less risky things that aided
the Jews—smuggling food into the ghettos, conveying warnings about
the death camps, providing false documents to enable especially
non-Semitic-looking Jews to pass for Gentiles. . . .

The Poles were unique among the people under German occupation to form an underground organization which specifically aided Jews. In late September 1942, Zofia Kossak, chairman of the Front for Reborn Poland, and Wanda Krahelska-Filipowicz, an activist in the Socialist Party, had a major role in forming the Provisional Committee for Assistance to the Jews. During its brief existence, the committee helped hundreds of Jews in the Warsaw area. Three months later, it was replaced by the Council for Aid to Jews (*Rada Pomocy Żydom*), or *Żegota*, a cryptonym derived from the Polish word for Jew, *Żyd*. . . .

Żegota carried out an impressive program of aid that webbed the entire country. It was involved in trying to find shelter, provide food and medical assistance, and give proper documents to Jews under its care. It also carried out an active campaign against blackmailers, informers, and the anti-Semitic propaganda of the Nazis. *Żegota* never seemed to lack for personnel, including members of the AK, in its activities.

One of the most critical aspects of *Żegota's* activities was the forging of documents which Jewish refugees needed. Using the printing press of the Democratic Party, *Żegota* produced in time an average of 100 forged documents every day. In less than two years, *Żegota* was responsible for making available 50,000 documents, 80 percent of which reached Jews without any cost to them. . . .

German determination to kill the Jews with the apparatus of terror at their disposal was still the dominant factor that Jews themselves recognized in limiting Jewish survival. As top Jewish leaders of the Jewish underground told Jan Karski, a Polish emissary who in 1942 gave an eyewitness account to western statesmen concerning the plight of the Jews: "We want you to tell the Polish government, the Allied governments and great leaders of the Allies that we are helpless in the face of the German criminals. We cannot defend ourselves, and no one in Poland can defend us. The Polish underground authorities can save some of us, but they cannot save the masses. . . . We are being systematically murdered. . . . Our entire people will be destroyed. . . . This cannot be prevented by any force in Poland, neither the Polish nor the Jewish Underground. Place this responsibility on the shoulders of the Allies." Dr. Emmanuel Scherer, who represented the Bund on the Polish National Council after the suicide of Zygielbojm, echoed the same sentiments: "I fully realize that the main part of the work is beyond the limited possibilities of the Polish state." *Żegota* officials recognized this and called for a general international effort to help save the remnants of European Jewry in 1943. "The needs are enormous," Żegota declared. But there was, as is well known, no international action along the lines Żegota suggested.

Most of the Jews who survived the German occupation of Poland were saved by Poles who were not connected with Żegota. Recent estimates of the number of Jewish survivors range from 40,000–50,000 to 100,000–120,000, though one estimate of the Polish underground at the time placed the figure at 200,000. Tadeusz Bednarczyk, who was active in the Polish underground and had close contact with the Warsaw Ghetto, estimated that 300,000 Jews survived the Nazis in Poland. Wladyslaw Zarski-Zajdler stated that at one point during the German occupation there were as many as 450,000 Jews sheltered by Poles, but not all of them survived the war. As for Warsaw itself, it is speculated that there were 15,000 to 30,000 Jews hiding in Warsaw during the period 1942–1944 and that 4,000 of them were beneficiaries of the work of Żegota. Żegota officials boasted aiding 40,000 to 50,000 Jews throughout Poland. As this study has suggested, it was the degree of Nazi control over Poland, not anti-Semitism, which was the decisive factor in influencing the number of Jews who survived the war. The Netherlands, which had few Jews and less anti-Semitism than Poland, experienced about the same percentage of Jewish losses as Poland. On the other hand, Romania, which had an anti-Semitic history, had a relatively low rate of Jewish losses.

It is equally difficult to draw precise conclusions concerning the number of Poles actively involved in aiding Jews. Ringelblum estimated that in Warsaw alone 40,000 to 60,000 Poles were involved in hiding Jews. As Polish scholar Wladyslaw Bartoszewski has pointed out, however, there were thousands of Poles who had been engaged in aiding Jews but, despite their best efforts, had been unable to save them. These people are not included in Ringelblum's guess. He estimates that "at least several hundred thousand Poles of either sex and of various ages participated in various ways and form in the rescue action." More recent research on the subject suggests that, 1,000,000 Poles were involved in sheltering Jews, but some authors are inclined to go as high as 3,000,000. Thus a significant minority of Poles helped the Jews during the German occupation. Poles were no different from western Europeans, where only minorities—in much less threatening circumstances—aided Jewish refugees. The Polish record of aid to Jews was better than many

Eastern Europeans—Romanians, Ukrainians, Lithuanians, Latvians—and, as Jewish historian Walter Laqueur has stated, "a comparison with France would be by no means unfavorable for Poland." . . . Estimates of the number of Poles who perished aiding Jews run the gamut from a few thousand to 50,000. . . .

One of the most controversial aspects of Polish-Jewish relations during World War II concerns the role of the AK prior to and during the Warsaw Ghetto uprising in April 1943. Prevailing historiography depicts the AK as a nest of anti-Semites reluctant to help the Jews and implies that had the AK given substantial assistance to them, the outcome of the struggle would have been different. As has been seen, the AK was a large umbrella organization housing numerous military organizations, reflecting, in political terms, a variety of attitudes. The extreme right-wing anti-Semites, the NSZ,[1] were not members of the AK during the greater part of the war. The leadership of the AK, like the Polish government in London, was not anti-Semitic, and its decisions concerning the Jews of the Warsaw Ghetto were influenced by considerations that, unfortunately, have not been given the emphasis they deserve. . . .

In comparison to the existing supply of arms in the AK, the amount of arms and ammunition given by the AK to the ZOB was small. In the city of Warsaw, the AK had immediately prior to the Ghetto uprising 25 heavy machine guns, 62 light machine guns, 1,182 rifles, 1,099 pistols, and 51 submachine guns. But the AK had only a few anti-tank rifles and anti-tank guns in its arsenal in Warsaw, and these were the types of weapons the Jews needed in order to prolong their struggle. Even Schwarzbart saw clearly that it was not merely a matter of giving the Jewish resistance more weapons. The critical problem for the Jews and the AK was the lack of heavy arms: "It is obvious that whatever the quantity of arms at their disposal, the Jewish fighters were doomed to be defeated eventually by the formidable war machine of the Germans. The only thing which could have been achieved by the possession of more and particularly of heavy arms would have been the inflicting of greater losses upon the German forces in the ghetto."

It would have been unreasonable to have expected the AK to divest itself entirely of these few heavy weapons that it would obviously

---

[1]"National Armed Forces," an extreme right-wing faction of the Polish underground. —Ed.

need for launching the long-planned general uprising when the Germans were at the point of military collapse. To be sure, the Poles could have given more pistols and rifles to the Jews, but smaller weapons of this type would not have altered the military situation in Jewish favor against the Germans. Moreover, it is not entirely clear how many of these guns were the personal weapons of members of the AK who, like soldiers anywhere, would have been reluctant to part with them. . . .

At no time did responsible Jewish leaders of the Warsaw Ghetto except perhaps Anielewicz, expect the AK to squander its strength and join the Jews in a suicidal uprising. Nor did they have the right to do so. . . . [A]ny uprising by the AK at the time would have been "pointless." This view was obviously shared by Sikorski, because as Poland's commander in chief he did not order major AK involvement in the Jewish insurgency. The only reasonable option open to the AK was to initiate diversionary attacks when the Jewish uprising began. Before the uprising began, the AK apprised the Jews of what it would do in this regard. To have attempted to do anything more would have unnecessarily eroded AK strength, depriving it of the men and resources they needed to take power in Poland at the time of German military collapse and before the Soviets took possession of the country. After all, the purpose of the Polish underground was not only to engage in anti-German conspiracy but also to help the Polish people survive the occupation into the postwar era. . . .

The word Holocaust suggests to most people the tragedy the Jews experienced under the Germans during World War II. From a psychological point of view, it is understandable why Jews today prefer that the term refer exclusively to the Jewish experience, thus emphasizing the distinctiveness of the wartime fate of the Jews. Yet, by excluding others from inclusion in the Holocaust, the horrors that Poles, other Slavs, and Gypsies endured at the hands of the Nazis are often ignored, if not forgotten.

From a historical point of view, no reasonable student of World War II can deny that Hitler's policy toward the Poles was also genocidal and that about as many Polish Christians as Polish Jews died as a result of Nazi terror. Without detracting from the particularity of the Jewish tragedy in which all Jews were victimized because they were Jews, it is time to speak about the forgotten Holocausts of World War II. By failing to broaden the scope of research on the Holocaust, we have allowed our perspective on it to become distorted, and this has led to simplistic and false conclusions about the subject. . . .

If novelists and publicists perpetuate distortions of the Poles and their history, one would at least hope for better in the writings of historians. Unfortunately, it is disquieting to read most writings on the Holocaust, because the subject of Polish-Jewish relations is treated so polemically. Preoccupied with the overwhelming tragedy of the Jews, Jewish historians, who are the major writers on the subject, rarely if ever attempt to qualify their condemnations of the Poles and their defense of the Jews. The result is tendentious writing that is often more reminiscent of propaganda than of history. Despite the scholarly pretensions of many of these works—and there is genuine scholarship in some of these books—they have contributed little to a better understanding of the complexity and paradox of Polish-Jewish wartime relations.

If a more objective and balanced view prevailed in the historiography on the Holocaust, there would be less said about Polish anti-Semitism and more about the problems that faced the Poles and their military and political leadership in dealing with the Germans. If the magnitude of the Polish tragedy were objectively presented, unrealistic and unhistorical judgments about the possibilities and opportunities available to the Poles to render greater aid than they did to the Jews would not be made.

Michael R. Marrus and Robert O. Paxton

Western Europeans
and the Jews

Nazi policy toward the Jews of occupied western Europe evolved in three phases, determined by far-flung strategic concerns of the Third Reich. In the first, from the outbreak of war in the west in April 1940 until the autumn of 1941, all was provisional: Nazi leaders looked forward to a "final solution of the Jewish question in Europe," but that final solution was to await the cessation of hostilities and an ultimate peace settlement. No one defined the Final Solution with precision, but all signs pointed toward some vast and as yet unspecified project of mass emigration. When the war was over, the Jews would leave Europe and the question would be resolved. Until that time the various German occupation authorities would pursue anti-Jewish objectives by controlling the movements and organizations of Jews, confiscating their property, enumerating them, and sometimes concentrating them in certain regions. Throughout this phase, the circumstances of Jews varied importantly according to various occupation arrangements worked out by Germany following the spectacular blitzkrieg of 1940.

In the second phase, from the autumn of 1941 until the summer of 1942, Hitler drew implications from a gradually faltering campaign in Russia: the war was to last longer than he had planned, and the increasingly desperate struggle against the Bolsheviks prompted a revision of the previous timetable and general approach to the Jewish problem. Now Nazi leaders were told to prepare for the Final Solution itself, which could not be postponed. The Jewish question had to be solved quickly, *before* the end of the war. Nazi Jewish experts soon adopted the new rhythm, and began urgent preparations. Henceforth, mass resettlement was taken to be impractical, and Jewish emigration was indeed forbidden. By the end of 1941, in a dramatic reversal of policy, Jews were no longer

Excerpted from Michael R. Marrus and Robert O. Paxton, "The Nazis and the Jews in Occupied Western Europe, 1940–1944," as appeared in *Journal of Modern History*, 54:4 (1982), pp. 687–714. Copyright © 1982 by the University of Chicago Press. Reprinted by permission.

permitted to leave German-controlled Europe. With the exception of Norway and Denmark, where the numbers of Jews were unimportant, the Jews were subjected to a concerted series of new harassments, beginning with segregation by means of a yellow star. More Jews were interned in camps, made ready for deportation to the east.

The third phase began in the summer of 1942, and continued to the end of the war in the west. . . .

The Final Solution was launched in the west in the summer of 1942, at a high point in the history of Hitler's continental empire. But one should not assume from the outstanding fact of German hegemony from the Atlantic to the outskirts of Moscow and Stalingrad that the Nazis had unlimited power everywhere in Europe. On the contrary, German forces were stretched thin, and nowhere more so than in western Europe. There were enormous new demands upon German manpower. After the blitzkrieg stalled in Russia at the end of 1941, Hitler ordered a transformation of the wartime economy of the Reich, building for a longer war which would require a vastly greater production of arms and equipment. Together with increasing calls for men by the armed forces, this meant a growing reliance upon foreign workers in Germany. By the end of 1941 there were close to 4 million of these, eventually to reach more than 7 million by mid-1944—20 percent of the German workforce—when 7 million more were working in their own countries for the German war effort. Despite this heavy reliance on foreign labor, there were few Nazi police and troops available in the west to handle the deportations of Jews. Without the extensive cooperation of indigenous police forces and other officials, the Germans were therefore incapable of realizing their plans for the murder of west European Jews.

Help came easily to the Nazis during the early stages of deportation. Participation by the Belgian police was extremely limited, but both the French and the Dutch police rounded up Jews, held them in camps, and saw the convoys off to the east. Frequently, the mere presence of the local gendarmerie helped lull the Jews who were taken away; certainly, their participation reduced apprehensions among the surrounding population by making the arrests seem as normal as possible. In addition to the police, who were the most directly involved, there were countless others—prefects and their subordinates, judicial officials, mayors, railwaymen, concierges—who had a part to play. The French government at Vichy authorized their involvement, and indeed welcomed a situation in which French and not German personnel exercised authority in the country. In Belgium and Holland the captive administrations, with each ministry headed by a secretary-general, carried on in a similar fashion, although municipal officials in Brussels took a clear stand against persecution after the yellow star was imposed in June. In all west European states there were local, homegrown fascists to join domestic or German police from the beginning in rounding up Jews—Jacques Doriot's Parti Populaire Français in France, Rexist and Flemish bands in Belgium, Anton Mussert's National Socialist movement in the Netherlands, and Quisling's Nasjonal Samling in Norway.

Such collaboration, especially that of ordinary officials who were not particularly sympathetic to nazism, reflected in part the momentum generated by two years of working with the Germans. During these two years officials had acquired the habits of a new chain of command, sometimes involving unpleasant tasks. Many could not conceive deporting Jews in any other context. Collaboration also reflected the disposition on the part of local authorities to view refugees harshly, particularly Jewish refugees. Since the Germans encouraged the rounding up of foreign Jews at the start, many bureaucrats lent a hand to what might simply be considered a long-standing national effort to rid their countries of unwanted outsiders. The proportion of foreign Jews was by far the highest in Belgium, where only 6.5 percent of the over 57,000 Jews enumerated by the Gestapo had Belgian citizenship. About half of the 350,000 Jews in France were noncitizens, as were 19 percent of Denmark's 8,000 Jews, and almost 16 percent of Holland's 140,000. In this regard, French authorities outdid any in Europe except the Bulgarians and possibly the Slovaks, by actually volunteering to hand over such unwanted Jews from *un-occupied* territory.

Collaboration was never complete, and in France, Belgium, and the Netherlands various officials showed signs of reluctance by the beginning of 1943. Only in Norway did this not pose a serious problem. There were almost twice as many German police in that country (3,300) than there were Jews, and so even when some of Quisling's men turned unreliable for the deportations, it was possible to send more than a quarter of the Jews from the port of Bergen to Auschwitz by the end of 1942. Proportionately, deportations went furthest in Belgium during the first three months of convoys, when close to 30 percent of the Jews were taken from that country. Yet many Jews fled successfully from Belgium into France or Switzerland, found hiding places provided by non-Jews, or procured false identity papers with which they could evade capture. Already in December 1942 Martin Luther was pressing for the inclusion of Belgian citizens, a sign that all was not quite going in Belgium as he had hoped. Thanks to the intervention of von Falkenhausen, responding to local appeals, Belgian citizens were not deported for about a year. In September 1943, when the first and only mass roundup of Jews of Belgian nationality occurred, there was once again a loud protest, and General Reeder ordered their release from the assembly camp of Malines. Once native French Jews were included in the shipments, the police in France proved less and less reliable; much the same was true in the Netherlands. Of course, the Germans were able to continue their work despite these problems with local authorities. Yet the job required more German effort than at the beginning, and the momentum of the first months of the Final Solution in the west could not be sustained.

The Germans encountered a very serious obstacle in 1943 owing to the position of the Italian government. Anti-Semitism had never struck deep roots among the Italian people, or even the Fascist Party, which had considerable Jewish support and membership during the 1920s and early 1930s. Mussolini himself did not particularly like Jews, but shared the indifference of most of his countrymen to a "problem" which did not exist in their society. In 1938, to bring Italy into ideological tune with the Reich, Mussolini opportunistically adopted a racist posture, and issued laws against the 50,000 Italian Jews. But persecution was mild in comparison with the Hitlerian version, involved many exceptions, and did not have the enthusiastic support of the Italian population. When in November 1942, in response to the Allied landings in North Africa, the Germans swept south across the demarcation line in France, the Italians moved west to the Rhone River and occupied eight French departments. To the Nazis it was bad enough that the duce had seemed unwilling to contribute his Jews to the contingents deported from western Europe since the summer of 1942; by the beginning of 1943 it became apparent that the Italians were also shielding French Jews as well. The Italian troops shared much of the anti-German sentiment of the increasingly war-weary Italian population, and in this climate the idea of a racialist crusade on behalf of Aryan civilization seemed even more alien and absurd than before. Italian occupation officers not only refused to turn Jews over to Vichy or the Germans, they also blocked the application of French anti-Semitic legislation. As with their occupation policy for Croatia and part of Greece, the Italians held firm, and by one means or another resisted every effort to bring them into line. Ribbentrop failed to convince Mussolini to change his policy when he visited Rome in March 1943, and the SS ground their teeth over the obstruction they encountered. The Italian zone of France became a haven for some 50,000 Jews, protected by *carabinieri* against both the Germans and the French police.

Unfortunately, this protection was not to last. It continued after the fall of Mussolini in July 1943, but could not survive the surrender of Italy to the Allies early in the autumn. The Italians evacuated their zone of France suddenly when the armistice was announced prematurely on September 8, too quickly to implement an evacuation scheme which had been negotiated by an Italian Jew, Angelo Donati. As the Italians left, the Germans moved in, and the Jews were caught. Very few escaped, and most were sent to Auschwitz in a matter of days.

Only now did the deportation of Italian Jews begin. Despite Hitler's restoration of an Italian fascist regime, the phantom Republic of Salo, the renewed persecution and the deportation of Jews from the parts of Italy outside Allied hands was entirely a German operation. Himmler pressed for the application of the Final Solution, and neither the severe difficulties associated with the worsening war situation in the peninsula nor the widespread opposition to the deportations among Italians, and even some Germans on the spot, prevented the dispatch of more than 8,000 Jews to the east.

As in Italy, the Germans knew that the Final Solution could be extended to Denmark only through their own efforts. Anti-Semitism had flared briefly in Denmark in the wake of surrender, as elsewhere in western Europe, but the Danish political leadership, continuing in place from before the war, remained adamantly opposed to all manifestations of anti-Jewish feeling. Danish Nazis were hopelessly divided among themselves, and politically incompetent. Nazism and anti-Semitism remained unpopular. For three years the Danes collaborated economically with the Reich, in exchange for which the Germans did not interfere in internal Danish affairs. When the German representative in Copenhagen, the traditionalist Cecil von Renthe-Fink, was replaced by the former police and military administrator Werner Best in November 1942, the latter searched imaginatively for some means to move against the Jews without unduly disturbing relations with a cooperative Danish government. No real opportunities appeared, however. Even the ambitious Martin Luther at the Foreign Office, never one to neglect an opportunity for pressing forward with Jewish persecution, felt unable to recommend a change in policy.

Until the summer of 1943, therefore, the Germans left the Danes alone with their Jews. The Jewish issue suddenly came to a head, however, with the general crisis in Danish-German relations that arose in August 1943. As political and social conditions worsened dramatically throughout the country, due largely to Danish protests against mounting German exactions, the occupation imposed a state of emergency. The government of Erik Scavenius resigned, leaving internal control of Denmark in the hands of its civil service. Taking advantage of the upheaval, Ministerialdirigent Werner Best triggered the persecution of local Jews, with the object of deporting them by sea, from Copenhagen.

This operation failed utterly, as is well known, and in the end the Nazis were able to lay their hands on only 475 of the close to 8,000 Jews in Denmark. During the first week of October 1943, within a matter of days, thousands of Danes organized a rescue expedition unprecedented in the history of the Final Solution, which transferred nearly the entire community of Jews across the Sund to Sweden in small boats. In part the impotence of the Germans flowed from internal divisions among the occupation authorities. Best failed to obtain the cooperation of the Wehrmacht in Denmark because of his rivalry with its commander, General Hermann von Hannecken, who opposed the deportations, and he failed also to win full authority to seize control of the Danish civil service because he was so distrusted in Berlin, particularly by Himmler, who seems for the moment to have had other priorities in mind than the deportation of a small number of Danish Jews. But most importantly, Best failed to get the support of the Danish administration and public opinion, without which the deportation could not succeed.

The source of this failure has often been pondered by those concerned with drawing some moral lesson from the terrible events we have been considering. The most important study of the rescue, by the Israeli historian Leni Yahil, discusses several explanations, but judges the decisive factor to have been "the special character and moral stature of the Danish people and their love of democracy and freedom." Hannah Arendt saw in the Danish response an exemplary demonstration of the efficacy of nonviolent resistance to tyranny. The Nazis, she wrote in *Eichmann in Jerusalem,* changed their entire posture when faced with open native opposition. "They had met resistance based on principle, and their 'toughness' had melted like butter in the sun." While not wishing to depreciate the significance and moral import of the rescue or strategies of nonviolence, it is well to remember that the community of Jews in that country was small, that the haven of Sweden was close (between five and fifteen miles across open water), that the Swedes were willing to accept all the Jews, and that the persecutions occurred in a country already seething with opposition to nazism. These conditions greatly facilitated the rescue operation, which would, indeed, have been impossible without them.

It is also worth considering how the timing of the Nazi attempt to implement the Final Solution in Denmark differed so sharply from the other cases in western Europe we have been discussing. The attack upon the Danish Jews coincided with a sharp reversal of occupation policy which, after three years of encouraging a model protectorate, suddenly subjected the entire state to humiliating subservience and oppression. The contrast is obvious with other west European countries, where deportations of Jews followed two years of habituation to anti-Jewish laws and policies, introduced at a time of national prostration and soul-searching following an overwhelming military collapse. Defenders of Jews everywhere in Europe claimed that the Jewish fate was part of the general fate of people conquered by Nazism. Unfortunately, it was not always easy to demonstrate how this was so, when the Jews were so sharply singled out. But in Denmark, as Yahil suggests, the victimization of Jews coincided exactly with a sudden political assault upon the entire Danish people.

Notably, all this happened when the Reich was in retreat, following the German defeats at El Alamein, Stalingrad, and Kursk, and the Allied landings in Italy. By the autumn of 1943, as the British and American air offensive against the Reich reached spectacular proportions, Hitler no longer seemed invincible—a sharp contrast with the beginning of the occupation in 1940, or the launching of the Final

Solution in the summer of 1942. The implication is clear: because of the delay in preparing deportations in Denmark, it was easier for Danes to perceive the attack on Jews as an attack upon themselves and hence to rally to their defense; it was also morally easier to challenge the power of the Reich, which by late 1943 showed signs of its eventual collapse.

Proper timing was obviously crucial to the success of opposition to Nazi Jewish policy. On one rare occasion in western Europe public protest came too soon—the Dutch workers' strike of February 1941, in solidarity with persecuted Jews. This was the first massive, open opposition anywhere in occupied Europe to Nazi anti-Semitism. The strike was crushed by overwhelming force, and to an important degree the courageous Dutch opposition continued for years to be demoralized by the brutally effective display of German power so early in the occupation. And the strike had no effect whatever on the substance of Nazi anti-Jewish activity in Holland, except perhaps to worsen the plight of native Jews. This resistance therefore seems to have come prematurely; on the other hand, resistance more often came too late to help at all. By the latter part of 1943 the unpopularity of the deportations of Jews caused problems for the Nazis in France, Belgium, and the Netherlands, precisely at the moment when protests against the conscription of the indigenous labor force to work in the Reich made local police less reliable. But by that time it was not possible to do more than slow the deportation machinery, and even then the rescue of Jews does not seem to have ranked high for resistance strategists in selecting targets. In any event, by late 1943 the great majority of Jewish deportees were already dead.

Assessment: The Holocaust in Western Europe

The Final Solution did not succeed in western Europe because the war ended too soon and the Nazis did not have time to complete their task. Nevertheless, the scale of destruction was staggering—some 40 percent of west European Jews killed. With 105,000 deported, or 75 percent of its Jews, the Netherlands suffered the greatest losses, both in absolute and relative terms. Belgium came next, with the murder of over 24,000, more than 40 percent of its Jewish population of late May 1940. Norway lost about the same proportion—760 Jews. In France 20 percent of the Jews—about 75,000—were murdered. Italy lost about 8,000, or 16 percent.

What accounts for these variations? Let it be clear at the outset that these figures do not reflect any absolute measure of Nazi capability, but rather the results of a program interrupted prematurely by the military reverses suffered by the Reich in the latter part of 1944. For the Nazis' will to destroy the Jews weakened only at the end of that year, among certain top leaders, in the face of impending defeat. So what we are really considering is the relative pace of deportations from west European countries.

We hope that enough has been said to caution against relying on any single factor to explain this. A recent effort by a sociologist to isolate, quantify, and assess the significance of variables which would account for the incidence of genocide in European countries failed notably to produce a clear answer because the work ignored the evolution of German strategy and certain basic problems associated with comparison. None of these variables makes sense outside of the particular experiences of individual states. The availability of a haven to which Jews could flee, for example, was unquestionably crucial in the rescue of Danish Jews, but did not prevent the proportionately high level of destruction in Norway, despite the existence of a thousand miles of frontier with Sweden. Concentration of Jews in one place clearly could be dangerous, as in the cases of Amsterdam and also Oslo, where the Jews could easily be identified and rounded up. But concentration in the port of Copenhagen, only a few miles from freedom, helped save the Danish Jews. Without it, the rescue could not have succeeded. Sheer numbers could be important. Clearly, the Nazis felt that Denmark, with a mere 8,000 Jews, could wait for the implementation of the Final Solution, whereas France, with the largest Jewish population in the west, received a high priority. But in France, owing to the circumstances of the military defeat in 1940 and the peculiar armistice arrangement with the Germans, the Jews remained scattered across a large and, relatively speaking, sparsely settled country. In view of the thin screen of German troops and police available for the job, it is not surprising that the proportion of deported Jews from France was relatively low, despite the valuable aid given the Germans by the Vichy government.

Generalizations break apart on the stubborn particularity of each of our countries. Nowhere is this more obvious than in considering the dominant religious traditions in western European states. Catholic Italy and Protestant Denmark provide the two outstanding cases of consistent popular resistance to the persecution of the Jews. Lutheran theologians made the earliest and most forceful denunciation of anti-Semitism in Denmark, which was decidedly not the case among their coreligionists in Germany. The notable lack of public protest against Jewish deportations from the Vatican, about which there has been so much discussion, does not seem to have affected the deep antipathy toward anti-Semitism among the Italian population, including the Catholic clergy. In the Netherlands, the Catholics and the Protestant Dutch Reformed Church were about equally divided in their numbers of adherents. When they were about to issue a joint public denunciation of the deportations in the summer of 1942, the Germans threatened reprisals unless they desisted. The Synod of the Dutch Reformed Church complied, but the Catholics did not, immediately resulting in the inclusion of Catholic Jews in shipments to the gas chambers. There has been anguished discussion about this episode ever since it occurred, but it seems unlikely that one can draw from it any useful generalization about how the behavior of particular denominations might have influenced the Final Solution.

Each case was different. It makes little sense to attempt to deduce laws about victimization from an examination of so few cases, in which the degree of particularity was so high. Our conclusion is more modest. It seems plain that German policy, and also the ability of the Nazis to apply their power, were decisive in determining how far the destruction process went by the time of liberation. Nazi policy in the first phase, when the European war was going well for the Germans, was governed by pragmatic considerations. During this period some groundwork was laid for a final solution, the outlines of which remained unclear and the timing obscure. Because conditions for occupation differed, and because of the lack of urgency, the degree to which the Jews were isolated from the surrounding population differed considerably, and remained incomplete. Then, in response to the changed war situation in the east, policy changed: the Final Solution was defined, and declared a compelling necessity. The second phase involved adjustment to these new circumstances, by sometimes feverish planning and preparations. In the third phase, from the summer of 1942, the plans were implemented. For a time all went according to projection. But by 1943 serious military setbacks suffered elsewhere by the Reich took their toll: the Germans were unable to supply sufficient men and railway transport to keep up the pace of the first deportations and to finish the job quickly. Geography, administrative difficulties, conflicts among German agencies, Jewish resistance, and the actions of some west Europeans all helped to slow the process of deportation at various points. But only the outcome of the military conflict itself could have a decisive effect upon the Final Solution.

Only the defeat of the Reich brought the trains to a halt. This is especially clear when one observes how long the shipments of Jews continued. The last regular deportation from Drancy, outside of Paris, left France for Auschwitz on July 31, 1944, almost two months after the Allied landings in Normandy; two more smaller convoys followed from France, the last departing on August 17, only a week before the first tanks of General Leclerc arrived to liberate Paris. The last convoy from Belgium left Malines for Auschwitz on July 31, with 554 Jews. The last convoy from Holland went to Auschwitz on September 3, with over 1,000 Jews. Deportations from northern Italy continued the longest of all, due to the tenacious and successful German resistance against the Allies: trains went to Auschwitz until October 24, when the death factory in Poland had only days left to function, and on December 14 to Ravensbrück and Flossenbürg; a final convoy of Jews went from Trieste to Bergen-Belsen on February 24, 1945.

Nechama Tec

Righteous Gentiles

[W]ho within the [Polish] gentile population was likely to stand up for the persecuted Jews, who traditionally had been viewed as "Christ killers" and who, for still unexplained reasons, continue to be blamed for every conceivable ill? More specifically, what characteristics did the large group of altruistic gentile rescuers share? What propelled them to engage in behavior that threatened their own lives?

A systematic examination of this group, in terms of social class, level of education, political involvement, degree of anti-Semitism, extent of religious commitment, and friendship with Jews reveals a very heterogeneous group. Some came from higher, some from lower classes. Some were well-educated while others were illiterate. Comparisons in terms of religious and political affiliations also show much diversity. Here and there a few characteristics and conditions suggest a partial explanation. For example, belonging to a certain class and espousing certain political preferences might push an individual toward or away from becoming a rescuer of Jews. Specifically, intellectuals and socialists had a slightly higher percentage of rescuers. But the differences in the percentages were not high enough to predict rescue.

A selective presentation of findings, and how these link the empirical with the theoretical, follows. I have identified one shared characteristic of these rescuers as individuality or separateness. It suggests rather consistently that these rescuers did not quite fit into their social environments; a condition of which they were often unaware. Individuality or separateness appears under different guises and its effect upon rescue seems to be related to other shared conditions and motivations.

Being an outsider, on the periphery of a community, whether one is aware of it or not, suggests fewer constraints. With individuality come fewer social controls and greater independence, factors that have other important implications. Freedom from social constraints and a high level of independence create opportunities to act in accordance with personal values and moral precepts, even when these are in opposition to societal expectations. In short, to the extent that people are less controlled by their environment and are more independent, they are more likely guided by their own moral imperatives, regardless of whether or not these imperatives conform to societal expectations.

While the rescuers in my study have rarely reflected upon their separateness, they had no trouble talking about their self-reliance and their need to follow personal inclinations and values. Nearly all of them (98 percent) saw themselves as independent. Jewish survivors also described their protectors as independent and motivated by particular personal values. In addition, a quality often mentioned in the testimonies and memoirs of survivors, one almost as prevalent as independence, was the rescuers' courage. Of the sample of Jewish survivors, the overwhelming majority (85 percent) described their helpers as courageous.

With the rescuers' view of themselves as independent came the idea that they were propelled by moral values not dependent on the support and approval of others but rather on their own self-approval. Again and again they repeated that they had to be at peace with themselves and with their own ideas of what was right or wrong.

To illustrate: Janka, a Righteous Gentile who saved ten Jews by hiding them in her apartment, said:

> *I have to be at peace with myself, what others think about me is not important. It is my own conscience that I must please and not the opinion of others. My father always told me that I should act in a way which should not embarrass me. . . . Public opinion is fickle, it depends on the way the wind blows. . . . At one point during the war I had to decide whether to follow my conscience or save myself. One day, Adaœ, the Jewish man who stayed with me, left and did not return. The Polish police came to search the house. We had a good hiding place and they did not find the others. They told me that Adaœ was at the police station. I was advised by all who knew about it to run away. The situation appeared hopeless. To try and save him would be suicidal. Adaœ looked very Jewish. Also, as a man his identity could be easily checked. [Only Jewish men were circumcised.] But I could not follow the advice of others. Instead, I went to the police station. They wanted a large sum of money which I managed to get. They also demanded that I give them a grand piano and some valuable paintings. I was ready to give them everything. [. . .]*
> *When I got Adaœ from the clutches of the police, I felt so light it was as if I had wings. I felt so gratified; I knew I acted correctly and that I had no reason to be ashamed of myself.*

Closely related to the rescuers' moral convictions and values was their enduring commitment to the protection of the needy. This commitment was expressed in a wide range of charitable acts extending over a long period of time. Evidence about selfless acts also came from survivors, most of whom described their protectors as good-natured and as people whose efforts on behalf of the needy were limitless and long-lasting. There seems to be continuity between the rescuers' history of charitable actions and their protection of Jews. That is, risking lives for Jews fits into a system of values and behaviors that included helping the weak and the dependent.

This analogy, however, has inherent limitations. Most disinterested actions on behalf of others may involve inconvenience, even extreme inconvenience. Only rarely would such acts suggest that the rescuer might have to make the ultimate sacrifice of his or her own life. For these rescuers, only during the war was there a convergence between historical events demanding ultimate selflessness and their already established predisposition to help.

For example, Maria Baluszko, an outspoken peasant who helped many Jews, said: "I do what I think is right, not what others think is right". At first she resisted telling me that her aid to Jews was an extension of a tradition that involved helping the poor and the destitute. When I touched upon her reasons for rescue she was at a loss. Then, instead of answering she asked: "What would you do in my place if someone comes at night and asks for help? [. . .] One has to be an animal without conscience not to help." I had no answer. Impassively, I waited for her to continue. Only at that point did she tell me: "In our area there were many large families with small farms; they were very poor. I used to help them; they called me mother. . . . I used to help all. . . . When I was leaving the place people cried. I helped all the poor all that needed help".

We tend to take our repetitive actions for granted. What we take for granted we accept. What we accept, we rarely analyze or wonder about. In fact, the more firmly established patterns of behavior are, the less likely are they to be examined and thought about. Therefore, in a real sense, the constant pressure of, or familiarity with, ideas and actions does not mean that we know or understand them. On the contrary, when customary patterns are accepted and taken for granted, this often impedes rather than promotes understanding.

Related to this tendency is another one. Namely, what we are accustomed to repeat we do not see as extraordinary, no matter how exceptional it may seem to others. Thus the rescuers' past history of helping the needy might have been in part responsible for their modest appraisal of their life-threatening actions. Their modesty was expressed in a variety of ways. Two thirds of the rescuers saw their protection of Jews as a natural reaction to human suffering and almost a third insisted that saving lives was nothing exceptional. In contrast barely 3 percent felt that their saving of Jews was extraordinary.

For example, Pawel Remba limped because of an injury he suffered smuggling Jews out of the Warsaw ghetto during the uprising. For this and other acts of kindness on behalf of Jews, he was awarded the Yad Vashem medal. When I interviewed Pawel he categorically denied that he or others like him were heroes: "I would absolutely not make heroes out of the Poles who helped. All of us looked at this help as a natural thing. None of us were heroes; at times we were afraid, but none of us could act differently".

Refusal to perceive the drama of these life-threatening and risky actions was expressed in other ways as well. Some of these rescuers omitted from their accounts events that would attest to noble and courageous aspects of their rescue. This tendency is apparent from a comparison of information collected from matched pairs of rescuers and rescued.

One such example is provided by the case of Ada Celka and the girl she had saved, Danuta Brill. I interviewed Celka in Poland. A governess by profession, during the war she shared a one-room apartment with her unmarried sister and a handicapped father. In 1942, a Jewish woman, an acquaintance, asked Celka to save her child, a girl of eight. When the girl, Danuta, came to share the tiny apartment, the neighbors were told that she was an orphaned relative. To my suggestion that keeping the Jewish girl must have entailed economic hardships, Celka reacted with a flat denial. She also failed to tell me about a few facts that would have enhanced her image.

I heard only from Danuta, whom I interviewed in the United States, that Celka had planned and almost succeeded in smuggling Danuta's parents out of a work camp and in placing them with a Polish family on a farm. This, according to the daughter, involved extraordinary efforts. Celka was not an influential person; she had few connections and no money. Her success in locating a peasant family could be ascribed to her willingness to try again and again, to her strong determination. Finally, all was ready, and detailed plans for smuggling the parents out of their work camp were set in motion. On the chosen day, Celka went to the appointed place next to the camp, but she waited in vain. The day before, Danuta's parents had been deported to a death camp.

Celka also never bothered to tell me that when food was scarce, which it often was, she fed her handicapped father first, and then Danuta. She and her sister ate only after her father and the girl had had enough.

Whereas Jews were glad, even eager, to praise their protectors, the rescuers were reluctant to talk about their noble aid. Even those who did so spoke only in timid and restrained ways. I had to prod and probe before any of them mentioned things that would put them in a particularly favorable light. Instead, they consistently underplayed the risks and sacrifices inherent in their actions.

Not only did most helpers deny that their aid to Jews was heroic, they became embarrassed when this possibility was suggested to them. To underplay the heroism of their actions, many of the rescuers emphasized the fears that they had experienced during their rescuing activities. The underlying assumption in such arguments was that fear was incompatible with heroism.

Felicja Zapolska was one of those rescuers who emphasized fear. She felt that "in general, those that helped were sensitive people who tried to overcome their fears. Everyone was afraid. Do not believe it if someone tells you that they were not afraid because it has to be a lie".

Others denied the exceptionality of their deeds. This they did by describing such deeds as expressions of duty, or by pushing the dangers into the background, or by depicting it as just another part of a dangerous environment. Some emphasized the great value of saving a life.

Given these matter-of-fact perceptions of rescue, it is not surprising that help often began in a spontaneous, unpremeditated way, either gradually or suddenly. In fact, more than three-quarters of the Jewish survivors reported that the aid they had received happened without prior preparation.

So strong was this need to help, so much was it a part of the rescuers' makeup, that it overshadowed other considerations. When asked why they had saved Jews, the rescuers overwhelmingly emphasized that they responded to the persecution and the suffering of victims and not to their Jewishness. What compelled them to act was the persecution, the unjust treatment, and not who the victims were.

This ability to disregard all attributes of the needy, except their helplessness and dependence, I refer to as universalistic perceptions. Evidence for the presence of these perceptions comes from a variety of sources. One of these shows that most rescuers (95 percent) felt that they were prompted to help by Jewish neediness. This is in sharp contrast to the 26 percent who claim to have helped because it was a Christian duty, or the 52 percent who saw their response as a protest against the Nazi occupation.

Clearly, more than one kind of motivation was involved. Of the Jewish survivors, an overwhelming majority (81 percent) concurred that Jewish suffering made these rescuers offer protection. Universalistic perceptions were also indicated by the fact that very few of these rescuers (9 percent) limited their help to friends. The rest gave help to all kinds of people, including total strangers. When the sample of Jewish survivors is consulted, a little over half of them report being protected by strangers and less than a quarter said that they had received aid from friends.

This tendency is further illustrated by the case of Dr. Estowski, who was deeply involved in aiding Jews and non-Jews alike. He helped in two capacities, both as a member of the underground and as an individual. How does he describe his protection of Jews?

> *Whoever came to us we always managed to help. I felt that it was my duty to help people. It was not because they were Jews. I had a simple obligation to help people. One had to help people. It was not for us a question of them being Jews or not, just anyone who needed help had to get it. Jews were in a specially dangerous situation; all of us who were helping were aware of this fact—that because of their difficult situation, they had to be helped the most. After all, a Pole could somehow help himself, but the Jew was in a more horrible situation and could in no way help himself.*

The compelling moral force behind the rescuing of Jews, the universal insistence that what mattered was the victims' position of dependence and exposure to unjust persecution, combined to make such actions universalistic. In a sense it was this moral force that motivated the rescuers, independently of personal likes and dislikes. Some of those I spoke to were aware that to help the needy in general, and the Jews in particular, one did not have to like them. Liking and helping, they knew, did not necessarily go hand in hand.

Mixed in with the preceding discussion of altruistic rescue and rescuers are six closely interrelated and shared characteristics and conditions. Together they provide a theoretical explanation of altruistic rescue and at the same time suggest a profile of these rescuers. A more casual view of rescuers from other countries suggests that these theoretical explanations apply to them as well. A brief summary of these ideas follows: (1) individuality or separateness, which means that they did not quite fit into their respective social environments; (2) independence or self-reliance to act in accordance with personal convictions, regardless of how these were viewed by others; (3) broad and long-lasting commitment to stand up for the helpless and needy and an enduring history of performing charitable acts; (4) tendency to perceive aid to Jews in a matter-of-fact, unassuming way. These attitudes came with consistently strong denials of any heroic or extraordinary qualities of their rescue; (5) unpremeditated, unplanned start of rescue. That is, rescue which was extended gradually or suddenly, even impulsively; and (6) universalistic perceptions about the Jews. Rather than seeing a Jew in those they were about to protect, they saw them as helpless and totally dependent on aid from others. Such perceptions come with an ability to disregard all attributes except those that express extreme suffering and need.

Buchenwald, April 1945. Jews and Gypsies are among the prisoners liberated by American forces. Photograph by Margaret Bourke-White / Time-Life Pictures / Getty Images

PART

VI Possibilities of Rescue

Variety of Opinion

[N]o rescue action was taken because no one, anywhere, had anything genuinely practical or effective to suggest, apart from winning the war even more quickly.

William D. Rubinstein

Pope Pius XII . . . could have communicated with church leaders . . . encouraging all of them to urge Catholics to provide shelter to Jews. The consequence would have been fewer Catholic collaborators and bystanders, on the one hand, and more Catholic rescuers and fewer victims, on the other.

Michael Phayer

It is very easy to claim that everyone should have known what would happen once Fascism came to power. But such an approach is ahistorical. . . . There was no precedent in recent European history for the murderous character of German National Socialism and for this reason most contemporaries were caught unprepared.

Walter Laqueur

Finally, we turn to reactions to the Holocaust by foreign governments and institutions. Word about the mass murders leaked to the outside world within months of their start. We will inquire into the responses of the Western Allies and the neutral Vatican and examine prospects of rescuing the victims or slowing their destruction. Why was so little done and still less accomplished?

William D. Rubinstein doubts that much more could have been done and criticizes those who have identified concrete failures to act. He takes issue with an influential 1984 book by David S. Wyman, *The Abandonment of the Jews,* which attacks President Franklin D. Roosevelt and his administration for indifference to Holocaust victims. Wyman argued that hundreds of thousands of Holocaust victims might have been saved had the United States taken twelve measures:

1. create a War Refugee Board in 1942, rather than wait until January 1944
2. pressure or negotiate with the Germans to release Jews
3. pressure the Axis satellites to release Jews
4. provide European havens and aid to released Jews
5. locate havens outside of Europe for the Jews
6. provide shipping to transfer Jews to havens
7. encourage and assist Jews to escape
8. provide large sums of money for these purposes
9. provide medical supplies and food to victims in the camps
10. pressure allied and neutral countries to assist Jews
11. bomb Auschwitz and the rail lines leading to it
12. disseminate publicity about the Holocaust, threatening the German leaders and warning the victims.

Rubinstein attempts to refute all of Wyman's points. In Rubinstein's view the Germans were implacable in their determination to kill as many Jews as possible and would not have yielded to outside pressures to treat them differently. Hence any lack of will among Western leaders to aid the victims was irrelevant. They simply could not be helped. Rubinstein is particularly combative on the subject of bombing Auschwitz. Not all scholars agree with him that it was infeasible to destroy the gas chambers or that no one at the time advocated the bombing. Rubinstein is certainly correct that bombing Auschwitz would not have destroyed the Germans' ability to continue the killings in other ways. But what might the political and psychological impact have been? In evaluating these arguments by Wyman and Rubinstein, we ought to be thoughtful about contingency in history. Is it ever legitimate to use the record of what actually happened to prove an argument about what might have happened?

Michael Phayer sheds light on the well-known silence of Eugenio Pacelli, who as Pope Pius XII led the Roman Catholic Church during World War II. Phayer shows that Pius XII was not, as the title of a recent best-selling book has it, "Hitler's Pope." He despised the Nazis, but he feared Soviet communism even more and considered Hitler a bulwark against it. That and his hope of using diplomatic methods to end the war gave the Pope tunnel vision, says Phayer. Pius XII, well informed about Nazi genocide, assisted thousands of Italian Jews to hide in Vatican buildings and Catholic convents and monasteries, and he personally interceded to save the Jews of Slovakia and Hungary, but he refused to make public or private statements instructing the faithful to aid Holocaust victims and oppose their tormentors. It was, Phayer concludes, a failure of personal courage and of Christian judgment. Interestingly, this and other indictments of Pius XII coincide with Vatican proceedings to elevate him to sainthood. In evaluating the critical views, one must keep in mind that from 1943 on the Vatican was entirely at the mercy of the Germans. It seems unlikely that an outspoken Pope would have been allowed to speak out for long. Should Pius XII have done so anyway, or did he do more good by keeping silent and maintaining Vatican neutrality?

Walter Laqueur questions people's ability to comprehend the Holocaust at the time it was happening. The Jews in Nazi hands, terrified and helpless, could not surmount the psychological obstacles to confronting their own extermination. Jews in the free world often denied the evidence before them out of vicarious participation in the horror of their coreligionists. Among the Allies, skepticism about stories that seemed inherently incredible and preoccupation with purely military objectives led to the same result. Perhaps nothing better illustrates this than the astonishment of American and British officers and newsmen upon the liberation of concentration camps in 1945. All had read and heard about Nazi atrocities, but they had not registered. Laqueur concentrates on the first year of the Holocaust, during which most of the victims died; however, the implications of his analysis apply to the entire period. They place issues of Jewish resistance and outside responses in arguably less moralistic light.

It should be clear from these essays that assessing prospects of rescue during the Holocaust depends on our understanding of several issues. Were the Nazis determined to kill all members of the targeted groups, or prepared under certain circumstances to relent? Were Allied and church leaders antisemitic, indifferent to the fate of the victims, or lacking in imagination about how to help them? Or were these leaders helpless to act? If helpless, was that because of psychological impediments to comprehending the Holocaust, or because there was literally nothing they could do except defeat the Third Reich as quickly as possible?

William D. Rubinstein

The Myth of Rescue

Do what? What could the Allies have done, what should the Allies have done, to rescue Jews from the Nazi Holocaust? A number of historians have made quite specific proposals and these should be carefully considered in the light of the arguments of this work. In considering any such proposal, one must at all times be aware of a crucial distinction between *what was actually proposed at the time* in the West and what has since been proposed, often many decades later, by historians who are able coolly to reflect on the events of the Holocaust, possessing knowledge well known today but unknown at the time. Proposals for rescue first made many decades later—that is, suggestions not actually made by anyone during the war itself—are *ipso facto* highly suspect if not historiographically illegitimate. An historical actor cannot reasonably be criticised by later observers for failing to do what no one thought of at the time; it is so easy to be wise after the event. Many of the proposals made by later historians fall into the category of those first proposed and advanced after the war ended. But it must be emphasised that no proposal for rescue advanced by later historians was actually practical, or represented a likely way to save the lives of any European Jews, even if it had been taken up and acted upon with gusto by the Allies.

The most complete list of suggestions of what might have been done was advanced by David S. Wyman in the conclusion of *The Abandonment of the Jews*.[1] This list has been reprinted several times and is often taken by other historians to represent a realistic programme of regrettable missed opportunities. In my opinion, however, not one of the points made by Wyman is valid: not one could have been implemented during the war, and most were only proposed, with hindsight, many years later. . . .

Point (1): no one advocated the establishment of the War Refugee Board in 1942, or at any time before about July 1943. Professor Wyman has, in my opinion, exaggerated the number of Jews rescued by the Board by a factor of at least 90 per cent. Even if the Board had come into existence in 1942, it is extremely difficult to see what it could have accomplished, given that Nazi-occupied Europe was entirely beyond the reach of the Allies at that time.

Point (2): Adolf Hitler's aim was to exterminate European Jewry, and it is inconceivable that he would have agreed to releasing them at any time after late 1940. It was precisely upon Hitler's instructions that the Nazi policy of exiling its Jews was transformed into one of imprisoning them, prior to genocide. Professor Wyman evidently does not really believe that "pressing Germany" to release its Jews would have had the slightest effect, and is reduced to urging that this would have "demonstrated to the Nazis" that America was "committed" to saving Jews. But Hitler believed that America (as well as Britain and Russia) was *controlled* by its Jews; every air raid on a German city surely demonstrated the Allies' commitment to "international Jewry."

The fact that until mid-1944 "it was far from clear to the Allies that Germany would not let the Jews out" is a manifest *non sequitur*. From late 1940, it was Germany's policy "not to let the Jews out"; it is also difficult to see why Professor Wyman believes that the blocking of the Horthy offer marked a turning point in Allied-thinking.

---

[1]See chapter introduction. — Ed.

"Ransom overtures," even if vigorously pursued, would inevitably have failed [because] Hitler would, sooner or later, have heard of them and instantly stopped their continuation. And the more Jews who were likely to be ransomed, the more likely Hitler was to have learned of any negotiations.

Point (3): greater pressure *might* have been brought upon the Axis satellites, but it is difficult to see what this could conceivably have achieved. No Jews were deported from Rumania or Bulgaria to extermination camps; no Jews were deported from Hungary to extermination camps until May 1944, when the Nazis convinced Horthy that they were being sent to Germany to work for the *Reich*. When, through precisely the kind of campaign that Wyman implies was never made, Horthy became convinced that Hungary's Jews were being sent to their deaths, he halted the deportations; for his efforts, the Nazis staged a *coup d'état* in large part because of his lack of cooperation over the Jewish question. If Horthy had put a stop to the deportations before, Hitler would have staged the *coup* earlier. Indeed, an earlier pro-Nazi *coup* would almost certainly have seen the deportation and extermination of Budapest's Jews, who were spared chiefly because the Soviet armies were closing in on Auschwitz. One of Hitler's few explicit statements on the Holocaust is that he was extremely keen to deport Budapest's Jews to their deaths. Since *no* Italian Jews were deported to Auschwitz before the Nazi seizure of power there in September 1943, while Mussolini appeared to be protecting them from deportation, Italy's Jews seemed to be safe from extermination. Mussolini, by the outbreak of the war a convinced anti-semite (if not yet genocidal) and a pro-Nazi, was certain to reject any entreaties by the Allies: he had declared war on the United States, not the other way round.

Points (4), (5), (6), (7), and (8) require little comment, predicated as they are on the Jews being allowed to emigrate from Nazi-occupied Europe in significant numbers during the war, something which was *ipso facto* impossible without a total change of heart by Adolf Hitler. It is worth reiterating that no Jews who successfully fled from Nazi-occupied Europe to the democracies were ever returned to Nazi-occupied Europe, Jews fleeing to Switzerland being the sole possible exception to this generalisation. Perhaps more pressure might have been brought to bear on Switzerland to take more refugees, but—despite its age-old history of neutrality—that country, surrounded on all sides by Axis Europe, was desperately afraid of a Nazi invasion, and there is no reason to suppose that, for fleeing Jews, the borders to Switzerland were any less well guarded by the Germans than anywhere else.

The 70,000 Jews of Transnistria[2] survived the war, but, ironically, any sign that Antonescu was actually in the process of allowing them to emigrate would certainly have come to Hitler's attention and led to an immediate despatch of Eichmann and the SS. The Jews of Spain were safe from the Nazis, whether they remained in Spain or in a "long-promised camp in North Africa." This is a particularly egregious example of illogical "pseudo-rescue."

There were repeated messages and warnings, on the BBC and by underground sources, of what the Nazis had in mind for Europe's Jews. The central difficulty with all such warnings is that Jews in Nazi-occupied Europe could do nothing to heed them.

Point (9) in Wyman's list, concerning food and medical aid, is yet another example of egregious illogicality. Neither food nor medical aid could have been brought to Jews in Nazi-occupied Europe. As equivocal as the role of the International Red Cross during the Holocaust may well have been, it had no powers to enter any ghetto or concentration camp. Contrary to Professor Wyman's assertion, the Jews of Europe suffered not from a "British blockade" but from a Nazi blockade; short of defeating the Nazi scourge, this particular blockade was unlikely to end.

Point (10) is similar to point (3) and is fallacious for the same reason: the Nazis would not have allowed it. There were no "neutral diplomatic missions" in Poland, the German-occupied territories of the Soviet Union, or indeed virtually anywhere from where Jews were deported to extermination camps; had there been any neutral diplomats in these places, it is extremely difficult to see what they might have done, since Hitler, the absolute master of continental Europe, saw the extermination of European Jewry as arguably the central goal of his life. . . . Raoul Wallenberg was successful—in so far as he was successful at all—in saving Budapest's Jews from the Hungarian Arrow Cross (and, occasionally, from the Nazi death marches). He did not save any of Hungary's Jews from deportation to Auschwitz, for the deportation of Hungarian Jewry to Auschwitz had ceased just as he arrived in Hungary. . . .

---

[2]The region of the western Ukraine under Rumanian control. After initial massacres, the surviving Jews were left unmolested. Ian Antonescu was the Rumanian dictator.—Ed.

There are several major difficulties with . . . assertions made by Wyman and the other historians who regard bombing Auschwitz as a classic lost opportunity. In the first place, no detailed suggestions as to how the bombings should be carried out were made by anyone until much later. With the hindsight of many decades, schemes such as these can readily be devised by armchair historians and strategists, but no one did so *at the time*, and it is therefore utterly pointless to attach blame for the failure to bomb Auschwitz or to regard it as in any sense a lost opportunity. Second, and even more importantly, Wyman and his school are not military historians, and have made no effort to take the realities of military strategy into accurate account. Their knowledge of military history, as seen by professional military historians, is superficial, out of date and decontextualised.

Recent military historians have looked at Wyman's claims about the possibility of bombing Auschwitz with critical eyes, and concluded that the options put forward were highly impractical and most unlikely to have succeeded. Kitchens' analysis, "The Bombing of Auschwitz Re-examined," is the most thorough, and refutes Wyman's suggestions as unrealistic at every point: it should be required reading for every student of this topic. . . .

The similarity of the dramatic Mosquito[3] operations to the problem of attacking Auschwitz's gas chambers and crematoria, however, is vague at best, and in a close comparison, Auschwitz emerges as a well-nigh invulnerable target. All of the notable low-level Mosquito raids from England were conducted across the North Sea or relatively flat north-western Europe, and none had to contend with navigating long mountainous stretches while flying at maximum range. Few, if any, of the special Mosquito raids attacked more than one building, while there were *five* discrete objectives at Auschwitz. Mosquito fighter-bombers had no defensive armament and could not dogfight with interceptors; flying unescorted they relied solely on surprise and lightning speed for success. These advantages would have been very hard to achieve and maintain while attacking multiple objectives with a force of perhaps forty aircraft, and in fact even the later special low-level Mosquito operations in Western Europe were escorted by P-51 Mustangs. Thus, flying over 620 miles in radio silence, crossing the Alps in some semblance of

[3]British precision light bombers.—Ed.

cohesion at low altitude, then sneaking through German air defenses with enough fuel to make a coordinated precision attack on five targets and return home beggars belief. . . .

Kitchens (and other recent military historians who have examined this question) shows, with proposal after proposal made by Wyman and others, that these were simply impractical and made by non-specialists with no real knowledge of Second World War military history.

There is also another matter, ethical and moral in nature, which must characterise any proposal to bomb Auschwitz: the fact that many Jewish and other prisoners held there would certainly have been killed in any bombing raid on the camp. Normally, this objection is dismissed on two grounds: they were going to die anyway, while Jews and others suffering under the Nazi yoke would have welcomed any bombing raid as evidence that the Allies had not forgotten their plight, even if it meant death for some in the short term. While there may be a hind-sighted element of truth in these claims — hindsighted because no one at the time either proposed bombing Auschwitz or consulted its victims and prisoners — other realities have also to be kept clearly in mind. Bombing the gas chambers and crematoria at Auschwitz was *not* like bombing a German armaments factory. . . .

. . . [A] degree of pinpoint accuracy was required which simply did not exist at the time. Because raids were often so inaccurate, the real possibility loomed, in any raid, of a "worst case scenario" in which the Allies killed numerous Jewish and other prisoners while failing to halt the murders in any way: for example, by Allied bombs falling on the camp's barracks rather than on the gas chambers. In 1944 there was every likelihood in the world of something such as this actually happening. In March 1944 — after a marked degree of improvement in bombing accuracy during visual attacks — only *13 per cent* of bombs dropped in an average American Air Force bombing raid fell within *500 feet* of their intended targets, and only 34 per cent *within 1,000 feet.* Accuracy then increased still further, but even in August 1944 only 44.5 per cent of all bombs dropped by the US Eighth Air Force landed within 1,000 feet of intended targets. (Most of even these targets, it must be realised, were in western Germany, much closer to the Western Allies, and not in remote southern Poland.)

That any bombing raid on Auschwitz might well have killed its prisoners without necessarily halting the extermination process is at the heart of accurately assessing any such proposal in the context of what was actually proposed at the time. The central assumption made by Wyman and others is that proposals to bomb Auschwitz were repeatedly made by Jewish groups and individual activists, and these were rejected by the American government on a variety of inadequate and even malevolent grounds. In fact, however, many Jewish groups *specifically opposed the bombing of Auschwitz*, when the issue was raised in mid-1944, precisely because any such raid was likely to kill the camp's imprisoned Jews. . . .

Because of the inaccuracy of bombing raids in 1944, if a raid had somehow been launched against Auschwitz in 1944 it is probable—even likely—that such a mission would have been seen, then and now, as a complete fiasco, an ill-considered and dubious exercise, carried out for political rather than for military reasons, in which many hundreds of Jewish and other captives were killed but which utterly failed to halt the Nazi death machine. If (as is likely) this proved to be the case, one can readily imagine what the attitude of today's historians of "rescue" would have been: the Allies would now be *blamed* for "killing Jews" in a foolish and unnecessary way. Indeed, it seems to me to be a near-certain bet that many of today's historians who are loudest in their criticism of the Allies for failing to bomb Auschwitz, seeing it as evidence (if for them any were needed) of Western anti-semitism and complicity in genocide, would then be equally vocal—or, probably, even more vocal—in criticising the Allies for having bombed Auschwitz and "killed Jews" without reason, seeing it as evidence (if for them any were needed) of Western anti-semitism, complicity in genocide and assisting the Nazis to kill the Jews.

Wyman's final point falls into the same category as the others, a curious mixture of criticising the Allies for what they actually did and urging the egregious. The Allies repeatedly made clear their "full awareness of the mass-murder program," and were bombing Germany by day and by night. Professor Wyman's suggestion that Jews in Nazi-occupied Europe somehow volunteered for transport to Auschwitz is the most curious point of all. Jews had absolutely no choice in the matter: the Germans may have depicted their fate as working for Germany in factories or as "transportation to the east," but whatever their purported destination, the SS was, ultimately, there to enforce the deportation of Jews with their full terror, brutality and utterly relentless inhumanity.

It must finally be noted that few (perhaps none) of the points on this list were made by any person, Jewish or non-Jewish, or by any organisation at the time, certainly not in the form suggested by Professor Wyman, whose proposals represent his thinking when he wrote *The Abandonment of the Jews* in 1984. As such, they are similar to any counterfactual historical speculation—what if Napoleon had won the Battle of Waterloo or if Lee had been victorious at Gettysburg?: food for endless, fascinating debate, but remote from the historian's task. In this case their pointlessness is compounded by the fact that not one suggestion, even with the superior wisdom provided by forty years' hindsight, was likely to have been successful. Professor Wyman may well recognise this, for immediately after presenting his list, he is careful to note that

> *None of these proposals guaranteed success . . . There was a moral imperative to attempt everything possible that would not hurt the war effort. If that had been done, even if few or no lives had been saved, the moral obligation would have been fulfilled.*

In my opinion, given what was either possible or actually proposed *at the time*, this moral obligation was being fulfilled every day the war continued and brought Europe closer to liberation.

Other suggestions, different in kind from those made by Professor Wyman, have also been made by others. It has been suggested by several historians that the Western Allies could have launched D-Day a year earlier, in mid-1943, when Germany was allegedly in a weaker position to resist an invasion than in June 1944, and swept on to Berlin in time to prevent the genocide of Hungarian Jewry. . . . According to this view, America had favoured a 1943 invasion and was forced into foot-dragging by Churchill and the British strategists; in 1943 Germany's Atlantic Wall and its designs for maintaining an impregnable "Fortress Europe" were less well advanced, while landing craft for an invasion could have been found by diverting these from the Pacific and the Mediterranean theatres. *If* D-Day had occurred a year earlier, and *if* its success had brought about a German surrender a year earlier, the lives of perhaps 600–700,000 Jews who perished during the last year of the war would have been spared.

There are, however, many reasons for questioning whether it was logistically possible for the Western Allies to have initiated a successful Second Front a year earlier, and more fundamental reasons for doubting whether this could have saved Hungarian Jewry. The weight of very recent military history has been to emphasise the enormous strength of the Nazi military regime and the equally enormous difficulties facing the Western Allies as they prepared for Operation Overlord, the Normandy invasion. Nazi submarine warfare was a real danger to Allied shipping until mid–late 1943; Nazi Germany was highly successful in its efforts to organise an economically unified Axis Europe; there were too few American troops in Britain and no "Mulberry" harbours to facilitate a cross-Channel invasion until 1944; most of all, perhaps, American strategic bombing of Germany's military-industrial infrastructure had not yet brought the Nazi war machine to its knees: its success began only in 1944.

Churchill and his British advisors, who controversially wished to delay a direct invasion of Europe until the last possible minute, were chiefly motivated by perceptions of the extraordinary fighting ability of the German military, and (with memories of the 1914–18 trenches clearly in mind) the near-certainty that Britain would bear tremendous casualties in any invasion which was premature. In 1945, when Germany was reduced to conscripting 15-year-olds and was utterly outnumbered and outclassed in every phase of warfare by the Allies, it still took the Soviet Union (with 12 million battle-hardened soldiers under arms) nearly 100 days to advance the 200 miles from central Poland to Berlin, a gain of just two miles per day; the Soviet conquest of Berlin cost the lives of 300,000 Russian soldiers. It is well known, too, that the Normandy invasion succeeded as well as it did because of wholly fortuitous factors (Erwin Rommel, the Nazi commanding general, was away in Berlin celebrating a birthday party) and through the efforts of a far-reaching attempt at deceiving the Nazis as to the main thrust of the Allied invasion whose success was certainly not guaranteed in advance.

More significant, however, is the fundamental fact that it was not the Western Allies who liberated either Hungarian Jewry or the extermination camps in Poland, but the Soviet army, and in mid-1943 — or even mid-1944 — the Soviet Union's front line was literally hundreds of miles to the east of these places. Soviet troops liberated Kiev, the capital of the Ukraine, only in December 1943 and did not reconquer even one inch of Polish territory until July 1944. Neither Auschwitz nor Budapest were liberated until January 1945. Even if a Second Front had been opened a year earlier, and even if it had proved remarkably successful at thrusting into German territory, the Nazis would have had ample time to exterminate virtually every Jew who actually perished during the war; indeed Hitler might well have speeded up the extermination process if he suspected that the end was approaching. Only an advance of the Soviet armies at a rate paralleling that of an imaginary Western thrust a year earlier than actually occurred, and vastly more rapid than in the actual course of the war as it unfolded, could have guaranteed the liberation of the surviving remnants of eastern European Jewry. Given the stubbornness of Nazi resistance, and such factors as the Russian winter, it is most unlikely, even in the most optimistic plausible scenario, that the Soviet armies could have regained eastern Europe before the SS had done its work.

Regret has also been expressed that Hitler was not assassinated. "Had Hitler been assassinated in 1943 or 1944, hundreds of thousands of Jews—if not more—would have been saved, so pivotal was his input in the Holocaust policy," Yehuda Bauer has written, and it is impossible to disagree with this assertion other than to add that without Hitler's ordering of the Holocaust, it would not have occurred at all. It is indeed puzzling that no well-planned, well-financed attempt at assassinating Hitler was ever made by either a Jewish source or by the Western Allies: while several rather amateurish efforts were made to assassinate Hitler, only the famous "Officers' Plot" of July 1944, headed by Lieutenant-Colonel Klaus von Stauffenberg, had an even remotely professional air about it. Had Jewish or anti-Nazi sources financed six or eight separate, unconnected assassination squads, cleverly organised and properly financed, it is difficult to believe that one of these would not have succeeded. Since 1950, four American presidents have been the victims of serious assassination attempts—one, of course, a successful attempt—despite massive security protection. Hitler, obviously, was at the centre of a totalitarian, militarised society, closely guarded by an elite secret service whose members were sworn to lay down their lives for the *Führer*. Yet Hitler also appeared continuously in the open air, and relied heavily upon public appearances and speeches for his continuing authority and mass appeal. Perhaps those who would have loved to see Hitler dead assumed that his successor would be even worse, but in fact it is unlikely in the highest degree that his probable successors such as Goering, Hess or even Goebbels would have ordered the Holocaust. Presumably, too, the wartime Allies feared that Hitler's assassination, if carried out under Allied instructions, would invite retaliation against Churchill and Roosevelt. Yet of all the roads not taken, assassinating Hitler would have been the most certain way of preventing the Holocaust or of stopping it once it began: even if Goebbels or Himmler had succeeded Hitler during the war, it is likely—as Yehuda Bauer has rightly argued—that they would not have murdered Jews with the single-mindedness of Hitler, if they continued to kill Jews at all. To be sure, if a Jew had assassinated Hitler, it is certain that the Nazis would have carried out a pogrom of unprecedented violence against any and all Jews they could find, although no amount of Nazi vengeance against the Jews could have been worse than what actually occurred. The fact that no serious, carefully planned attempts were made by Jewish or Western anti-Nazi groups is evidence of how little the true menace of Hitler, or his utter centrality as the driving force in the Holocaust, was appreciated.

If the State of Israel had come into existence ten or fifteen years earlier, would this have helped in a central way? Self-evidently, a very significant number of Jews trapped in Nazi-occupied Europe would have fled there prior to Hitler's invasions of their countries; if Palestine/Israel had survived the war unscathed, presumably those Jews, too, would have survived the war. Yet, as we have seen previously, it is easy to overestimate the potential clientele for Zionism among eastern European Jewry prior to the Holocaust; *at the time, even when* Nazi Germany existed, most Jews were adherents of other ideologies—Bund Socialism, Strict Orthodoxy, Marxism—which were explicitly anti-Zionist, and showed no interest in migrating to the Hebrew-speaking *Yishuv*,[4] economically primitive and under constant Arab threat. Some historians have also argued that had Israel existed during the war, it might have saved Europe's Jews in other ways. For instance, Lucy S. Dawidowicz, seldom a proponent of overly sanguine "might-have-beens" of Holocaust rescue, nevertheless stated without qualification that:

> *Without political power Jews had no chance for survival. Had a Jewish state existed in 1939, even one as small as Israel today, but militarily competent, the terrible story of six million dead might have had another outcome. As a member of the Allied nations, contributing its manpower and military resources to the conduct of the war, a Jewish state could have exercised some leverage with the great powers in the alliance. Even though it would not have diverted Hitler from his determination to murder the Jews, a Jewish state might have been able to wield sufficient military and political clout to have inhibited Slovakia, Rumania, and Croatia from collaborating with the Germans in that murder. A Jewish state could have persuaded neutral countries to give Jewish refugees safe passage. A Jewish state would have ensured a safe haven. A Jewish state would have made the difference.*

It is genuinely surprising to read—alas—such a naive and improbable statement in the writings of an author as astute and intelligent as

[4]The Jewish population of British-administered Palestine.—Ed.

Lucy S. Dawidowicz. Unfortunately, even if Israel had existed and attempted to use its "military and political clout" to change the anti-semitic policies of "Slovakia, Rumania, and Croatia," it was Hitler and Hitler alone who had the final say about the fate of the Jews in these places: he could — and doubtless would — have intervened to ensure the deportation of Jews from these countries, just as he did in Hungary. Indeed, had an independent Jewish state existed in Palestine during the war, the fate of the Jews might have been very different, but not in the way imagined here: Hitler might well have made its conquest and destruction a much higher priority than it was actually given. Rommel had only ten divisions in North Africa; with the destruction of Israel and the extermination of perhaps 1 million Jews there as his goal, Hitler might have agreed to give him twenty, thirty or whatever number of Axis divisions was necessary for a successful drive through Egypt (incidentally seizing the Suez Canal) to Palestine, doubtless fanning Arab anti-British and anti-Jewish nationalism every inch of the way. Given what we know about Hitler, which possibility was the more likely?

With great and genuine regret, we reach the final conclusion of this work: turn where you will, turn to any proposal for rescue you wish, one will invariably find either that it was wholly impractical (and, very likely, irrelevant) or not actually proposed by anyone at the time. I simply know of no exceptions to this conclusion, and certainly of no plans for rescue action which were actually capable of saving any significant number of Jews who perished. While this conclusion must be deeply depressing to some readers, it also suggests very strongly that both the governments of the Western democracies and the Jewish communities of the democracies must be viewed much more favourably: no rescue action was taken because no one, anywhere, had anything genuinely practical or effective to suggest, apart from winning the war even more quickly. Those excuses which are sometimes offered for the lack of a rescue policy — ignorance of genocide, Jewish community powerlessness, anti-semitism and anti-Zionism in the democracies, and so on — were, even if true, essentially irrelevant to the basic fact that rescue was impossible. Conversely, it cannot be emphasised too strongly that the responsibility for the Holocaust lies solely and wholly with Adolf Hitler, the SS and their accomplices, and with no one else. In searching for a rational explanation of modern history's greatest crime, it is important that we not assign guilt to those who were innocent.

Michael Phayer

The Silence of Pope Pius XII

Pope Pius XII could not have halted the Holocaust, but even without a public protest, he could have communicated with church leaders throughout Europe, admonishing those who disdained the Jewish people and encouraging all of them to urge Catholics to provide shelter for Jews. The consequence would have been fewer Catholic collaborators and bystanders, on the one hand, and more Catholic rescuers and fewer victims, on the other. . . .

[In 1941 two] German bishops, having heard that 10,000 Jews would be sent from Austria to the General Government in Poland, asked each other "whether the episcopacy should intervene for them out of humanitarian concern or whether this must be left up to Rome to do." Catholic bishops felt the need of a coordinated policy.

It was not as if Germany's bishops were out of touch with the Holy See. Pius's letters to individual prelates during the war years number well over a hundred. . . . But Pius never divulged to them the horrible news that the Vatican had learned in 1942 and confirmed in 1943, namely, that Germany had built extermination centers in occupied Poland where millions were being murdered. Rather, Pius commiserated with German bishops about their bombed-out cities and churches, recalling with fondness his years in Germany and the particular churches, now in ruins, where he had celebrated this or that holy day liturgy. When the war turned against Germany, Pius assured its church leaders that he was praying daily, almost hourly, for peace.

But he almost never said a word about the Jews. Writing to Bishop Preysing, Pius said in April of 1943 that he was heartened to hear that Berlin Catholics were showing empathy for the city's Jews. To fend off Preysing, who pressured him more than any other Catholic bishop to speak out about the Holocaust, Pius adroitly put the blame on the United

States. Recalling that a few years earlier in 1939 Bishop Preysing had urged him to assist emigrating Jews, Pius said that he "didn't want to mention all the difficulties the United States made for Jewish immigration." Of course, it is true that the United States had been painfully negligent in the matter, not even admitting the allowed quota of Jews. But the difference between disallowing immigration of foreign nationals and persecuting and killing one's own citizens need not be belabored. The pope used the United States as a dodge for failing in what Bishop Preysing believed was his responsibility.

At times, lack of communication became miscommunication. In November 1943, Cardinal Bertram of Breslau wrote the Vatican secretary of state asking what could be done to provide the last sacraments for those being condemned to death and summarily executed in occupied Poland. Instead of telling Bertram that it would be impossible to get permission to provide the last sacraments for the victims because Germans were murdering them by the tens and hundreds of thousands, Maglione assured him that the Vatican was doing everything it could through local church officials (in Poland) to get permission to spend the sacraments. There was clear intent here to conceal the facts about genocide.

Nor did the Holy See share its information about the Holocaust with Catholic resistance movements that were trying to save Jews. Volume eight of the Vatican's World War II documents contains numerous reports from French bishops and Nuncio Valerio Valeri that briefed the Holy See on their statements opposing Vichy antisemitic policies, made known the courageous rescue work of the Témoignage Chrétien group, and gave voice to their fears for the Jews. But one looks in vain in this and subsequent volumes of the documents for any kind of response from the Vatican regarding Jews. It would have been quite possible to share information about the Holocaust with Zegota in Poland, with Catholic resistance movements in greater Germany that were centered in Berlin and Vienna, and with the Témoignage Chrétien circle in France. Historian Gerhard Weinberg believes that had Pope Pius spoken out about the murder of the Jews, many more Catholics would have had the courage to hide them. Such encouragement, even given privately, would certainly have bolstered the work of the four groups mentioned here. . . .

How could the Holy See have supported the work of these groups? Rescue work required organization and numbers as much as courage.

Because of food rationing and the frequent relocation of refugees, rescue work was more of a group than an individual activity. The French newsletter *Cahiers du Témoignage Chrétien* sought to inspire people to become active by reminding readers of Pius XI's "Spiritually we are Semites" statement and by urging action. "The church cannot disinterest itself in the fate of man, wherever his inviolable rights are unjustly threatened." The *Cahiers* was clandestinely delivered to all French bishops and to thousands of priests and laypeople—even Pétainists read it. As early as the end of 1942 the *Cahiers* affirmed, based on information from Cardinal Hlond, that hundreds of thousands of Jews had been murdered in gas chambers; in 1943, it reported that Hitler intended to exterminate all the Jews of Europe. Had the newsletter received confirmation of this information from the Holy See, or had it received encouragement from Pius XII similar to that of his predecessor, some French bishops would have continued after 1942 to protest the deportation of Jews, and more French Catholics would have become involved in rescue work. No, the Holocaust would not have been stopped, but as Elie Wiesel has written, "the trains rolling toward [Auschwitz] would have been less crowded."

The Zegota rescue circle in Poland had no need of Holocaust information; they had firsthand knowledge of the gruesome details. But the papacy could have assisted them with money. Since Polish Catholics had been the first victims of Nazi aggression and had felt totally abandoned by the papacy, any Vatican support of Jews, when their hour of desperation came, may have angered Poles. As we have seen, however, after the battle of Stalingrad, Polish church leaders became reconciled to Pius's ways. Certainly, more Poles would have been swayed to help rescue Jews if they had known the work had Rome's blessing. Zegota had need of money because Polish Catholics would not always harbor a Jew altruistically, and even if they would, they often did not have the money needed to feed extra mouths. . . .

. . . During the war years, the Vatican budget for its operations in Europe fluctuated between 1.3 and 2.2 million dollars. By converting some of the dollars into Swiss francs, the Vatican could finance its work in Nazi-occupied Europe. Clearly, the Holy See could have supported rescue operations. As it was, Zegota and Témoignage Chrétien depended solely on the Polish government-in-exile and on American Jewish organizations for infusions of cash. . . .

To find the actual reasons for Pius XII's silence about the Holocaust, we must look . . . toward two concerns of utmost importance to the pope: his desire to play the role of a diplomatic peacemaker, savior of western Europe from communism, and his fear that Rome and the Vatican, entirely defenseless, would be obliterated by aerial attacks before the war came to an end.

Years after the end of the war, Robert Leiber, the German Jesuit who was one of Pius's closest confidants, made clear the connection between the pope's silence about the Holocaust and his diplomacy. The reason that Pius XII did not speak out about the murder of the Jews, Leiber confided to the Dutch historian Ger van Roon, was that he wanted to play the peacemaker during the war. To safeguard his credentials for such a role, the Holy See had to preserve Vatican City's status as an independent state and neutral government. Pius's role model in this respect was Pope Benedict XV, whose efforts to negotiate a European peace during World War I had impressed a younger Eugenio Pacelli. There would have been nothing negligent about this policy had it not kept Pius from dealing adequately with the Holocaust. In his postwar report to the British Home Office, Minister Francis Osborne said that Pius had at his disposal two strong weapons against Nazi criminality—"excommunication and martyrdom." Pius did not use these, Osborne said, because he wanted to be the mediator of a negotiated peace. Thus, the Englishman, Osborne, a close observer of Pius, and the German, Leiber, his trusted adviser, are in full agreement on this point. . . .

A negotiated peace became an overriding concern for the Holy See. Before Stalingrad, Pius believed that the Americans should help the Russians, but with reservations, so that hostilities on the eastern front remained far from Germany. After the battle of Stalingrad and the successful Allied invasion of southern Italy in July 1943, Pius hoped that England and the United States would abandon the Russians so that Germany could deal with the Communist threat. Ideally, he hoped England would recognize the danger to the Christian west that communism posed, and conclude a separate peace with the Axis powers. This would pay a second dividend: Rome would no longer be threatened with air raids.

When Germany switched ambassadors to the Vatican in 1943, Pius tried to impress the departing Diego von Bergen and the newly appointed Ernst von Weizsäcker with his belief in a powerful Germany to withstand the Marxist threat from the east. If the Nazis would just live up to the terms of the Concordat,[1] Pope Pius could support a German mission against Russia. After his first private audience with the pope, Weizsäcker reported to Berlin that "hostility to Bolshevism is, in fact, the most stable component of Vatican foreign policy," and that "the Anglo-American link with the Soviet Russia is detested by the [Holy See]."

The combination of Russian successes on the eastern front, the invasion of Italy by Anglo-American forces, and the fall of Mussolini (July 1943) led to a very noticeable increase in Communist activity in Rome and northern Italy, where a number of Catholic priests were murdered by Communist guerrillas. This disturbed Pope Pius, particularly because of vehement anti-church Communist propaganda. Still, the Vatican refrained from promoting a separate Italian peace with the Allies, because it would necessarily weaken Germany. The radical cure for Italian communism lay in the defeat of Communist Russia.

But Communist agitation in Rome was close to home, and it rested uneasily on Pius's mind. It would necessarily have reminded him of the the tumultuous days in Munich at the end of the Great War when he had himself faced down a gun-toting Red revolutionary. Pius's concern over Italian Communist activity coincided with Germany's concern about Rome's Jews, whom they wished to "resettle." When the roundup of hundreds of Jews took place in October 1943 just outside Vatican city, Ambassador Weizsäcker and other Germans held their breath to see if the pope would protest. He did not, but three days later he requested that Germany increase its police manpower in Rome in order to cut down on Communist agitation.

The same priority of concerns was reflected several months later, in December 1943, when a Vatican consultation about Germany was intercepted by Berlin or allowed to leak out by the Holy See. Reichssicherheitshauptamt (Reich Security Main Office) chief Ernst Kaltenbrunner sent a memorandum to Joachim von Ribbentrop, German minister for foreign affairs, which reported that the main obstacles to a loyal relationship between the church and National Socialism lay in the latter's euthanasia and sterilization policies. The murder of the Jews was left out of the equation.

---

[1]A 1933 treaty between the Vatican and Nazi Germany that promised religious freedom to German Catholics. — Ed.

Pius XII's response to the Allies' Casablanca ultimatum for an unconditional surrender was to call for a peace of justice rather than a peace of force in his 1943 Christmas address. Sitting on the diplomatic sidelines, Pius referred derisively to the "Big Three" in conversation with Germany's Ambassador Weizsäcker. Pius had been upset with Germany when Hitler negotiated a non-aggression pact with Russia and invaded western Europe, but when the dictator returned to his quest for Lebensraum and invaded Russia in 1941, the pope became visibly emotional in conversation with the Spanish ambassador about what appeared to be the German defeat of the Communist menace. Because in Pius's mind Germany remained the last line of defense against Russian communism, the pope frequently discussed schemes for a negotiated peace with Weizsäcker.

The troubling aspect of Pius's preoccupation with diplomacy was that Jews would continue to be murdered as peace negotiations were under way. Hundreds of thousands of Jews were murdered during the time period between the battle of Stalingrad and the end of the war. Instead of confronting Weizsäcker with these crimes, Pius discussed peace negotiations with him. The subject of the Jews and their fate never came up. During 1943, Pius's attention remained riveted on his church and the potential danger to it from aerial attacks and from communism. Historian Saul Friedlander asks,

> How is it conceivable that at the end of 1943 the pope and the highest dignitaries of the church were still wishing for victorious resistance by the Nazis in the east and therefore seemingly accepted by implication the maintenance, however temporary, of the entire nazi extermination machine?

Pius would necessarily have been aware of the ongoing murder of the Jews because of reports about it to the Holy See and appeals for him to intervene. This continued almost to the end of the war, when international efforts, which involved the Holy See, got under way to save Hungarian Jews from deportation to Auschwitz. A high-ranking official in the secretariat of state, Monsignor Domenico Tardini, told the German ambassador that the United States would probably object to his (latest) proposal for negotiations because of the Holocaust (the "Jewish matter"). While Weizsäcker fished Vatican waters for negotiations, the Allies pressed Pius to speak out about the Holocaust.

Although Catholics and non-Catholics inside and outside the diplomatic corps reminded Pius of his role as a moral leader with reference to the Holocaust, he concentrated on diplomacy, often to the exclusion of genocide. The pope allowed the Vatican to become involved with German resistance in an attempt to overthrow Hitler. Later, when Italy wearied of the war, Pius again violated the Vatican's neutrality by allowing England's minister to the Holy See to be an intermediary between England and Italy. But when it came to the Holocaust, strict diplomatic rules were adhered to. The Holy See did not allow its diplomatic offices to involve themselves in the negotiations with England and the United States that were necessary to ensure safe passage across the Mediterranean for the Jews in the Italian zone of France, who were desperately seeking to avoid deportation to Auschwitz.

As the Holocaust lingered on into the latter years of the war, Pius wearied of hearing about the Jews. "I remember," Polish ambassador to the Vatican Kazimierz Papée recalled, "when I came to see the Holy Father for . . . perhaps the tenth time in 1944; he was angry. When he saw me as I entered the room and stood at the door awaiting permission to approach, he raised both his arms in a gesture of exasperation. 'I have listened again and again to your representations about Our unhappy children in Poland,' he said. 'Must I be given the same story yet again?'" Even though ambassador Papée and western diplomats repeatedly pressed Pius about the Holocaust, the pope omitted time and again to discuss it with Germany's Ambassador Weizsäcker, who would later be found guilty of war crimes against Jews at the Nuremberg Trials.

The correspondence and dispatches of the German ambassador and the American envoy to the Vatican make it clear that Pope Pius's second great concern was the possible bombing of Rome, not the murder of the Jews. With the Holocaust in full force, the Vatican's diplomatic staff and the pope himself devoted most of their energy to ensuring that neither Germany nor the Allies would bomb Rome. This became possible for the Allies after General Erwin Rommel's Panzerkorps had been pushed out of northern Africa, allowing English and American troops to cross the Mediterranean and occupy Sicily. Driving German forces from mountainous southern Italy proved a more difficult task, one that lasted from the summer of 1943 to the summer of 1944. During these months of acute danger, the Holy See communicated directly with Envoy Taylor or Chargé d'Affaires Tittman no fewer than thirty-four times in an effort to forestall the bombing of Rome. . . .

President Roosevelt . . . promised that no American aircraft would drop bombs over the Vatican. The Holy See continued to press the issue relentlessly, both through Envoy Taylor and through the apostolic delegate to the United States, trying to exact promises that Vatican property outside Vatican City would also not be harmed. Roosevelt, somewhat exasperated, finally gave instructions that the apostolic delegate should be informed that "war is war," and that with the Germans in charge of the city of Rome, no further promises would be forthcoming. The Holy See responded that if Vatican property were indeed bombed, the pope would protest publicly. No such threat was ever made regarding the murder of the Jews.

It exasperated observers, both inside and outside the Vatican, that the pope would be so concerned over what had not yet taken place and so little concerned over the ongoing murder of the Jews. Cardinal Tisserant remarked as early as 1940 that the pope dwelt too much on the danger of Rome's being bombed and not enough on the affairs of the church. In September, Myron Taylor told Montini that the "deplorable inhumanities in Germany against civilian populations are even more reprehensible than the attacks on all her neighbors whom she invaded." Minister Osborne put it to the Vatican secretary of state more bluntly on December 14, 1942: "Instead of thinking of nothing but the bombing of Rome, [the Holy See] should consider [its] duties in respect to the unprecedented crime against humanity of Hitler's campaign of extermination of the Jews."

Bishop Preysing, writing to Pius from heavily bombed Berlin, adopted the perspective that Minister Osborne found lacking in the pope. "Even more bitter [events than the air raids] face us here in Berlin with the new wave of Jewish deportations that were put in motion just before the first of March [1943]." Preysing then asked the pope to speak out again about the Holocaust. Six months later, in October 1943, Pope Pius was confronted with the precise choice that Bishop Preysing had put to him so pointedly—deportation of Jews versus aerial bombardment. It was at that time that the Reich Security Main Office moved to deport the Jews of Rome to Auschwitz.

When the catastrophe struck the Roman Jews, the bombing of the Basilica of San Lorenzo, which took place in July, still weighed heavily on the pope's mind. . . .

. . . The evening of the day on which San Lorenzo was bombed, Pope Pius wept as he prayed the rosary while looking out over the city of Rome from his Vatican quarters. When Vatican City itself became the victim of an air raid, the Holy See assumed, incorrectly as it turned out, that an American plane was to blame. Because of all of the destruction by the Allies, Ambassador Weizsäcker could report to Berlin that Germany was winning the propaganda war. How could this be, survivor and historian Saul Friedlander has asked, at a time when the pope was aware of the nature of Hitler's regime?

In his correspondence with Bishop Preysing, Pope Pius made no secret of his priorities. Responding to the Berlin prelate, who had urged the pope to address the Holocaust, Pius asserted that the most pressing problem facing him lay in maintaining the absolute trust of Catholics, regardless of which side they fought for, so as to ensure the church's unity. Pius felt that if Rome became contested by Germans on one side and Anglo-Americans on the other, this trust would be in jeopardy. Pius also defended his policy by saying that he was conscience bound to bring all the pressure he could muster on the Allies not to bomb Rome. Catholics the world over, he said, saw the Eternal City as the center of Christendom and the birthplace of the church. As such, Rome symbolized the universal nature of the church. Should this symbol be destroyed, Pius affirmed, faith and hope among Catholics would be shaken.

What Pope Pius told Bishop Preysing, he could not tell the rest of the world. The fortunes of the war made the threat of Allied bombardment greater than bombardment by Germany so long as Pius remained silent about the murder of the Jews. The Holy See dared not link its concern over the possible bombing of Rome to its silence about the Holocaust because of the implication that the murder of Europe's Jews was a lesser priority.

Earlier Pius had assured Bishop Preysing that he was doing all that he could for the persecuted Jews, that he deeply sympathized with them, and that he prayed for them. The pontiff asserted that what he had said about the persecution of the Jews in his 1942 Christmas address[2] "was short but well understood," and he said that he intended to speak out again when the circumstances were right. Whatever circumstances the pope had in mind evidently never came to pass.

The inconsistencies of papal policy relative to the Holocaust may best be understood in the light of Pius's assumptions and priorities. These

---

[2]The Pope had broadcasted a general statement of sympathy for those who "by reason of their nationality or race are marked down for death or gradual extinction." —Ed.

were, first, that the welfare of Catholic states took precedence over the interests of Jews. The Holy See used diplomacy rather than (public) moral strictures to attempt to curtail the involvement of Slovakia and Croatia in genocide. Pius XII did not want to undercut popular support for the fledgling governments of these new Catholic countries by threatening their leaders with excommunication. The same policy held in western Europe for Catholic Vichy France. The Vatican avoided interfering with the "resettlement" of Jews after a sharp government warning following the courageous statements of a number of French bishops.

Second, the long-term danger that communism potentially held for the church preoccupied Pope Pius. His assumption that Germany would be the west's defense against bolshevism ensured that Pius's diplomatic course would be rocky, since Hitler instigated both the Second World War and the Holocaust. But Pius stayed his course inflexibly. The Vatican warned Slovakian leaders that "resettlement" meant perdition for its Jews, but only months later Pius allowed the Germans to "resettle" the Jews of Rome without uttering a word. Earlier, before the German occupation of Italy, the Vatican and officials in Mussolini's government had cooperated smoothly to save Jews. When the Germans took control of the country, the Vatican refrained from even approaching them on behalf of Jews.

Pius's assumptions and priorities are clearly set forth in his letters to Bishop Preysing in 1943 and 1944. He wanted his German friend from Weimar years to know that he cared about the Jews, but that his first concern was for the Catholic church, its universality and unity. Pius may have feared that communicating throughout the church word of the murders perpetrated by the Catholic Ustasha,[3] the complicity in genocide of Catholic Slovak priest Tiso, and the crimes of Catholic Austrians and Germans committed against Catholics in Poland would deeply divide the church. But this apprehension does not explain the Vatican's deceleration of information about the murder of the Jews.

Pius XII harbored a personal ambition to play an important role in world diplomacy, and he felt duty bound to shield the visible center of Catholicism from destruction. Standing amid the ruins of the Basilica of San Lorenzo, Pope Pius said, "Almost in the center of Rome . . . is our Vatican City, an independent state and an independent neutral

---

[3]The regime that controlled Croatia, a German satellite state during the war. — Ed.

state, which shelters priceless treasures, sacred not only to the Apostolic See but to the whole Catholic world." The Vatican's "priceless treasures" were not worth the lives of millions of Jewish men, women, and children, but in Pius's view what those treasures stood for were worth those lives.

Pius XII's priorities put Jews at mortal risk. Thousands, perhaps tens of thousands, of additional Jews would have eluded Hitler's death camps had the Holy See accelerated rather than decelerated information about genocide. Did Pope Pius think the church so fragile that, should he speak out, it would not survive the war, even though it had survived the fratricidal Great War intact? Should the possible bombardment of Rome have been Pius's primary concern, or, as Bishop Preysing pointed out, should not the moral issue of the murder of the Jews have taken precedence? Were the churches and other structures of Rome and the Vatican really the nerve center of Catholic faith that Pius believed them to be? Was the possible future clash between Christianity and atheistic communism more important than the slaughter of the Jews who were being murdered in eastern Europe, and who would continue to be murdered while Pius hoped for a negotiated settlement to the war that would favor genocidal Germany, the church's defender from Russian communism? . . .

Pius XII's leadership failures inevitably affected how Catholics in high and low stations reacted to the Holocaust. The centuries of pogroms and antisemitism notwithstanding, the murder of the Jews was an unprecedented event that struck Catholics, especially in eastern Europe, as an apocalyptic event in some sense. Germans, hoping not to be held responsible for the Holocaust, did not wish to hear news of it. Elsewhere in Europe, the Nazi terror had the same effect on people to a greater or lesser extent, depending upon the degree of collaboration in each region. Only very strong papal leadership could have broken through these several obstructions to rally more Catholics to the cause of the Jews, who were traditionally regarded as outsiders.

The necessity for incisive leadership was most obvious in Catholic Hungary. Eastern European bishops often held leadership positions in both the church and the state prior to the Holocaust. Acting on cultural animosity toward Jews, they helped to enact antisemitic legislation as parliamentarians during the interwar period. Hungary's Cardinal Serédi played this role, and then turned a blind eye to the murder of the Jews during the course of the Second World War. Were these prelates unable to see or to regret that what they had done before the war led ineluctably to what happened to the Jews during the war? When they persisted in their antisemitic convictions, did they think that the Nazis were the hand of God punishing his Chosen People? Since some eastern European bishops showed a correct and courageous attitude toward the persecuted Jews, we may assume that a sharp Vatican rebuke toward callous members of the Slovakian, Croatian, and Hungarian hierarchy would have had some effect.

Those bishops who harbored no ill will toward Jews—and they were numerous in western Europe, including Germany—tried to rescue them. We have seen that this occurred in Italy, France, Belgium, and Germany, although not uniformly throughout the land. Many bishops believed that in the face of Nazi ruthlessness, Catholics could accomplish more by sheltering a few Jews than by a public protest against their mass slaughter. But the postwar statement of Cardinal Frings to the effect that the passivity of German bishops before the Nazis resembled the passivity of Christ before Pilate is completely lacking in credibility. A number of bishops would very likely have spoken out if Pope Pius himself had done so or had encouraged them to do so. Pius XII's limitations as a church leader register here clearly, because, while claiming that when bishops spoke they spoke for him, he failed to tell them about the death camps in eastern Europe. In the absence of Vatican leadership, no European bishop had the courage to follow the example of Berlin priest Bernhard Lichtenberg and protest publicly.

We must look lower down the hierarchical ladder to find the Catholics who sacrificed the most for the Jewish people. Bearing in mind that they were only a tiny minority of all Catholics, we find that priests, nuns, and laypersons, rather than bishops, were prepared to intervene on behalf of Jews. A walk along the Avenue of the Righteous at the Yad Vashem memorial in Jerusalem gives witness to the number of Polish Catholics who sacrificed themselves, even their lives, for Jews. Operating through convent and monastery networks, within diocesan structures, through individual parish communities, through their own organizations such as Zegota, or, quite simply, as individual believers, hundreds, if not thousands, of Catholics throughout Europe came to the assistance of Jews. On the basis of their efforts, we may speculate that if there had been effective leadership on the part of the Holy See or on the part of bishops, the Catholic church could have organized a much more extensive and effective underground rescue operation.

We must not exaggerate about what might have been accomplished. Regardless of who the pontiff was, the centuries-old tradition of antisemitism, dating back to the Fathers of the Church, if not to the Gospels themselves, could not have been reversed quickly enough either to forestall the Holocaust or to cause the majority of Catholics to come to the rescue of the Jews. In the middle of the war, Pope Pius wrote to Bishop Konrad Preysing that his pontificate was the most difficult of modern times. There can be no doubt about that. No other pope had to deal simultaneously with the problems of communism, world war, and genocide. Nevertheless, it remains lamentable that the murder of the Jews found a low place among Pope Pius's concerns. The pope's Cold War policies, giving precedence to the danger of communism over justice for Holocaust war criminals, speak volumes about his priorities. Had either Pius XII's predecessor or his successor led Catholics during the Second World War, historians would have more words of praise and fewer words of regret for the history of the church during the Holocaust.

Walter Laqueur

The Failure to Comprehend

[T]here is one main pitfall in a work of this kind: the temptations of hindsight. Nothing is easier than to apportion praise and blame, writing many years after the events: some historians find the temptation irresistible. But the "final solution" more perhaps than any other subject should be approached in a spirit of caution and even humility. It is very easy to claim that everyone should have known what would happen once Fascism came to power. But such an approach is ahistorical. Nazism was an unprecedented phenomenon. In Fascist Italy, with all its evils, it is also true that during the twenty years of its existence some twenty enemies of the state (or of Mussolini) were actually executed, and of those some had, in fact, engaged in terrorist action. There was no precedent in recent European history for the murderous character of German National Socialism and for this reason most contemporaries were caught unprepared.

To understand this reluctance not only in Britain and the United States but also inside Germany and even among the Jews themselves to give credence to the news about the mass murder, one ought to consider the historical impact of the atrocity propaganda in the First World War. While this had not, of course, been the first war in which allegations had been made of widespread massacres and unspeakable cruelty, such propaganda campaigns had never before been conducted systematically on such a large scale. Both sides engaged in such propaganda, but the British and French with much greater effect than the Germans who felt aggrieved that they were losing the battle of words even though they had made a valiant effort to charge their enemies (and especially the Cossacks in East Prussia) with every possible crime.

Western allegations of German atrocities began with the violation of Belgian neutrality by the Germans in August 1914. The Germans, it was said, had ravished women and even young children, impaled and crucified men, cut off tongues and breasts, gouged eyes and burned down whole villages. These reports were not only carried in sensationalist newspapers but also endorsed by leading writers. . . .

Some readers probably remembered these stories when in June 1942 the Daily Telegraph was the first to report that 700,000 Jews had been gassed. For when the First World War had ended it soon appeared that many of these reports had either been invented—and some of the inventors admitted this much—or grossly exaggerated. The invasion of Belgium had indeed been a war crime, many Belgian civilians had been executed by the Germans on charges of armed resistance which were frequently unproven and there was a considerable amount of wanton destruction. But neither had the Allies always been wholly innocent and, in any case, it was a far cry from these acts to the allegations previously made with regard to German outrages. In the mid-twenties, Austen Chamberlain, the Foreign Secretary, admitted in Parliament that the story of the corpse factory had been without foundation. And as late as February 1938, on the eve of another war, Harold Nicolson said, also in the House of Commons, that "we had lied damnably," that the lies had done Britain tremendous harm and that he hoped that he would not see such propaganda again. Thus, when in late 1941 and 1942 information was again received about mass murder, about the use of poison gas and the manufacture of soap from corpses, the general inclination was to disbelieve it, frequently with reference to "lessons" from the First World War: no one wanted to be misled for the second time within one generation. Two vital circumstances were ignored: above all the fact that Nazi Germany of 1942 was a political regime very different from the Emperor's Reich of 1914, and secondly that even in the First World War, albeit in different conditions, large-scale killings had taken place in distant parts—the Armenian massacres. The atrocity propaganda of the First World War acted as a deterrent; it was not the only psychological obstacle making the acceptance of the horrible news so difficult, but certainly a very important one. Even what happened before 1939 in Germany and Austria could not be reasonably considered at the time the logical prelude to genocide. Hence the reluctance of the Jews both inside Europe and outside to believe the information about the "final solution." Accusations have been levelled against the Poles, the Western Allies and the Soviet leaders, against the Vatican and the Red Cross and almost everyone else for having betrayed the Jews. This study concerns itself not with the question of rescue but with the transmission of information. For all these countries and organizations the Jewish catastrophe was a marginal issue. This is particularly true for the main strategists of the war against Nazi Germany. Their paramount aim was to win the war against Hitler. Everything else was a matter of little interest and low priority. Winning the war in 1942 was bound to be more than a part-time preoccupation for the outcome was as yet by no means certain.

But *tout comprendre* is not necessarily *tout pardonner*. When all allowances have been made, when all mitigating circumstances have been accorded, it is still true that few come out of the story unblemished. It was a story of failure to comprehend, among Jewish leaders and communities inside Europe and outside, a story of failure among non-Jews in high positions in neutral and Allied countries who did not care, or did not want to know or even suppressed the information.

It will be asked whether it really would have mattered if the world had accepted the facts of the mass murder earlier than it did. No one knows. Quite likely it would not have made much difference. The Jews inside Europe could not have escaped their fate, those outside were too weak to help, and the neutrals and the Allies might not have done more than they did in any case, which, as is known, was very little indeed.

But there is no certainty. It is unlikely that many of those killed in 1942 could have been saved. Militarily, Germany was still very strong, its hold on its allies and satellites unbroken. There were, however, ways and means to rescue some even then. They might or might not have succeeded, but they were not even tried. It was a double failure, first of comprehension and later of seizing the opportunities which still existed. . . .

The evidence gathered so far shows that news of the "final solution" had been received in 1942 all over Europe, even though all the details were not known. If so, why were the signals so frequently misunderstood and the message rejected?

1. The fact that Hitler had given an explicit order to kill all Jews was not known for a long time. His decision was taken soon after he had made up his mind to invade Russia. Victor Brack, who worked at the time in Hitler's Chancellery, said in evidence at Nuremberg that it was no secret in higher party circles by March 1941 that the Jews were to be exterminated. But "higher party circles" may have meant at the time no more than a dozen people. In March 1941, even Eichmann did not know, for the preparations for the deportations and the camps had not yet been made. First instructions to this effect were given in Goering's letter to Heydrich of 31 July 1941. The fact that an order had been given by Hitler became known outside Germany only in July 1942 and even then in a distorted form: Hitler (it was then claimed) had ordered that no Jew should be left in Germany by the end of 1942. But there is no evidence that such a time limit had ever been set. It would not have been difficult, for instance, to deport all Jews from Berlin in 1942, but in fact the city was declared empty of Jews by Goebbels only in August 1943. Witnesses claimed to have seen the order, but it is doubtful whether there ever was a written order. This has given rise to endless speculation and inspired a whole "revisionist" literature—quite needlessly, because Hitler, whatever his other vices, was not a bureaucrat. He was not in the habit of giving written orders on all occasions: there were no written orders for the murderous "purge" of June 1934, for the killing of gypsies, the so-called euthanasia action (T4) and on other such occasions. The more abominable the crime, the less likely that there would be a written "Führer order." If Himmler, Heydrich or even Eichmann

said that there was such an order, no one would question or insist on seeing it.

2. The order had practical consequences, it affected the lives or, to be precise, the deaths of millions of people. For this reason details about the "final solution" seeped out virtually as soon as the mass slaughter started.

The systematic massacres of the *Einsatzgruppen* in Eastern Galicia, White Russia, the Ukraine and the Baltic countries became known in Germany almost immediately. True, the scene of the slaughter was distant and it took place in territories in which at the time civilians and foreigners were not freely permitted to travel. But many thousands of German officers and soldiers witnessed these scenes and later reported them and the same is true of Italian, Hungarian and Romanian military personnel. The German Foreign Ministry was officially informed about the details of the massacres; there was much less secrecy about the *Einsatzgruppen* than later on about the extermination camps. The Soviet Government must have learned about the massacres within a few days; after several weeks the news became known in Western capitals too, well before the Wannsee Conference. The slaughter at Kiev (Babi Yar) took place on 29–30 September 1941. Foreign journalists knew about it within a few days; within less than two months it had been reported in the Western press. The massacres in Transniestria became known almost immediately. Chelmno, the first extermination camp, was opened on 8 December 1941; the news was received in Warsaw within less than four weeks and published soon afterwards in the underground press. The existence and the function of Belzec and Treblinka were known in Warsaw among Jews and non-Jews within two weeks after the gas chambers had started operating. The news about the suicide of Czerniakow, the head of the Warsaw *Judenrat*, reached the Jewish press abroad within a short time. The deportations from Warsaw were known in London after four days. There were some exceptions: the true character of Auschwitz did not become known among Jews and Poles alike for several months after the camp had been turned into an extermination centre. At the time in Poland it was believed that there were only two types of camps, labour camps and extermination camps, and the fact that Auschwitz was a "mixed camp" seems to have baffled many.

3. If so much was known so quickly among the Jews of Eastern Europe
    and if the information was circulated through illegal newspapers and
    by other means—there were wireless sets in all major ghettos—why
    was it not believed? In the beginning Russian and Polish Jewry were
    genuinely unprepared, and the reasons have been stated: Soviet Jews
    had been kept uninformed about Nazi intentions and practices, Pol-
    ish Jews believed that the massacres would be limited to the former
    Soviet territories. At first there was the tendency to interpret these
    events in the light of the past: persecution and pogroms. The Jewish
    leaders in Warsaw who learned about events in Lithuania and Latvia
    in early 1942 should have realized that these were not "pogroms"
    in the traditional sense, spontaneous mob actions, nor excesses
    committed by local commanders. There are few arbitrary actions in
    a totalitarian regime. The *Einsatzgruppen* acted methodically and
    in cold blood. The majority of Jewish leaders in Eastern Europe did
    not yet realize that this was the beginning of a systematic campaign
    of destruction. The whole scheme was beyond human imagina-
    tion; they thought the Nazis incapable of the murder of millions.
    Communication between some of the ghettos was irregular; Lodz
    ghetto, the second largest, was more or less isolated. But rumours,
    on the other hand, still travelled fast. If the information about the
    "final solution" had been believed it would have reached every cor-
    ner of Poland within a few days. But it was not believed and when
    the "deportations" from Polish ghettos began in March 1942 it was
    still generally thought that the Jews would be transported to places
    further East.

    The illegal newspapers and other sources conveyed disquieting
    news, and the possibility that many would perish was mentioned.
    But the information was contradictory. Most people did not read the
    underground press and there were no certainties. Perhaps the Nazis
    did after all need a large part of the Jewish population as a labour
    force for the war economy; perhaps the war would soon be over;
    perhaps a miracle of some sort or another would happen. Rumours
    are rife in desperate situations and so is the belief in miracles.

    After July 1942 (the deportations from Warsaw) it is more and
    more difficult to understand that there still was widespread confusion
    about the Nazi designs among Jews in Poland, and that the rumours
    were not recognized for what they were—certainties. Any rational

analysis of the situation would have shown that the Nazi aim was the destruction of all Jews. But the psychological pressures militated against rational analysis and created an atmosphere in which wishful thinking seemed to offer the only antidote to utter despair.

4. Of all the other Jewish communities only the Slovaks seem to have realized at an early date some of the dangers facing them. (So did the Romanians but their position was altogether different.) But even they failed to understand until late 1943 that the Nazis aimed at killing all Jews. The other communities (including German, Dutch, Danish, French, Greek Jews, etc.) seem to have lived in near ignorance almost to the very end. These communities were isolated, the means of information at their disposal limited. But with all this, most Jews in Europe, and many non-Jews, had at the very least heard rumours about some horrible events in Eastern Europe and some had heard more than rumours. These rumours reached them in dozens of different ways. But they were either not believed or it was assumed that "it cannot happen here." Only a relatively small minority tried to hide or escape, aware that deportation meant death. Nazi disinformation contributed to the confusion among the Jews. But the Nazi lies were usually quite threadbare and they cannot be considered the main source of the disorientation.

5. Jewish leaders and the public abroad (Britain, America and Palestine) found it exceedingly difficult in their great majority to accept the ample evidence about the "final solution" and did so only with considerable delay. They too thought in categories of persecution and pogroms at a time when a clear pattern had already emerged which pointed in a different direction. It was a failure of intelligence and imagination caused on one hand by a misjudgment of the murderous nature of Nazism, and on the other hand by a false optimism. Other factors may have played a certain role: the feeling of impotence ("we can do very little, so let us hope for the best"), the military dangers facing the Jewish community in Palestine in 1942. If the evidence was played down by many Jewish leaders and the Jewish press, it was not out of the desire to keep the community in a state of ignorance, but because there were genuine doubts. As the worst fears were confirmed, there was confusion among the leaders as to what course of action to choose. This was true especially in the US and caused further delay in making the news public. In Jerusalem the turning point came with the arrival

of a group of Palestinian citizens who had been repatriated from Europe in November 1942. The leaders of the Jewish Agency, who had been unwilling to accept the written evidence gathered by experienced observers, were ready to believe the accounts delivered by chance arrivals in face-to-face meetings.

6. The Polish underground played a pivotal role in the transmission of the news to the West. It had a fairly good intelligence-gathering network and also the means to convey the information abroad through the short-wave radio and couriers. Most of the information about the Nazi policy of extermination reached Jewish circles abroad through the Polish underground. The Poles had few illusions about the intentions of the Nazis and their reports gave an unvarnished picture of the situation. They have been accused of playing down the Jewish catastrophe in order not to distract world opinion from the suffering of the Polish people, and of having temporarily discontinued the transmission to the West of news about the killing of the Jews. The Polish underground, needless to say, was mainly preoccupied with the fate of the Polish people, not with that of a minority. But it did not, on the whole, suppress the news about the mass killings in its bulletins and the information transmitted abroad. There was one exception — the period in late July, August and early September 1942 (the deportations from Warsaw), when the London Government-in-exile, either on its own initiative or following the advice of the British Foreign Office, did not immediately publicize the news received from Warsaw. The evidence is conflicting: the information was certainly played down for some time but there was no total blackout. There was delay in London but no more than the delay among the Jewish leaders who also disbelieved the information when they first received it. It cannot be proved whether or not the London Polish Government-in-exile did show the members of the National Council all the material received. But Zygielbojm and Schwarzbart certainly had access to all essential information. The Polish Government was the first to alarm the Allied governments and world public opinion but it was accused of exaggeration, as were the Jews at a later date. From this time up to the end of the war the number of victims given in the official declarations of the Allied governments was consistently too low. Even after it had been accepted in London and Washington that the information about the mass slaughter was correct, the British and

US governments showed much concern that it should not be given too much publicity.

7. Millions of Germans knew by late 1942 that the Jews had disappeared. Rumours about their fate reached Germany mainly through officers and soldiers returning from the eastern front but also through other channels. There were clear indications in the wartime speeches of the Nazi leaders that something more drastic than resettlement had happened. Knowledge about the exact manner in which they had been killed was restricted to a very few. It is, in fact, quite likely that while many Germans thought that the Jews were no longer alive, they did not necessarily believe that they were dead. Such belief, needless to say, is logically inconsistent, but a great many logical inconsistencies are accepted in wartime. Very few people had an interest in the fate of the Jews. Most individuals faced a great many more important problems. It was an unpleasant topic, speculations were unprofitable, discussions of the fate of the Jews were discouraged. Consideration of this question was pushed aside, blotted out for the duration.

8. Neutrals and international organizations such as the Vatican and the Red Cross knew the truth at an early stage. Not perhaps the whole truth, but enough to understand that few, if any, Jews would survive the war. The Vatican had an unrivalled net of informants all over Europe. It tried to intervene on some occasions on behalf of the Jews but had no wish to give publicity to the issue. For this would have exposed it to German attacks on one hand and pressure to do more from the Jews and the Allies. Jews, after all, were not Catholics. In normal times their persecution would have evoked expressions of genuine regret. But these were not normal times and since the Holy See could do little—or thought it could do little—even for the faithful Poles, it thought it could do even less for the Jews. This fear of the consequences of helping the Jews influenced its whole policy. The position of the International Red Cross was, broadly speaking, similar. It had, of course, fewer sources of information than the Catholic Church and less influence. But it also magnified its own weakness. It was less exposed, in fact, to retaliatory action than it thought, and while its protests might well have been to no avail, it could have made known directly and indirectly the facts it knew. Some of its directors did so.

The neutral governments received much information about the "final solution" through many channels. There was no censorship in Sweden (except self-censorship) and in 1942 Swiss press censorship did not prevent publication of news about the fate of the Jews. Not all Swiss newspapers showed an equal measure of understanding and compassion, and the Swedish press had instructions not to report "atrocities," but their readers could have had few doubts about the true state of affairs by late 1942.

9. Neither the United States Government, nor Britain, nor Stalin showed any pronounced interest in the fate of the Jews. They were kept informed through Jewish organizations and through their own channels. From an early date the Soviet press published much general information about Nazi atrocities in the occupied areas but only rarely revealed that Jews were singled out for extermination. To this day the Soviet Communist Party line has not changed in this respect: it has not admitted that any mistakes were made, that the Jewish population was quite unprepared for the *Einsatzgruppen*. It is not conceded even now that if specific warnings had been given by the Soviet media in 1941 (which were informed about events behind the German lines) lives might have been saved. As far as the Soviet publications are concerned the Government and the Communist Party acted correctly—Soviet citizens of Jewish origin did not fare differently from the rest under Nazi rule, and if they did, it is thought inadvisable to mention this. The only mildly critical voices that have been heard can be found in a few literary works describing the events of 1941–2. Some Western observers have argued that the (infrequent) early Soviet news about anti-Jewish massacres committed were sometimes dismissed as "Communist propaganda" in the West and that for this reason the Soviet leaders decided no longer to emphasize the specific anti-Jewish character of the extermination campaign. This explanation is not at all convincing because Soviet policy at home was hardly influenced by the *Catholic Times*, and it should be stressed that domestically even less publicity than abroad was given to the Jewish victims from the very beginning.

In London and Washington the facts about the "final solution" were known from an early date and reached the chiefs of intelligence, the secretaries of foreign affairs and defence. But the facts were not considered to be of great interest or importance and at least some of the officials did not believe them, or at least thought them exaggerated. There was no deliberate attempt to stop the flow of information on the mass killings (except for a while on the part of officials in the State Department), but mainly lack of interest and disbelief. This disbelief can be explained against the background of Anglo-American lack of knowledge of European affairs in general and Nazism in particular. Although it was generally accepted that the Nazis behaved in a less gentlemanly way than the German armies in 1914–18, the idea of genocide nevertheless seemed far-fetched. Neither the *Luftwaffe* nor the German navy nor the Afrika Korps had committed such acts of atrocities, and these were the only sections of the German armed forces which Allied soldiers encountered prior to 1944. The Gestapo was known from not very credible B-grade movies. Barbaric fanaticism was unacceptable to people thinking on pragmatic lines, who believed that slave labor rather than annihilation was the fate of the Jews in Europe. The evil nature of Nazism was beyond their comprehension.

But even if the realities of the "final solution" had been accepted in London and Washington the issue would still have figured very low on the scale of Allied priorities. 1942 was a critical year in the course of the war; strategists and bureaucrats were not to be deflected in the pursuit of victory by considerations not directly connected with the war effort. Thus too much publicity about the mass murder seemed undesirable, for it was bound to generate demands to help the Jews and this was thought to be detrimental to the war effort. Even in later years, when victory was already assured there was little willingness to help. Churchill showed more interest in the Jewish tragedy than Roosevelt and also more compassion but even he was not willing to devote much thought to the subject. Public opinion in Britain, the United States and elsewhere was kept informed through the press from an early date about the progress of the "final solution." But the impact of the news was small or at most shortlived. The fact that millions were killed was more or less meaningless. People could identify perhaps with the fate of a single individual or a family but not with the fate of millions. The statistics of murder were either disbelieved or dismissed from consciousness. Hence the surprise and shock at the end of the war when the reports about a "transit camp" such as Bergen-Belsen came in: "No one had known, no one had been prepared for this."

Thus the news about the murder of many millions of Jews was not accepted for a long time and even when it had been accepted the full implications were not understood. Among Jews this frequently caused a trauma in later years which in extreme cases led to the belief that every danger facing Jews, individually or as a group, had to be interpreted in terms of a new holocaust. Such a distortion of reality is psychologically understandable, which does not make it any less dangerous as a potentially disastrous political guideline. The impact among non-Jews has been small. There have been, after all, many intelligence failures throughout history. Optimists could still argue that one failure should not inspire pessimism and strengthen the argument for worst case analysis. As the long term (1910–50) British diplomat rightly said, his record as an inveterate optimist has been far more impressive than that of the professional Cassandras forever harping on the danger of war. He had been wrong only twice. . . .

It has been said that in wartime there are no "strategic warnings," no unambiguous signals, no absolute certainties. Not only the signals have to be considered but also the background noise, the interference, the deception. If even Barbarossa and Pearl Harbor came as a surprise, despite the fact that the eyes of the whole world were scanning the horizons for such signals—and despite the fact that there was much evidence and many warnings to this effect—is it not natural that European Jewry was taken unaware? But there was one fundamental difference: Barbarossa and Pearl Harbor were surprise attacks, whereas the "final solution" proceeded in stages over a long period. Some have claimed in retrospect that *Mein Kampf* and Hitler's speeches should have dispelled any doubts about the Nazis' ultimate murderous intentions. But this is wrong. The "solution of the Jewish question" could equally have meant ghettoization or expulsion to some far-away place such as Madagascar. It was only after the invasion of the Soviet Union that there was reason to believe that large parts of European Jewry would not survive the war. At first there were only isolated rumours, then the rumours thickened and eventually they became certainties. A moderately well informed Jewish resident of Warsaw should have drawn the correct conclusions by May 1942 and some of them did. But the time and the place were hardly conducive to detached, objective analysis; the disintegration of rational intelligence is one of the recurrent themes of all those who have written about that period on the basis of inside knowledge.

Democratic societies demonstrated on this occasion as on many others, before and after, that they are incapable of understanding political regimes of a different character. Not every modern dictatorship is Hitlerian in character and engages in genocide but every one has the potential to do so. Democratic societies are accustomed to think in liberal, pragmatic categories; conflicts are believed to be based on misunderstandings and can be solved with a minimum of goodwill; extremism is a temporary aberration, so is irrational behaviour in general, such as intolerance, cruelty, etc. The effort to overcome such basic psychological handicaps is immense. It will be undertaken only in the light of immediate (and painful) experience. Each new generation faces this challenge again for experience cannot be inherited.

The reaction of East European Jewry can only be understood out of their specific situation in 1942. But there are situations which cannot be re-created, however sophisticated the techniques of simulation, however great the capacity for empathy and imagination. Generalizations about human behaviour in the face of disaster are of limited value; each disaster is different. Some of those who lived through the catastrophe have tried in later years to find explanations. But while their accounts are of great interest, they are no longer *a priori* reliable witnesses. Their explanations are rooted in a different situation and this is bound to lead to a rationalization of irrational behaviour. The "final solution" proceeded in stages, chronologically and geographically. This should have acted as a deterrent, but it did not, on the whole, have this effect. There were no certainties, only rumours, no full picture, only fragments. Was it a case of a "people without understanding," which had eyes and ears but saw not and heard not? The people saw and heard but what it perceived was not always clear, and when at last the message was unambiguous it left no room for hope and was therefore unacceptable. It is a syndrome observed by biblical prophets and modern political leaders alike, that it is natural for man to indulge in the illusions of hope and to shut his eyes against a painful truth.

But it is not natural for man to submit passively to a horrible fate, not to try to escape, however great the odds against success, not to resist, even if there is no prospect of victory. True, there are explanations even for paralysis, but later generations can no longer accept them—hence the abiding mystery. Total hopelessness (the psychologists say) results in inaction; when there is no exit, such as in a mine or a submarine disaster, this leads to resignation.

The reaction of Dutch or Hungarian Jews can be compared to that of people facing a flood and who in contradiction of all experience believe that they will not be affected but are individually or as a group invulnerable. Some social psychologists will argue that such a denial of a threat betrays a fear of not being able to cope with it. But if such an explanation was true for some it certainly did not apply to others. They genuinely did not know what was in store for them. Danish Jews were perfectly able to escape to Sweden and if they did so only at the very last moment the reason was that they genuinely believed that they would not be deported. Equally, to give another example, the Jews living in Rhodes could have fled without difficulty to Turkey and would have done so had they known their fate in Auschwitz. But they did not know. Other Jewish communities were indeed trapped but their situation was still not identical with that of the victims of a mine disaster. Comparisons are only of limited help for understanding human behaviour in unique situations. In many cases the inactivity of Jews, individuals and groups, was not the result of paralysis but on the contrary of unwarranted optimism. . . .

One of the questions initially asked was whether it would have made any difference if the information about the mass murder had been believed right from the beginning. It seems quite likely that relatively few people might have been saved as a result and even this is not absolutely certain. But this is hardly the right way of posing the question, for the misjudgment of Hitler and Nazism did not begin in June 1941 nor did it end in December 1942. The ideal time to stop Hitler was not when he was at the height of his strength. If the democracies had shown greater foresight, solidarity and resolution, Nazism could have been stopped at the beginning of its campaign of aggression. No power could have saved the majority of the Jews of the Reich and of Eastern Europe in the summer of 1942. Some more would have tried to escape their fate if the information had been made widely known. Some could have been saved if Hitler's satellites had been threatened and if the peoples of Europe had been called to extend help to the Jews. After the winter of 1942 the situation rapidly changed: the satellite leaders and even some of the German officials were no longer eager to be accessories to mass murder. Some, at least, would have responded to Allied pressure, but such pressure was never exerted. Many Jews could certainly have been saved in 1944 by bombing the railway lines leading to the extermination centres, and of course, the centres themselves. This could have been done without deflecting any major resources from the general war effort.

It has been argued that the Jews could not have escaped in any case but this is not correct: the Russians were no longer far away, the German forces in Poland were concentrated in some of the bigger towns, and even there their sway ran only in daytime—they no longer had the manpower to round up escaped Jews. In short, hundreds of thousands could have been saved. But this discussion belongs to a later period. The failure to read correctly the signs in 1941–2 was only one link in a chain of failures. There was not one reason for this overall failure but many different ones: paralyzing fear on one hand and, on the contrary, reckless optimism on the other; disbelief stemming from a lack of experience or imagination or genuine ignorance or a mixture of some or all of these things. In some cases the motives were creditable, in others damnable. In some instances moral categories are simply not applicable, and there were also cases which defy understanding to this day.

Suggestions for Additional Reading

Only a few of the most important studies of the Holocaust can be included here. This brief bibliography is restricted to literature available in English and does not include any of the works excerpted in this volume.

General Surveys and Reference Sources

Michael Berenbaum, ed., *A Mosaic of Victims: Non-Jews Persecuted and Murdered by the Nazis* (New York: 1990).

Doris L. Bergen, *War and Genocide* (Lanham, Maryland: 2009).

Guenter Lewy, *The Nazi Persecution of the Gypsies* (New York: 2000).

Donald Niewyk and Francis Nicosia, eds., *The Columbia Guide to the Holocaust* (New York: 2000).

Leni Yahil, *The Holocaust: The Fate of European Jewry, 1932–1945* (New York: 1991).

Documents and Readings

Lucy S. Dawidowicz, ed., *A Holocaust Reader* (New York: 1976).

Raul Hilberg, ed., *Documents of Destruction* (Chicago, 1971).

Richard J. Levy, *Anti-Semitism in the Modern World: An Anthology of Texts* (Lexington, Mass.: 1991).

John Mendelsohn, ed., *The Holocaust: Selected Documents in Eighteen Volumes* (New York: 1982).

Historical Background

Saul Friedländer, *Nazi Germany and the Jews* (New York: 1997).

Steven T. Katz, *The Holocaust in Historical Context* (New York, 1994).

Donald Kenrick and Grattan Puxon, *The Destiny of Europe's Gypsies* (New York: 1972).

Albert S. Lindemann, *Esau's Tears: Modern Anti-Semitism and the Rise of the Jews* (New York: 1997).

Ezra Mendelsohn, *The Jews of East Central Europe Between the Two World Wars* (Bloomington, Indiana: 1983).

George Mosse, *Toward the Final Solution: A History of European Racism* (London: 1978).

Donald L. Niewyk, *The Jews in Weimar Germany* (New Brunswick, N.J.: 2001).

Bruce F. Pauley, *From Prejudice to Persecution: A History of Austrian Anti-Semitism* (Chapel Hill, N.C.: 1992).

Leon Poliakov, *A History of Anti-Semitism*, 4 vols. (New York: 1965–1986).

Peter G. J. Pulzer, *The Rise of Political Anti-Semitism in Germany and Austria* (Cambridge, Mass.: 1988).

Hitler and the Nazi State

Karl Dietrich Bracher, *The German Dictatorship: The Origins, Structure and Effects of National Socialism* (New York: 1970).

Christopher R. Browning, *The Origins of the Final Solution* (Lincoln, Neb.: 2000).

Philippe Burrin, *Hitler and the Jews: The Genesis of the Holocaust* (London: 1994).

Robert Gellately, *The Gestapo and German Society: Enforcing Racial Policy* (Oxford: 1990).

Ulrich Herbert, ed., *National Socialist Extermination Policies* (New York: 2000).

Eberhard Jäckel, *Hitler's Weltanschauung: A Blueprint for Power* (Middletown: 1972); and *Hitler in History* (Hanover, N.H.: 1984).

Ian Kershaw, *Hitler, the Germans, and the Final Solution* (New Haven: 2008).

Robert Koehl, *The Black Corps: The Structure and Power Struggles of the Nazi SS* (Madison: 1983).

Wolfgang Sofsky, *The Order of Terror: The Concentration Camps* (Princeton, N.J.: 1997).

Survivors' Accounts

Moshe Garbarz, *A Survivor* (Detroit: 1992).

Raul Hilberg et al., eds., *The Warsaw Diary of Adam Czerniakow* (New York: 1979).

Judith Isaacson, *Seed of Sarah* (Urbana, Ill.: 1990).

Gerda Klein, *All But My Life* (New York: 1971).
Primo Levi, *Survival in Auschwitz* (New York: 1969).
Frida Michelson, *I Survived Rumbuli* (New York: 1979).
Filip Müller, *Eyewitness Auschwitz* (New York: 1981).
Emmanuel Ringelblum, *Notes from the Warsaw Ghetto* (New York: 1974).
Gisella Perl, *I Was a Doctor in Auschwitz* (Salem, N.H.: 1992).

Ghettos and Camps

Yitzhak Arad, *Ghetto in Flames: The Struggle and Destruction of the Jews in Vilna in the Holocaust* (Jerusalem: 1980).
Hannah Arendt, *Eichmann in Jerusalem* (New York: 1963).
Yisrael Gutman and Michael Berenbaum, eds., *Anatomy of the Auschwitz Death Camp* (Bloomington Ind.: 1994).
George M. Kren and Leon Rappoport, *The Holocaust and the Crisis of Human Behavior* (New York: 1980).
Wolf Gruner, *Jewish Forced Labor Under the Nazis* (New York: 2006).
Isaiah Trunk, *Judenrat: The Jewish Councils in Eastern Europe Under Nazi Occupation* (New York: 1977).

Jewish Resistance

Reubin Ainsztein, *Jewish Resistance in Nazi-Occupied Eastern Europe* (New York: 1974).
Yehuda Bauer, *They Chose Life: Jewish Resistance in the Holocaust* (New York: 1973).
Yisrael Gutman, *The Jews of Warsaw, 1939–1943: Ghetto, Underground, Revolt* (Bloomington, Ind.: 1983).
Shmuel Krakowski, *The War of the Doomed: Jewish Armed Resistance in Poland, 1942–1944* (New York: 1984).
Annie Latour, *Jewish Resistance in France* (New York: 1981).
Dov Levin, *Fighting Back: Lithuanian Jewry's Armed Resistance to the Nazis, 1941–1944* (New York: 1985).
Yuri Suhl, ed., *They Fought Back: The Story of the Jewish Resistance in Nazi Europe* (New York: 1975).
Nechama Tec, *The Bielski Partisans* (New York: 1993).

Victims and Bystanders

David Bankier, *The Germans and the Final Solution* (Oxford: 1992).

Randolph L. Braham, *The Politics of Genocide: The Holocaust in Hungary* (New York: 1981).

Helen Fein, *Accounting for Genocide: National Responses and Jewish Victimization During the Holocaust* (New York: 1979).

Saul Friedlander, *The Years of Extermination* (New York: 2007).

Jan T. Gross, *Neighbors: The Destruction of the Jewish Community of Jedwabne, Poland* (Princeton, N.J.: 2001).

Radu Ioanid, *The Holocaust in Romania* (Chicago, 2000).

Michael R. Marrus and Robert O. Paxton, *Vichy France and the Jews* (New York: 1981).

Bob Moore, *Victims and Survivors: The Nazi Persecution of the Jews in the Netherlands, 1940–1945* (London: 1997).

Emmanuel Ringelblum, *Polish-Jewish Relations During the Second World War* (New York: 1976).

Nechama Tec, *When Light Pierced the Darkness: Christian Rescue of Jews in Nazi Occupied Poland* (New York: 1986).

Leni Yahil, *The Rescue of Danish Jewry* (Philadelphia: 1969).

Susan Zuccotti, *The Italians and the Holocaust* (New York: 1987).

Rescue

Yehuda Bauer, *Jews For Sale? Nazi-Jewish Negotiations, 1933–1945* (New Haven, Conn.: 1994).

Saul Friedlander, *Pius XII and the Third Reich: A Documentation* (New York: 1966).

Martin Gilbert, *Auschwitz and the Allies* (New York: 1981).

Sharon Linnea, *Raoul Wallenberg: The Man Who Stopped Death* (Philadelphia: 1993).

Michael J. Neufeld and Michael Berenbaum, eds., *The Bombing of Auschwitz: Should the Allies Have Attempted It?* (New York: 2000).

Monty N. Penkower, *The Jews Were Expendable: Free World Diplomacy and the Holocaust* (Urbana, Ill.: 1983).

Bernard Wasserstein, *Britain and the Jews of Europe, 1939–1945* (London: 1979).